D0889746

BOOKS BY HUGH DELANO

EDDIE

HUGH DELANO

EDDIE

Atheneum   New York   1976

Library of Congress Cataloging in Publication Data
Delano, Hugh.   Eddie.
Summary: A biography of hockey player Eddie Giacomin, all-star goalie
of the New York Rangers.
1. Giacomin, Eddie.   2. Hockey.   [1. Giacomin, Eddie.
2. Hockey—Biography]   I. Title.   GV848.5.G52D44
796.9'62'0924 [B] [92] 75-38345
ISBN 0-689-10715-3

AUTHOR'S NOTE

The memory is vague. I don't remember the date or the score of the game. But I remember the goalies.

Turk Broda played goal for the Toronto Maple Leafs. He had a large belly and curly blond hair and a bored look on his round face when he scraped away the ice chips in his goal crease.

Chuck Rayner was the goalie for the New York Rangers. He had thick, wavy black hair. When he circled the rink in the warm-up, I could see the lumpy red scar tissue around his eyes. The bulky pads strapped to his legs and the protective vest he wore under his sweater made his chest bulge, and he seemed almost grotesque.

I was thirteen years old when I went to the old Madison Square Garden to see my first hockey game. It cost $4.50 for a seat by the ice and 70 cents to sit in the side balcony. I remember some of the names—Bones Raleigh, Edgar Laprade, Tony Leswick, Buddy O'Connor, Teeder Kennedy, Gus Mortson, Fleming Mackell, Max Bentley, and Tod Sloan.

I didn't watch the game. I watched the goalies. I was fascinated by them. They made it look so easy when they stopped pucks that flew at their faces at speeds of more than 100 miles per hour or dived and sprawled fearlessly into a scramble of skates and sticks. Their bare faces reflected the frantic tension and intensity of the position they played.

I liked the sound the puck made when it thumped against the goalie's padded legs or the cracking sound that signified a stick save. I saw the look of utter helplessness and shame in the goalie's eyes as he lay motionless in front of the net and the flashing red goal light became a beacon of his failure to stop the puck.

Goaltending seemed to be the essence of daring bravery in all of sports.

I fell in love with goaltending on that first night in Madison Square Garden.

When the river that wound its way through my hometown occasionally froze in the winter, kids gathered to play hockey until it was dark. Only a few had skates and sticks and pucks and knew how to skate. Most of us slipped and skidded along the ice in our shoes.

Hockey in suburban New Jersey in the late 1940s did not enjoy the widespread popularity it does today. Few sporting-goods stores stocked pucks or sticks, and there seldom was ice on the river.

Lack of ice never became a problem. We played hockey on the icy sidestreets in our shoes and galoshes. It was hockey in the most peculiar form. We took the hard-glass coasters from under the legs of our beds and used them for pucks until they hit the curb and shattered. I made a makeshift goalie's stick from scrap lumber and wrote "Mr. Zero" down the shaft.

Frankie Brimsek was the goalie for the Boston Bruins. I was "Mr. Zero" in galoshes and baseball catcher's shin guards stopping a glass puck on a snow-covered street. It was a beautiful fantasy.

The walls of my bedroom suddenly became covered with magazine pictures of Brimsek, Broda, Rayner, Harry Lumley, Bill Durnan, and a goalie with a name I loved—Sugar Jim Henry. I never found a picture of the Chicago Black Hawks' goalie. But I knew his name: Emile "the Cat" Francis.

At night Bert Lee and Ward Wilson broadcast Ranger games on radio station WMGM. I kept a notebook of all the goalies' records—of the saves they made and the ones they didn't make.

"Mr. Zero" had one great advantage over me: he could skate. I could, too—just barely.

So I had to apply my zest for goaltending to other sports in later years. I became the goalie for my high-school and college soccer teams. The soccer goal cage was wider than a hockey goal cage, but at least the goalie stood on his own two feet instead of balancing on a pair of skates. Regretfully, my goals-against average in soccer was what I wished my batting average could have been as a high-school and college baseball catcher.

I never really understood what made goaltending so intriguing. It must be the inherent danger of the position and the courage men must have to play the most hazardous position in sports. There is a balletlike quality in the way goalies defend their nets. The physical ordeal of a man strapping himself into heavy equipment to become a clay pigeon seems the most courageous act in sports.

Goalies are a breed apart from other athletes. They risk injury and disgrace every moment they play. It is a lonely job. The mental tension is tremendous. The responsibility to their team is greatest. The goalie is the last soldier to stop the enemy attack and time and again is more victimized by the mistakes of others than by his own. In the final result, it is the goalie who is most often blamed for defeat and least appreciated in victory.

Perhaps people are fascinated by the brave, masked men in the goal for the same reason they watch steeplejacks, construction workers walking on steel beams high above the city streets, or circus performers on the high wire.

The first time I met Eddie Giacomin was in 1970 in the dressing room at the Rangers' training camp in Kitchener, Ontario. I had watched him sweat and strain under the weight of his heavy equipment at practice. He seemed to do everything more vigorously than the other players.

I wanted to tell him of my admiration for goaltending, but that would have been unprofessional.

I wondered why a man who played as demanding and tiring a position as goalie felt it necessary to exert himself so much in practice with such a long season ahead.

"Here," he said sharply, thrusting all of his cumbersome equipment into my hands. "Now you know. This stuff weighs forty pounds. If I'm going to have to wear it when I play this season, then I better work hard in practice to be in shape, or I'll never make it through the year."

Then he looked at me and laughed.

"I guess you don't know anything about being a goalie, eh?"

Hugh Delano
Cranford, New Jersey

ACKNOWLEDGMENTS

In writing this book, it was inevitable that assistance was needed from many persons who at one time or another were involved in the life and hockey career of Eddie Giacomin.

The author is grateful to Emile Francis, general manager and former coach of the New York Rangers, who gave willingly of his time. Also to such players, coaches, and hockey personalities as Jean Beliveau, Rod Seiling, Vic Hadfield, Jean Ratelle, Pete Stemkowski, Bernie Parent, Ross Brooks, Eddie Westfall, Al Arbour, Red Sullivan, John Muckler, John McLellan. Johnny Gagnon, Fern Flamen, Ted Irvine, Bruce MacGregor, Dale Rolfe, Ken Hodge, Don Awrey, Steve Brklacich, Terry Reardon, Jack Riley, Marcel Pelletier, Gilles Villemure, Rod Gilbert, Ron Stewart, and Brad Park.

Special thanks for their valued help, too, go to John Halligan, Janet Halligan, and Arthur Friedman of the New York Ranger staff and to Ron Andrews, Norm Jewison, and Bob Casey of the National Hockey League. And, finally, to Eddie Giacomin himself, to his wife Marg, and to Marylou Delano.

INTRODUCTION

The most important trade I ever made was getting Eddie Giacomin. We needed a goaltender to build our team around and to get the New York Rangers out of last place and to where we have been the last nine years—battling for first place and in the Stanley Cup playoffs every year. I've had to discipline quite a few players as coach but I've never had to discipline Eddie Giacomin. He is the most dedicated and determined man I ever saw.

EMILE FRANCIS
General Manager, New York Rangers

When I think of Eddie Giacomin, I think of him as the player who was the most vital in changing the image of the New York Rangers from a last-place team into a championship contender for the last nine years. In many ways, he represents the true spirit and determination of the New York Rangers.

WILLIAM M. JENNINGS
President, New York Rangers

I have played both against Eddie Giacomin and with him as a teammate, and now he's the goaltender on the team I coach. I consider him to be one of the greatest competitors in the game of hockey. He came up the hard way and has been rewarded with a record that speaks for itself. He still has that one great ambition—to win the Stanley Cup. I know he's not going to stop trying until he reaches that goal. That's what makes him so valuable to the New York Rangers.

RON STEWART
Coach, New York Rangers

I call Eddie Giacomin the relentless worker. He's had to work his tail off to get where he is today. But even though he's become successful he hasn't stopped working, and he's the same good guy he's always been. Success hasn't changed or spoiled Eddie. He's a good team man. He's a good friend to all the guys on the team. He's respected by his rivals wherever he goes in hockey. He's a good family man and a guy who really seems to love playing hockey.

BRAD PARK
Former Captain, New York Rangers

He is only a well-made man who has a good determination.

EMERSON

The greatest test of courage on earth is to bear defeat without losing heart.

INGERSOLL

To strive, to seek, to find, and not to yield.

TENNYSON

All my life people have been telling me I couldn't make it.

EDDIE GIACOMIN

CONTENTS

ILLUSTRATIONS

An album of photographs follows page 138.

EDDIE

The Night Eddie Refused to Leave the Game

"THE SKIN WAS RIPPED AND HANGING LOOSE
AND HIS GLOVE WAS FILLED WITH BLOOD."

HE sat on a wooden bench inside the small cubicle in the corner of the dressing room in Chicago Stadium. His wiry, salt-and-pepper hair was tousled and matted to his scalp. Beads of sweat ran down the gaunt features of his face. He looked thin and weary, drained of all mental and physical energy, and his chest heaved as he gasped for breath.

"Things have never been easy for me," Eddie Giacomin said softly. "I guess they never will be. I've always had to do things the hard way. All my life people have been telling me I couldn't make it."

The New York Rangers' goaltender seemed forlorn and almost pathetic. He still wore his rumpled red hockey pants, and the bulky brown leather pads strapped to his legs were blotched with dark perspiration stains. The suspenders he wore were slipped down over his shoulders and hung at his sides. There was a smear of blood across the front of the damp undershirt that clung to his sweaty body.

"Let's have a look at it," said the elderly man in the brown felt hat who bent over Giacomin.

Eddie raised his left arm and extended his hand. The doctor grasped the wrist gently and Eddie winced with pain. Slowly, tenderly, Frank Paice, the Rangers' trainer, began to unwind the bloodstained bandage encasing Eddie's hand.

When he finished, the ugly gash across the back of the hand above the knuckles was revealed. The deep wound had been pulled closed with five heavy black stitches. The hand was red, swollen, bruised, and caked with bits of dried blood.

Eddie reached down with his right hand for the green towel at his feet and mopped his face dry. It was hot in the crowded dressing room the night of April 18, 1971. The only noise at that instant was the hiss of the shower.

One by one, the players walked to and from the shower, pausing to look down at their wounded goalie. Their faces reflected admiration and respect.

Seven minutes had elapsed in the second period of the first game of the Stanley Cup playoffs between the Rangers and the Black Hawks when Bobby Hull intercepted a clearing pass from defenseman Tim Horton inside the New York blue line.

The crowd had been boiling with excitement because of the emotionally frantic tempo of play and roared its approval as the big, blond left wing drew back his stick to slap the puck toward the Rangers' goal cage.

Hull shot and the hard black puck became a blur as it flew toward Giacomin from forty feet away. Eddie lunged forward and made a difficult sprawling save with the catching glove on his left hand. He had to trap the puck against the ice in front of the goal crease because his defense momentarily had left him unprotected and Hull was charging toward the net, searching for the rebound of his shot.

In a flash, Hull darted across the ice in front of the goal crease and inadvertently skated across Giacomin's left hand.

The razor-sharp blade of his left skate cut through the back of the leather glove between the knuckles and upper wrist, ripping open a deep gash on the back of the goalie's hand.

"I knew right away he'd cut me," said Eddie. "I could feel the skate cut and grind down into my hand. There was a burning sensation, like I'd been stabbed, and a lot of blood inside my glove. It hurt like hell."

Emile Francis, the Rangers' general manager and coach, and Paice ran from the bench across the ice to where Giacomin lay writhing in pain and clenching his teeth. Referee Bruce Hood stopped play and soon most of the Rangers and Black Hawks milled about near the fallen goaltender.

Francis motioned to Gilles Villemure on the bench, and New York's back-up goaltender climbed over the boards and began unlimbering his legs so he could replace his injured teammate in goal.

Francis told Giacomin he was too badly hurt to continue playing and was coming out of the game.

"No way I'm coming out," said Eddie, looking up at his coach.

The wounded goalie could easily have asked to come out of the game. Or he could have asked to go into the dressing room and have his wound cleaned and stitched. That would have caused a fifteen- or twenty-minute delay in the game until he returned.

Eddie did neither.

"Put a bandage on it, Frank, and I'll be O.K.," he told Paice.

The trainer bandaged the throbbing, bleeding hand at the bench, and in less than five minutes Giacomin was back in goal and the game had resumed.

The Black Hawks led, 1-0. They might easily have scored three or four more goals in the final thirteen minutes of the second period. They rained shot after shot at Eddie but the injured goalie stopped them all.

He was in pain and his glove was filled with blood from the wound.

"The bandage didn't hold too well and my hand hurt pretty badly," he said. "I knew I'd have to get stitches between the second and third periods because the blood kept oozing out into my glove. I was determined I was going to hang on until they stitched me up."

During one stoppage of play near the end of the period, after Giacomin had made three spectacular saves, Brad Park skated over to Eddie. The bandage on Eddie's bleeding hand had come off and Park saw his teammate's wound.

"My god, it must have been a quarter of an inch deep and the skin was all ripped and hanging loose," said the young defenseman, shaking his head in amazement at the goalie's courage. "You could look down in the cut and see the muscles and tissue. Eddie's glove was filled with blood. What a bloody mess. It made me sick to look at it."

A doctor closed the wound with five stitches between the second and third periods. He advised Eddie not to continue playing. Francis again asked the goaltender if he wanted to leave the game.

"No way I'm coming out," replied Eddie.

Giacomin turned back every shot the Black Hawks took at him during the remainder of the game. His injured hand was swollen and throbbing with pain. But he kept going. Jean Ratelle tied the score with 3:16 remaining in the third period. Pete Stemkowski won it for the Rangers, 2-1, with a goal after ninety-seven seconds of sudden-death overtime.

Why had Giacomin insisted on staying in the game even though he was badly injured and in pain?

"I've had to come through the back door all my life," he said. "Nobody ever opened the front door and let me in. Being here in the playoffs means too much for me to quit, because it took me so long to get here."

He smiled and the twinkle in his hazel eyes made it seem

as though he were laughing at his fate. "But you know me. Just when it looks like I'm down and out, I always bounce back up again, eh?"

Eddie looked at his bandaged hand and shrugged. "Now I'll have something to show my kids when I'm old. I can say, 'Hey, see this scar? Bobby Hull did that.' Not a bad guy to have cut you, eh?"

Later that night several of the Rangers gathered at a bar near the Bismarck Hotel. "I know this sounds corny," said Park. "But when I looked back at Eddie making all those saves with all that pain in his hand, it made me play even harder. Guts. That's what he's got. Guts are what Eddie Giacomin's all about."

Ratelle talked about Eddie's courageous act at breakfast the next morning in the hotel. "We probably shouldn't have won the game," said the soft-spoken center. "Chicago had more chances to score than we did. Eddie kept us in the game and when he got hurt and wouldn't quit, it made all of us determined we would not let him lose. Eddie was so badly hurt and yet he was keeping us in the game with great saves. I would have felt ashamed if we had not won because of what he was doing for us. I always knew Eddie was a great goaltender but I never really knew how great until now."

Rod Gilbert said: "Eddie Giacomin deserves the Red Badge of Courage for what he did."

Ted Irvine was deeply moved and inspired by Giacomin's courage. "It was one of the bravest things I've seen a man do in a hockey game," he said.

"Eddie could have come out of the game and no one would have blamed him," said Park. "But the fact that he stayed in there, with his hand cut open and bleeding, showed the rest of us just how much this game and his team means to him. He brought us all together when we were losing and gave us the spirit we needed to win the game."

Even the Black Hawks were impressed by Eddie's courage. The one word they used to describe him was "guts."

Bobby Hull used the word and said he was sorry and hoped Eddie understood it was an accident. Billy Reay, Chicago's feisty coach, said Giacomin's bravery gave the Rangers the psychological lift they needed to win and turned the outcome of the game around. "Giacomin was outstanding," said Reay.

"It took a lot of guts for him to do what he did," said Tony Esposito, the Black Hawks' goaltender. "Most guys would have come out of the game if they got cut as badly as he did. But if you know anything about Eddie Giacomin, you shouldn't be surprised. He's a hell of a competitor and a tough son-of-a-gun to put out of action."

As Esposito spoke, his hands still shook as he unlaced his goaltending equipment. Despite his success, the Chicago goalie is a jittery, nervous man, who cannot conceal the tension and pressure that goes with the most demanding job in sports.

"The mental strain is always there," he said of goaltending. "I go into some games so shook up that it's almost unbearable. There are other goaltenders with different temperaments who don't get half as shaky. They are the lucky ones."

Goalies have one thing in common: to stop the small, hard rubber puck shot at them at terrifying speeds without being injured or maimed for life. When their team wins, the goalie often is taken for granted and the goal-scoring forwards and defensemen receive the most credit. When their team loses, it is the goalie who is blamed for the defeat because he did not stop the puck from entering the goal cage.

Many goalies have suffered nervous breakdowns from the pressure of their profession and have been driven out of the game. Some are blithe spirits. Others are men who become moody and experience deep depressions. Roger Crozier of

Buffalo has suffered from ulcers and undergone surgery for pancreatitis as a result of being a goalie. Glenn Hall, one of the greatest goalies in the history of the game, often became sick and threw up before games.

"Goaltending can be hell," Jacques Plante once said. "How would you like it if every time you made a mistake in your job, someone turned on a red light so 20,000 people knew you had made a mistake and could criticize you?"

"The goaltender has the most nagging mental pressure of all the positions in hockey. The other guys can let off steam by banging into people or rushing up and down the ice. The goaltender just stands there and must stop pucks shot at speeds of 125 mph with his body," said Gerry Cheevers, a former Boston goalie now playing for the Cleveland Crusaders of the World Hockey Association.

When Crozier temporarily retired from hockey in 1967, he said his nerves were at the breaking point. "I'll be in a nut house in three weeks if I continue. If I had some other way to make a living, there's no way I would be a goalie."

During the 1975 Stanley Cup playoff final against the Philadelphia Flyers, Buffalo's Gerry Desjardins said: "We all must be crazy to be goaltenders. If I could go back and start my career over again, I'd never be a goalie. I'd be a forward or a defenseman, or I wouldn't play hockey at all."

Desjardins's arm bears a jagged scar from the shoulder to the elbow. Twice he broke the arm in collisions with the metal goal post while defending the net.

"Sometimes when I am asleep at night in bed with my wife, I wake up in a cold sweat and I am kicking my legs," said Gilles Meloche of the California Seals. "My wife asks me what's wrong and I tell her, 'Don't worry. I'm just stopping pucks in my sleep.'"

Emile Francis, a former goaltender, described goaltending this way: "When most players make a mistake, they can slink back to the bench and hang their heads in shame. But not the goalkeeper. He has no place to hide. If he makes a mistake, he has to stand there in front of his net and take it. It's a tough way to make a living."

No one knew that better than Eddie Giacomin on the night that Bobby Hull's skate ripped open a gash in his hand.

Few expected Eddie to show up for practice the next morning. But he was there. And he grew irritated when his teammates flipped soft, easy shots at him in shooting drills because they were concerned about his injured hand.

"Damn it. Come on, you guys," Eddie barked from behind his mask. "What are you waiting for? Let's see some real shots, eh?"

He had spent a sleepless night in his hotel room after the game, soaking his throbbing hand in ice water. Few thought he would play in the second Playoff's game, but he did. Even though his hand still hurt and the wound had become infected.

After Sunday night in Chicago, when Hull's skate tore open Giacomin's hand, Francis stood in the dimly lighted corridor outside the Rangers' dressing room and took a long drag on his Lucky Strike.

"Eddie Giacomin is the most determined man I ever saw," said the coach. "He's had to work hard for anything he ever got. He wasn't born with a silver spoon in his mouth. This was his finest hour."

The coach ground out the stub of his cigarette on the cement floor and smiled. "But if you know Eddie Giacomin's background, you wouldn't be so surprised by what you saw him do here tonight."

Chapter 2

Growing Up in Sudbury and the "Midnight" League

"SORRY, SON. WE CAN'T USE YOU."

EDDIE Giacomin relaxed in a chair by the window in an Atlanta hotel room and propped his feet on the table. Outside the afternoon sun was bright and warm. He could look down from the fourteenth floor and see the people on the busy streets and sidewalks below.

He had gone to Mass earlier in the day and then to the 11 A.M. team meeting and practice. At 1 P.M. he and his teammates ate their pregame steak in one of the hotel's private dining rooms. Eddie went for a stroll in the balmy spring weather and then returned to his room for a nap.

In a few hours he would stop in the hotel coffee shop for a light snack with roommate Walt Tkaczuk and then board the team bus and go to the Omni and play goal for the Rangers against the Atlanta Flames.

He was offered a beer but he politely declined. "I'd love a beer but not before I play. After the game, it'll be different," he said with a smile creasing his face.

He looked out the window at the people passing by below. "Did you ever look at people in a crowd and wonder who they are and what they do and where they came from or how their backgrounds made them what they are?" he wondered out loud.

Eddie came from Sudbury, an industrial city of factories and hard-working, middle-class people, located in the mining region of northern Ontario. His upbringing and his family background made him what he is today.

"My parents came over to Canada from the old country looking for a better life, and they found it through hard work," said Eddie.

Generation after generation of the Giacomins had eked out a living on land worn from centuries of tilling in a small village in northern Italy near the Yugoslavian border.

Tony Giacomin emigrated to Sudbury and got a job as a construction worker in the Depression years. Life was hard and he did not make much money, but he worked hard and became a foreman at his plant in nearby Gatchell, Ontario. His wife, Cecile, gave birth to five children. Their first was a boy whom they called Jiggs. Next born was Rollie. Eddie was born June 6, 1939, and then Tony and Cecile Giacomin became the parents of two daughters, Gloria and Ida.

Tony Giacomin was a big man in many ways. He weighed almost 260 pounds. He raised his children in the tradition of the old country and taught them to appreciate the life they had and to work hard. He was strict. He believed in discipline. He believed nothing worthwhile in life came easily or without hard work and sacrifice. He commanded respect from his sons and saw to it that Eddie and his brothers and sisters shared family responsibilities and went to church and to school without fail.

"My father worked hard, real hard, all his life, and I feel fortunate that I grew up with the kind of background I had.

We never had much money, but we had a lot of pride and love in our family," said Eddie.

Al Arbour also grew up in Sudbury. Although he was seven years older than Eddie, he knew the Giacomin family.

"Sudbury was a mining town, a factory town of about 50,000 people in those days," said the man who became coach of the New York Islanders. "They were honest, hard-working people who lived there. It was a very sports-oriented town. Sports were really the only outlet or relaxation and enjoyment in Sudbury."

Jiggs was eleven years older than Eddie. Rollie was six years older than his younger brother. Jiggs and Rollie both gravitated toward sports and became outstanding athletes in school and with local football, baseball, and hockey teams.

"Everybody in Sudbury knew the Giacomin boys," said Arbour. "If there was a game going on somewhere, they'd be in it."

As the little brother, Eddie idolized his older brothers. He always tried to follow in their footsteps. He had a special fondness for Rollie, because he was the goaltender on a local team and later played for the Montreal Royals and Sudbury Wolves of the Eastern Professional League and had a chance to sign with the Montreal Canadiens of the National Hockey League.

"Rollie was a great goalie and he could have made it as a pro, but he had a job in the plant and a family to support," said Eddie.

Rollie used to take Eddie along with him on road trips and the younger boy would watch in awe as his brother played goalie.

"I remember watching Rollie play and how much I admired him," said Eddie. "I wanted to be a goalie, just like he was. The teams he played with weren't always very good and he had to work hard and make a lot of saves. I remember the applause he got. Most of the kids I knew wanted to be forwards so they could score goals. Playing forward was more fun and most kids didn't want any part of being a goalie. But being a goaltender was what I wanted. You always seemed to be the key man. You were always in the action, always in the game. I liked that."

There was not enough money for Eddie to buy his own goalie's equipment, but there was always goaltending equipment around the house because of Rollie.

"Whenever Rollie couldn't find his goalie equipment, he knew where to look; I had it," said Eddie, laughing.

Eddie first put on a pair of his brother's old, discarded skates when he was about five years old. In Canada, boys often learn to skate before they walk or learn to ride a bicycle.

"I was the world's worst skater," said Eddie. "When I was small, I'd go to where the older kids were playing hockey and just hang around and watch. If one side needed a goalie, I'd volunteer. Sometimes the older kids let me play just to get me out of the way."

Eddie laughed. "I was a hockey nut by the time I was ten years old. My mind wasn't set on school, the way it should have been, because all I could think about was playing hockey."

Eddie and several of his friends formed their own six-team National Hockey League with a ball-bearing hockey game and fantasized that they were the Montreal Canadiens, Toronto Maple Leafs, Detroit Red Wings, Chicago Black Hawks, Boston Bruins, or New York Rangers in after-school or weekend games in Eddie's house or in his back yard.

"All we talked about was hockey," said Eddie. "I made my own rink on the empty lot next to our house on Morrison Avenue."

The empty lot became a beehive of sports activity for Eddie and his friends. They played sports in the lot after school until it was dark and on the weekends and throughout the summer.

"We played what the kids today call street hockey, but we called it foot hockey," said Eddie.

In the summer Eddie and his friends spent most of their time in the empty lot playing baseball. Hardball or softball; it didn't matter.

"My father had a garage at the end of the lot and we painted lines on it," said Eddie. "You had to hit one line for a single, another for a double, another for a triple, and another for a home run." One of Eddie's closest boyhood friends, who was always in the lot, playing baseball or hockey, was Norm Clement.

"He became a priest. Now he's the assistant bishop in North Bay," said Eddie.

"It probably sounds corny, but I grew up sleeping, eating, and dreaming hockey," said Giacomin, smiling. "It was always my hope, my big dream, that I'd be able to make it to the National Hockey League some day."

On Saturday nights after supper, Rollie and Eddie would go into their room and turn on the radio to listen to the broadcast of the Toronto Maple Leafs' games.

"That was one of my greatest thrills and nicest memories as a kid," said Eddie.

"They had this announcer on the CBC. His name was Foster Hewitt. To kids in Canada, he was like Mel Allen or Red Barber were to Yankee or Dodger fans in the United States. We'd turn on the radio and wait to hear him say, 'Good evening, hockey fans across Canada, this is Foster Hewitt speaking to you from the gondola high above Maple Leaf Gardens. . . .' "

In his own mind, Eddie became Turk Broda, Bill Durnan, or Chuck Rayner playing goal in Maple Leaf Gardens.

"When he said that, it always sent a chill up and down my spine," said Eddie. "Me and my brother just sat there, not saying a word, trying to imagine what it was like playing there. Playing for the Maple Leafs. Being in goal."

Eddie attended Our Lady of Perpetual Help, a parochial grammar school now named St. Anthony's. He attended Our Lady of Perpetual Help Church and became an altar boy.

"Our priest was Father Brennan. He's still there. I don't think I was ever one of his favorite altar boys," said Eddie.

When Eddie was twelve years old he got what he calls "one of my thousands of jobs to try to earn money." He worked at Cecutti's Bakery and the owner of the bakery, Cookie Venderman, took Eddie along as his helper when he made deliveries in his truck to customers.

"I learned to drive when I was twelve or thirteen," he said. "Cookie let me drive his truck down the street when he was making a delivery, but I made sure I never took the truck out of first gear."

When he was fourteen, Eddie joined a midget-league hockey team in Sudbury. He borrowed Rollie's equipment so he could play goalie, but the team already had a good goal-tender so Eddie often played on the forward line.

"I scored four goals in one game as a left wing but I couldn't wait until they put me back in goal," he said.

When he was sixteen, Eddie got a chauffeur's license and drove a five-ton gravel truck.

"I'd drive ten to sixteen hours a day just so I could make more money," he said.

In Canada the best teen-aged hockey players joined the burgeoning web of junior teams that were sponsored by National Hockey League teams and spread across the country into almost every city and town. Junior hockey resembled a minor-league baseball farm system in the United States, only junior hockey players in Canada technically were amateurs.

Teams were classified as either Junior A or Junior B. The best players played in Junior A. The less skilled had to be content to play in Junior B and hope they might improve enough to make Junior A. It was the only route to becoming a professional hockey player, and if they were lucky, eventually reaching the National Hockey League.

There was no chance for a boy who was not considered good enough to play Junior Hockey to become a pro.

Eddie was playing with local teams in Sudbury. He was small in size but big in heart, and he wanted to play Junior Hockey. Even the local teams he played with had sponsorship affiliation with an NHL team. The Detroit Red Wings were the NHL team that had first claim to Eddie.

In the fall of 1954, when he was fifteen, Eddie went to a Detroit junior-tryout camp in Michigan. There he met Terry Sawchuk, who twice had won the Vezina Trophy as the National Hockey League's leading goaltender. He also met Gordie Howe, the Red Wings' great star.

"It was an ego trip for me just to be there," said Eddie. "It gave me my first big thrill; I played Ping-Pong with Gordie Howe."

The thrill didn't last long. A man from the Detroit organization called Eddie aside and told him he might as well go back home to Sudbury.

"He told me I just wasn't good enough to play junior hockey and that I'd never make it. He said I should forget about being a goalie," said Giacomin.

Eddie was crestfallen. Gordie Howe could have helped console him if only he had known. The brawny right wing who became the highest scorer in hockey history went to a New York Ranger tryout camp as a boy and was told he would never make it, either.

The Rangers learned in later years that they had made a grave mistake in misjudging Howe. The Red Wings would learn they were making a mistake in rejecting Eddie Giacomin.

Eddie went back to Sudbury. He worked as a mechanic's helper in an acid plant. He worked as an electrician's apprentice.

His father told him, "Forget about playing hockey and stick to school and your job." Big Tony Giacomin didn't know it but his son Rollie was telling Eddie just the opposite.

"My father never pushed me into doing anything, but he was from the old country and he believed in hard work," said Eddie. "He thought getting a job and working hard and going to school and studying were all I should be doing. He couldn't see the game of hockey. He couldn't understand how you could make a living playing hockey. He wanted me to give up my idea of becoming a hockey player."

Tony Giacomin had good reason for that. All he knew was that his eldest son, Jiggs, had come home three times with broken collarbones from playing hockey.

"Rollie wouldn't let me quit playing goalie," said Eddie. "He pushed me. He told me I could make it. He really encouraged and influenced me. I learned to play goal by watching him."

So Eddie kept on going to school and working—and playing hockey. He played goalie for a Detroit-sponsored team in the Sudbury Juvenile League. The team had an unusual name, John Baby's. The coach, John Baby, was a stocky man from Sudbury, who had been a pro defenseman in the American, Pacific Coast, and United States hockey leagues.

Eddie was eighteen when a local hockey scout told him that the Detroit Red Wings were conducting tryouts in Hamilton for the Junior A Hamilton Red Wings of the Ontario Junior Hockey Association. John Baby drove Eddie from Sudbury to Hamilton but had to return to his job.

"I had a strike against me already," said Eddie. "All the kids who came to try out for the team had their coach or the men who had scouted them along with them to push for them. I was by myself. The guy who scouted me wasn't there. I had no one to push for me or see that I got a fair chance to make the team."

Giacomin realized he was competing against heavy odds. Most of the candidates for the Hamilton Red Wings had already played some form of Junior Hockey. They were far more experienced than Eddie. They had the benefit of better training, as well as having played against stronger competition in their formative years.

Playing in local leagues in Sudbury hardly qualified Eddie to compete against better trained players. But he worked hard and thought he was doing well.

The Hamilton Red Wings had two goaltenders whom they prized. One was Carl Wetzel, a Detroit-born boy. The Detroit Red Wings hoped he someday would play in the NHL in the city in which he was born. The other goalie was sixteen-year-old Dennis Jordan. He was highly publicized and also was a cinch to make the team.

Eddie got bad news one day. "Sorry, son," said a man named Johnny Mitchell from the Detroit Red Wings' organization. "We can't use you. If you've got a job back home, I think you better stick to it and forget about being a goalie."

The words hurt.

"They had eleven goalies at their tryout camp, and I was the third last to be cut and told to go home," said Giacomin. "They had to keep Wetzel because he was from Detroit and I knew they wanted to keep Jordan as soon as I got to camp."

Jordan never reached the National Hockey League. Wetzel played one game with Detroit in 1965 and had an 8.00 goals-against average and played five games with the Minnesota North Stars in 1968 and had a 4.00 average.

By then Eddie Giacomin already had been an NHL All Star and played in the Stanley Cup playoffs.

But on that day in Hamilton, when he was told for the second time in his life that he would never make it as a goalie, Eddie felt as though he never would achieve his aim.

He returned to Sudbury to his job and decided that if the Detroit Red Wings had no use for him in their organization, he wanted to be free of them. Under existing rules, he had to sit out one year and not play for a sponsored team to become a free agent.

"I played in what you might call an 'outlaw' league," he said.

The league in which he would play the next three years was the Sudbury Commercial League. It was the kind of league known throughout the United States as the "industrial" league, a "recreation" league, or, to some, a "bar" league, which is a team sponsored by a bar, business, or fraternal group.

In Canada it was known as the "midnight" league.

Every Canadian city or town had its midnight league. It was the last and loneliest refuge for local hockey players who were not considered good enough for Junior Hockey. The men and boys who played hockey in the midnight leagues did so only for recreation or because they loved to play the game. They had no place in Junior Hockey and no future as pros.

"Stick to your job at the plant. You got two years' seniority," Tony Giacomin told his son.

Eddie stuck to his job at the plant, but he also played in the Sudbury Commercial League after work, tending goal for the Bell Telephone Company team.

"I had to pay to play hockey while others got paid to play," he said.

The midnight league was aptly named. Because at midnight the games still could be going on.

"We had to buy our own sweaters to play on the team, and each guy had to chip in two or three bucks so we could use the ice for games," said Eddie. "We had to scrape the ice ourselves before the game and nobody ever came to see us play. People were all home in bed asleep when we were playing hockey."

Games usually started at 9 p.m. Teams scheduled to play then were more fortunate than those whose games started at eleven o'clock or midnight and ended as late as 1 or 2 a.m. the next morning.

"Guys would finish their shift work at the plants, grab a quick bite to eat, put on their makeshift uniforms, and drive to the rink to play hockey," said Giacomin.

Hockey was not the only sport in Eddie's life.

He excelled in football and baseball and played on the semipro level when he was seventeen. He was an outstanding quarterback for the Sudbury Hardrocks in the fall and an outfielder who batted .400 and ran the bases with speed and hustle for the Copper Cliff Redmen. His brothers before him had been good athletes in all sports, and Eddie was following in their footsteps.

"Eddie was a hell of a quarterback," said Al Arbour. "He could throw the football. He played in a fast semipro league when he was just a kid of seventeen. Most of the guys he played against were bigger and older, and a few of them had played in the Canadian Football League."

In baseball, Giacomin's hitting, fielding, and running were considered good enough for a St. Louis Cardinals' scout to express interest. Eddie never followed it up. He still wanted to be a goalie.

Cam Church coached the Sudbury Hardrocks. He offered Eddie a football scholarship to attend San Fernando College, a small institution in California. All Eddie had to do was go back to high school for another year.

"I had hockey on my mind more than school," he said. "Besides, I didn't think I was big enough to play college football."

So he turned down the chance for a football scholarship and kept hoping he would get a chance to play hockey.

Hockey, however, was not the only interest in Eddie's life. There was a pretty blond girl in town. He had known her since he was in school. Her name was Margaret Wilder, but her friends called her Marg.

"She went to Sudbury High School when I went to Sudbury Tech. I knew who she was but that was about all. I was working at Canadian Industries when a friend of mine named Bill Dorosh, who lived down the street, asked me to double-date with him and the girl he was going out with," said Eddie.

Marg Wilder was Eddie's date. They were married in their hometown on June 16, 1962, in Our Lady of Perpetual Help Church after Eddie finally became a pro goalie with Providence.

But at the time of his first date with Marg, Eddie was still playing hockey at midnight in the industrial league. He had almost reached the point where he was seriously beginning to wonder if he was wasting his time trying to become a professional goaltender.

Chapter 3

A Telephone Call from Washington

"ARE YOU ROLLIE GIACOMIN?"

WINTER in Sudbury. Outside the wind whipped through the city and the March air was cold. The atmosphere was heavy with sulphur fumes from the factories. Inside the house on Morrison Avenue, it was warm and comfortable and the supper dishes had been cleared from the table.

The break for which Eddie was waiting came when the telephone rang. Leo Gasparini was calling. He wanted to speak with Rollie Giacomin.

"Rollie. This is Leo. They need a goalie down in Washington for a couple of weeks. Can you make it?" he asked.

"I can't go, Leo," said Rollie. "I'm on shift work at the plant and I already took holiday time off. My boss won't give me any more time off. But hold the line. I think I can help you out."

Rollie cupped his hand over the phone and called his brother. "Eddie, they need a goalie in Washington. I can't take off from work. I'll tell them you'll go, O.K.?" Rollie said to his younger brother.

Gasparini was a well-known sports figure in Sudbury. He coached the Falconbridge Hockey Club and he knew Big Tony Giacomin and his three boys, Jiggs, Rollie, and Eddie. When someone needed a hockey player they called Leo Gasparini. He knew the kids in town and he always managed to come up with someone when a team needed a player. He knew Rollie Giacomin had experience and was the practice goalie for the Sudbury Wolves.

The Washington Presidents of the Eastern League had only eight games left in their 1958–59 schedule. They had gone through eight goaltenders that season. Don "Bibber" O'Hearn was the only goalie they had left and he had gone home to Niagara Falls.

Andy Branigan, the Washington coach, was desperate. He had phoned Gasparini in the afternoon to ask for help. "You know any goalies around Sudbury who can come down to Washington?" he asked.

"Yeah. The Giacomin boys. One of them's nineteen, the other's twenty-six," said Gasparini.

"We want the one who's twenty-six and has some experience," said Branigan.

Rollie still had his hand over the phone and was trying to convince Eddie to go to Washington. Leo Gasparini was getting impatient.

"Eddie. I'm telling you. Go," said Rollie. "It's the chance you've been waiting for. Don't blow it. You can do the job. It's only for a couple of weeks."

At first Eddie was hesitant. Twice he had been rejected when he tried out for the Junior A team. Twice he had been told he was wasting his time and would never make it as a goalie. He did not want to be hurt again. He had a job at the plant. He could play hockey in the midnight industrial leagues without fear of being told he was not good enough.

Rollie would not let him refuse the opportunity that was waiting. He convinced his brother to go.

"Leo's waiting. I've got to give him an answer now," said Rollie.

"O.K., I'll go if you say so," said Eddie.

"Hey, Leo. Tell them they've got a goalie. Eddie will go," Rollie told Gasparini.

Eddie was nervous. He did not know what to expect. He had never been to the United States. He had never flown before. He was in the airport in Toronto. He was nineteen years old. And he was scared.

When he arrived in Washington, he hailed a cab. "I want to go to the hockey arena," he told the driver.

"Which hockey arena?" asked the driver.

Eddie did not know there were two hockey arenas in the city. "The arena where the Washington Presidents play," he told the driver.

Purely by luck the driver knew the Presidents played at the old Uline Ice Arena on Third and M Streets in northeast Washington.

"The arena was in a really bad part of the city. A high-crime area, I guess you'd call it," said Giacomin.

So at three o'clock in the afternoon Eddie stepped out of a taxi and walked through the front door of the arena.

"There I was with my goalie stick, my hockey bag, and a clothes bag," he said. "There was no one around."

Finally he saw a face at a ticket window. "Are you Rollie Giacomin?" the man asked Eddie.

"Not really, but I'm his brother," replied Eddie.

The man at the ticket window looked Eddie up and down. He did not seem impressed. Eddie asked where the team was.

"They're in Johnstown, Pennsylvania. Won't be back until tomorrow," he was told.

The man at the ticket window told Eddie to leave his gear

in the dressing room and report back to the rink tomorrow. He suggested he try to get a room at the Dodge Hotel.

"There I was, not a penny of U.S. money to my name and scared out of my boots," said Eddie.

He got a room on the twelfth floor of the hotel and sat down to look out the window. He could see the Capitol Building. But his mind was not on United States history. It was on food.

"I was hungry as hell," he said.

If it had not been for a sympathetic hotel desk clerk, the young goalie might have sat in his room all night and listened to his stomach grumble.

"The desk clerk knew a restaurant where some of the hockey players ate and referred me to that," said Eddie.

Giacomin telephoned Branigan the next day. He didn't say he was Rollie Giacomin and he didn't say he was Eddie Giacomin. The coach told him to report to the arena for practice.

Branigan was a veteran defenseman of the minor-league hockey wars and had played briefly with the old New York Americans in the National Hockey League. He was a no-nonsense guy. He was anxious for his new goalie to arrive. He had been told by Leo Gasparini that Rollie Giacomin was twenty-six years old and a rugged 200-pounder.

The coach got the shock of his life when he saw Eddie. "Who are you?" he barked at Eddie.

"I'm Eddie Giacomin. I'm Rollie's brother. He couldn't come so I took his place," Eddie said sheepishly.

Branigan stared at Eddie. At first he seemed too startled to speak. "I was expecting a bigger guy," he said, frowning.

"Yes, sir," said Eddie, who was a skinny 140 pounds.

"How old are you?" asked Branigan.

"Nineteen," said Eddie.

"I was expecting an older guy, too," said the coach.

Branigan was in a quandary. Bibber O'Hearn was in Niagara Falls. The Presidents needed to win six of their last eight games to make the playoffs. He was unimpressed by Giacomin's appearance. He decided to find another spare goaltender and hope Bibber O'Hearn showed up again quickly.

The Presidents were a team of hard-boiled, hard-living veterans, most of them in their thirties. To them Eddie was an oddity, a fresh-faced nineteen-year-old kid.

The veterans wasted no time taking advantage of Eddie. They made him their "gopher."

"I became their errand boy," said Eddie. "It was 'go for this,' 'go for that.'"

The veterans liked to gather for nightly card games in the hotel rooms or apartments they shared. They asked Eddie to tag along—for a purpose.

"They'd have these twenty-four-hour card games that would never end," said the nervous rookie. "I don't know how they could drink and play cards all night and still play hockey. They made me their messenger boy. I was afraid to move. They'd keep me up with them all night. They had me tending bar for them, running out to get them cigars and sandwiches, and cooking pots of chili."

The old gunfighters on the team could take the late hours and hard drinking. The kid goalie from Sudbury could not.

"I'd be dead at practice the next day," he said.

Finally the veterans grew fond of Eddie and let up on him. Lloyd Hinchberger and Moose Lallo, a big, tough defenseman, took the kid under their wings.

The Presidents, meanwhile, had been eliminated from playoff contention. Eddie had worked hard in practice. He was a likeable young guy. His attitude was good. Bibber O'Hearn still had not rejoined the team.

There were only four games left in the season. Branigan had nothing to lose. He decided to give Eddie a chance to play a game. He owed that much to Leo Gasparini for sending the kid down. And why not? He was curious to see how the skinny kid from Sudbury would hold up under fire.

They did not concentrate on defense in the Eastern League. It was a scorer's league and that made it especially difficult for the goaltenders. Fifty-shot games were common. So were brawls and fights. The league was struggling to make a buck and the few fans who showed up for games liked to see fights and high-scoring games.

Eddie knew he could not count upon much support from his defensemen or much backchecking from the forwards. He had heard the players talking. Many of them were closing in on 20-goal seasons in the final few days of the schedule. They would be looking to score goals, not prevent them, in the final four games of the season.

Giacomin was nervous as he put on his equipment and green-gold-and-white Washington Presidents' uniform in Uline Arena's dingy dressing room before playing his first game.

"I wasn't just nervous. I was scared as hell," he said.

He won his first game, 5-1. He played so well that Branigan decided to let him play the next game. He won that game, too, 8-6. Bibber O'Hearn still was missing. So Branigan let Eddie play the last two games of the season. He won them both.

Now his two-week season was over. He had played four games and won them all. He had allowed only thirteen goals. He was glad Rollie convinced him to go to Washington to play goal.

"If it hadn't been for my brother, I never would have gone," said Eddie. "He's the one who gave me the chance. He's the one who said I should go. He was always the one encouraging me to stick with hockey and not give up even when it seemed hopeless."

Branigan told Eddie he was pleased with the way he had

played. He didn't make any promises but he told Eddie to keep in touch and to stay in shape during the summer. Eddie had the feeling there might be a place for him in hockey after all.

For a change, someone was telling Eddie that he had a future as a goalie instead of telling him, "Forget it, kid, go back to your job in Sudbury." It was a nice feeling.

Giacomin did not know it at the time, but Lou Pieri and Terry Reardon had driven down from Providence to watch two of the games he played in Washington. Pieri owned the Providence Reds of the American League and Reardon was his general manager. The Reds had a working agreement with the Washington Presidents and the owner and the general manager were trying to line up players for next season. They were looking for a young goaltender who was willing to start his apprenticeship at the bottom and work his way up.

Eddie would be hearing from the Providence Reds before the summer was over.

He would also be in a hospital bed, in terrible pain, hearing a doctor say he would never play hockey again.

At three o'clock on a morning in May of 1959, a fire was raging in the kitchen of the house in which Eddie and his parents and brothers and sisters lived in Sudbury.

Ida Giacomin was the first to awaken and smell the smoke. Eddie's younger sister was terrified. But without hesitation she ran through the flames and thick black smoke to awaken her brothers, who shared the bedroom next to the kitchen.

Rollie Giacomin leaped from his bed in a flash and Eddie, clad in his shorts, was right behind him. The smoke made their eyes sting and water and made them cough. They could feel the intense heat and see the ugly orange flames across the hall in the kitchen.

A deep fry-pan, filled with cooking grease, had been left

sitting on a burner of the electric stove. The burner had not been turned off, and since the red warning light on the stove was burned out, the family had gone to bed without knowledge of the danger in their kitchen.

"The grease in the big pot on the stove got so hot it exploded," said Eddie. "The curtains caught fire and then the whole kitchen was in flames. The house could have burned up if my sister hadn't awakened in her bedroom and smelled the smoke."

Eddie's brother was the first to reach the inferno in the kitchen. He grabbed the red-hot fry-pan, but the heat so severely burned his hands that he quickly dropped it.

Eddie, who was right behind Rollie, could not see what his brother was doing because of the smoke.

The hot, burning grease spilled down Eddie's legs, and he screamed out in pain.

"I set the world's high-jump record the minute the hot grease hit me," he said. "I can't remember anything but the pain. Terrible pain. Like it had ripped the skin right off my legs down to the raw bone. I never felt anything so bad in my life. All I could do was scream."

Eddie's first reaction was to run outside the house. By now his father had torn down the burning curtains, stomping the fire out on the kitchen floor with his feet.

"I just sat there on the porch steps with my legs burning, feeling like they were on fire, and kept screaming," said Eddie. "Rollie was there next to me. His hands were burned pretty bad. All I remember is him putting on my pants, throwing me into the car, and driving four miles to the hospital emergency room."

In the hospital they had to cut the trousers from Eddie's burned legs.

"That hurt even worse," he said. "When they cut the pants off, a lot of my skin came off with them because all the grease that burned me made my pants stick to my legs. The smell of my own burning flesh was awful. It stank. It made me sick."

Giacomin, only a few weeks from his twentieth birthday, was worried about his father.

"My father put out the fire with his bare hands, and they got pretty badly burned," he said. "But do you know, he was at work the next morning. He's a strong-willed man. He worked hard all his life and he didn't believe a man should miss a day on the job."

The diagnosis on Eddie was not good: first-degree burns on his left leg, hip, and buttocks. Second-degree burns on his right ankle. He spent one month in a hospital bed and then had to undergo therapy for his burned legs. The pain of healing was only slightly less than that of being burned. Worse yet, doctors feared he would need skin grafting on his legs.

"They had to keep sticking needles in my legs to kill the pain. I knew that if they had to do a skin graft, it would be impossible for me to play hockey or any other sport again. I began to wonder if I'd ever walk again," said Eddie.

The treatment for the burns was as distasteful as it was painful.

"They had to take off the dead skin that was so badly burned, and it left my legs raw," said Eddie. When he was able to leave his hospital bed, Giacomin was told to sit in the sun and expose his burned legs to the air.

Hospitalization and burn treatment created a period of both mental and physical torture for Giacomin. He finally had been given a chance as a minor-league goaltender with the Eastern League Presidents only a few months ago. He had succeeded in playing well. Now he wondered if his career was over.

The doctors who visited him daily were not optimistic. "You'll be O.K., but, of course, you won't be able to play sports anymore," the doctor told Eddie one day.

"My heart sank when I heard him say that. Until then I was trying to keep up my hope and my confidence, but after that I figured I'd never play hockey again," he said.

Eddie experienced a period of deep depression and self-pity following what the doctors told him. Then one day a letter came from Providence. The Providence Reds were inviting Giacomin to their training camp in September. They were offering him a job to play hockey. They offered him a $500 bonus to sign a contract with them.

"Things weren't going well, and I was feeling pretty depressed until that letter came to me in the hospital," said Giacomin. "The news that they wanted me to come to training camp picked me up right away. I felt great."

The feeling vanished almost as quickly as it had come. Eddie looked at his burned legs and felt the pain in them.

"The chance of a lifetime for me and look at where I am," he said. "The tears rolled out of my eyes and down my face."

Then one day a nurse wheeled another patient into Eddie's room. He was a boy, about eight years old, with a cheerful kind of smile.

"The poor little guy. His whole back was burned when an oil burner blew up, and he had to lie on his stomach," said Giacomin.

Eddie and the boy became friends. He visited Eddie in his room almost daily and when Giacomin was permitted to walk, he visited the boy in his room.

"My whole outlook suddenly changed because of that boy," said Eddie. "I was feeling sorry for myself until I met him and then I looked at him. I thought to myself: 'I'm nothing compared to him. He's worse off than I am. I should be walking out of here.'"

Eddie's voice grew somber as he spoke of the badly burned boy. "I made it out but the kid never did."

"Before I saw that kid, I was feeling sorry for myself,

thinking, 'why me?' " said Giacomin. "Maybe it sounds corny but it's true: if it hadn't happened, if I had not seen that little boy, I probably would not have found the determination or the inner strength I needed to go on. Seeing him made me realize that I wasn't so bad off, after all."

The doctors still told Eddie that he should forget about playing any sports. They told him he must wear bandages on his burned legs for a year.

"I was determined I was going to go to training camp," said Eddie. "But once again someone was telling me I'd never make it. In my own mind, I knew I had to give hockey another try."

By the end of summer Eddie was playing baseball. By September he was playing football. By the end of the month he was preparing to go to the Providence Reds' training camp.

Chapter **4**

Life in the Eastern League: It Was a Tough Place to Play

"YOU HAD TO LOVE THE GAME."

EDDIE had to make certain he always arrived at the rink before the other players when he reported to the Providence Reds' training camp for the 1959–60 season.

The Providence team did not know of the severe burns the twenty-year-old goaltender had suffered on his legs, ankles, and buttocks less than six months ago in the kitchen fire in his home. Nor did they know he had spent most of the summer in the hospital and was told he should not play hockey.

"I had to keep it hushed up," said Eddie. "I didn't want it to ruin my chances of playing hockey."

Giacomin's burned legs were healing slowly and surely, but they still were scarred and tender and caused him considerable pain.

"I wore Ace bandages on my legs when I went to training camp, but they weren't enough to stop the bleeding," said Eddie. "I'd get to the rink early, slip out of my clothes, and sneak into my long underwear to cover up the bandages that were full of blood."

Eddie had toughened up his legs by running and playing baseball and football in the last weeks of summer in Sudbury before going to training camp. Sometimes the pain from the burns was almost unbearable. But he refused to give up. He was not certain himself if he could play hockey, but he had to find out for himself and take advantage of the chance given him.

He was scared at training camp that the coach would discover his burned legs and send him home. Blood kept seeping through his bandages and the ice-level temperature felt as though it were twenty degrees below zero.

"My feet would get so cold that I'd have to take handfuls of snow from the ice and throw it on my toes to thaw them out after practice," said Eddie.

"If the people in Providence ever knew what my legs were like in the first place, they would have told me to forget about coming to training camp," he said.

Giacomin did not make the team in Providence. He lacked experience and was not yet ready for the fast competition in the American League. But his willingness to work left a lasting impression with Terry Reardon, the general manager, and Phil Watson, the coach.

The only question was: Where would Eddie play?

The Reds had a working agreement with the New York Rovers of the Eastern League, but, at the moment, the Rovers did not need a goaltender. Nor did the Washington Presidents, the team Eddie had first played with last season impersonating his brother, because it had folded temporarily.

"Providence didn't know what to do with me," said Giacomin. "They tried to find me a job playing goal somewhere, so they called Johnstown to try to find a place for me."

The Johnstown Jets were in the Eastern League. They played in a town in Pennsylvania made famous by a big flood. Steve Brklacich, the player-coach, said, "Sure, send the kid down and we'll look at him."

Eddie took a bus to Johnstown. He did not stay there long.

"Eddie looked pretty good and we were ready to sign him, but then we got the word that Eddie Johnston had just been reinstated as an amateur," said Brklacich. "Johnston had been a pro and had a lot more experience as a goalie than Giacomin."

Giacomin was told to report to the Johnstown Jets' general manager's office at 5 P.M. He thought he was going to be offered a chance to play for the team. The ironic twist was that Johnny Mitchell was Johnstown's general manager. He was the man who had rejected Eddie when he tried out for the Hamilton Red Wings' Junior A team. Their paths would across again five years later in Providence.

Mitchell gave Giacomin the bad news: he had decided to sign Johnston as goaltender instead of Giacomin.

"Sorry, son," said Mitchell, "but here's a bus ticket back to Providence."

Giacomin was downcast. Also annoyed. It was the second time in his life he had heard the "Sorry, son" regrets from Mitchell and had been told he was unneeded and unwanted.

Eddie feared his lack of experience and background as a Junior A player as a youth in Canada were working against him. To make a bad day seem even worse, he had to wait seven hours in the terminal before he could get a bus back to Providence.

Fortunately for Eddie, Providence was finally able to find him a job as goaltender. He was sent to Commack, Long Island, to join the Rovers. Oddly, Andy Branigan, his coach in Washington, now coached the Rovers. Giacomin started off by sharing the goaltending with a veteran named George

Wood, but eventually he took over as first-string goalie.

It would have been easier for a young rookie goaltender to break in with a team such as Johnstown. The Jets won the first of their three straight league championships in 1959–60. The Rovers, meanwhile, were a dreadful last-place team. They won only nineteen of sixty-four games and their defense gave away goals as rapidly as Monte Hall dispenses prizes on television's "Let's Make a Deal" game show.

Eddie played fifty-one games, gave up 206 goals and had a 4.04 goals-against average. Somehow he managed to post three shutouts. It was not a very impressive goaltending record. But it was a start.

"That's all I wanted," said Eddie. "Just the chance to get started."

Playing in the Eastern League was an experience unlike any other. It was a throwback to the lowest level of minor-league Class D baseball in which players lived, traveled, and played the sport they loved in relative obscurity in small towns.

"Any guy who was willing to put up with life in the Eastern League really had to love the game of hockey," said John Muckler. "It was a battle for survival more than anything else."

Muckler was one of Giacomin's Rover teammates in Eddie's first season of 1959–60. He later became the Rovers' player-coach and today is the general manager and coach of the New York Rangers' Providence farm team.

"My first contact with Eddie was with the Rovers," said Muckler. "I was one of his defensemen. Maybe I shouldn't admit it. Poor Eddie. He didn't see much defense played in front of him. We were a pretty bad team and finished dead last."

In addition to the Rovers on Long Island, the Eastern League had a continually changing network of teams, stretching from Greensboro and Charlotte, North Carolina, to Washington, Philadelphia, Johnstown, Pennsylvania, New Haven, and Clinton, New York.

Officially, the Eastern League was comprised of amateurs but actually it was semipro. Most of the players earned ninety dollars a week and many of them had outside jobs. They were paid four dollars a day in meal money on the road.

"You couldn't feed a dog on that kind of money," joked Ross Brooks, a fellow goaltender who fought for survival in the league. "That stupid league. No, I shouldn't say that. The Eastern League was a great place to learn, especially for a goaltender. There was no money to speak of and the life was brutal, but it gave a heck of a lot of us, guys like Eddie and me, a chance to play. If a goalie could survive life in the Eastern League, he could survive anywhere."

Most of the players in the league were older than Giacomin. They were tough, hard-boiled men in their late twenties and thirties. No one really knew why they played. Few of them ever escaped until their legs, bodies, minds, and digestive systems wore out. Few of them ever reached the National Hockey League. They played because they were hockey players and the Eastern League gave them a chance.

Most of the teams carried only thirteen players. There were as few as three defensemen on some teams and only one goaltender. Forwards and defensemen often logged as much playing time as a goaltender. The league had a rule in which one or two of the newer goalies were designated as the league's emergency goalie. When the goalie on another team became sick, injured, or shell-shocked, they asked for the emergency or traveling goalie.

Eddie was one of the league's emergency goalies during the season. When the Clinton Comets' goaltender was injured, Giacomin was sent to Clinton as a replacement until the team's regular goalie could play again.

Clinton was a dismal town near Utica in upstate New

York. The team played in a dreary little rink with little heat and chicken wire separating spectators from the ice. Where the stands ended, the side boards began, and the platform seats directly above the boards were popular with players for one reason.

"You got a good look at girls with pretty legs," said Eddie. "It was funny how so many guys would always freeze the puck up against the boards so they could take a quick peek at the girls," he said, laughing.

As a goalie, Eddie saw more pucks than legs.

He played with Clinton for one month. He even shut out his old Rover teammates twice. Once he was hit in the face with the puck and was knocked cold.

"I woke up in a hospital the next day and had no idea about who won or lost the game or where I was," he said.

When Clinton's regular goalie recovered from his injury, the Comets said they had no more use for Giacomin. But the Rovers did. He had played well for a team with a better defense and his goals-against average reflected it. The Rovers were glad to get him back.

"I think my month in Clinton is where I started to get my goaltending together," said Eddie. "Things started to fall into place for me."

It is hard to say which was worst for the players in the league: the arenas in which they played, the lack of money, travel accommodations, or the food they ate.

"Guys playing today in the NHL can't appreciate how good they have it," said Brklacich, now the Rangers' player personnel director. "They make all that big money, fly in chartered jets, eat the best food, and live in the best hotels."

Life in the old Eastern League in no way resembled life in the major leagues.

Eastern League teams traveled on road trips in battered buses, which often broke down, or in cars owned by the players. Sometimes a player had to drive the shabby team bus. Often the players would take turns serving as the team's trainer or equipment man and had to pack the team's equipment into cars and buses for road trips.

"The teams that had station wagons or buses were the lucky ones," said Brklacich. "That way you get most of the players into a couple station wagons or one bus."

The worst part of the travel was that many of the teams in the league were located so far apart. A game in Clinton one night and a game in Charlotte the following night meant approximately 600 miles of driving with little or no sleep for the players.

"The games were mostly on weekends," said Brooks. "You might have to drive from Johnstown to Washington to play on a Friday night, then get on the bus or into cars right after the game and drive all night, get in early the next morning, and play Saturday night in Clinton. Then you'd have to do the whole thing over again: drive to Long Island and play a game Sunday afternoon."

Hotel accommodations and restaurants?

Brooks and Muckler laughed almost simultaneously.

"Some of the hotels we stayed in were so bad guys were better off sleeping on the bus or in the back of the station wagon," said Brooks.

"There was one really bad hotel, I think it was in Johnstown, where they had four beds in one room for the players," said Muckler.

Since the players usually were broke, they brought along brown bags stuffed with sandwiches and fruit to eat and drank beer while they played cards as their battered old bus bounced, rumbled, and shook across dark country roads leading from one city to another.

"There weren't that many turnpikes or super highways in those days," said Muckler. "We had to ride the backroads."

Players in the National Hockey League now have an

average salary of $75,000, eat in the finest restaurants, and receive twenty-two dollars a day meal money.

"In the Eastern League, we'd stop in the middle of the night and eat at all-night diners and hamburger joints along the highway," said Muckler.

The rinks in most Eastern League cities often resembled condemned buildings. Many were small and dingy with poor lighting and bad ice. Dressing rooms were cramped and dirty and reeked with sweat. Showers often were mildewed, and if they worked at all, it was likely the water would be cold instead of hot.

Eastern-League games generally were played before crowds of only a few hundred spectators. The fans were rabid but often drunks among the crowd made life miserable for players, especially the goaltenders, by cursing, heckling, or throwing things at them. The fans liked to see rough, tough hockey and many games erupted into brawls, either on the ice among the players or in the stands among the fans.

"You really had to love the game to play in the Eastern League," said Muckler.

Eddie Giacomin did.

But it usually seemed as though the game did not love Eddie.

"Boy, did he ever get bombed playing for us," said Muckler.

The Rovers' arena in Commack was a cement-block building that could accomodate 4,000 persons, but the team was weak and crowds often were no more than 600. The building was poorly heated and fans and players alike in Long Island Arena often felt half-frozen during a game.

"They used to flood the ice with a hose. Some nights it was like playing in a lake," said Muckler.

Eddie was too busy stopping pucks to worry about the lack of heat or watery ice in the building.

"He'd get 50 or 60, sometimes as many as 70, shots against

him a night," said Muckler. "Eddie was well coordinated, quick as a cat, and made some amazing stops purely on his reflexes, but as a goalie he was as green as grass. He was just starting out and he didn't know much about the science of being a goaltender. He liked to roam and sometimes he came as far out as the blue line to try to get the puck. He was young and inexperienced, but I could see the raw material and the dedication was there."

Typical of the traumatic life in the Eastern League was an experience that happened to Giacomin and three of his unlucky Rover teammates on a Saturday afternoon in Greensboro. The Rovers had played Friday night and then had to drive from North Carolina to Long Island for a game Sunday afternoon.

"Andy Branigan got us all together and said we'd pile into the four cars we had and stick close together for the trip to Long Island," said Eddie.

The Rovers loaded their equipment into the overstuffed cars and started out on the long trip. One of the cars never got far.

"We all pulled up to a traffic light on the outskirts of town," said Giacomin. "I smelled something burning. Then a truck pulls up alongside us and the driver yells, 'Your car's on fire.'"

The four Rovers in the burning car never moved so fast in their lives.

"We jumped the hell out of that car and put the fire out. It was in the engine and all the wires were burned out," said Eddie.

Meanwhile, the three other cars full of Rovers had pulled out when the light turned green, leaving behind one goalie, two defensemen, a forward, and one smoldering old car.

"Norm Ryder was the driver but the car belonged to Red Barrett, one of our defensemen," said Giacomin. "Red had a broken leg and couldn't play, but he did what a lot of guys in the league did: he let the team use his car for road trips so he could make some money. He had it written in his contract that he'd get mileage money when the team used his car."

Eddie and his buddies were frantic. The four of them pooled their money and came up with only eighty dollars. They couldn't get their car repaired until eleven o'clock that night and were left with only ten dollars, hardly enough money for gas.

"Everything was going smooth until we hit the New Jersey Turnpike," said Eddie. "We were pushing it pretty good; Norm must have been doing ninety miles an hour. Suddenly we hear a siren and see a flashing red light in the mirror. The state police stopped us and we got a speeding ticket."

That wasn't all of the misadventure from Greensboro to Long Island.

"The muffler fell off the car," said Eddie.

By now Eddie and his friends knew they would not reach Commack by game time. They phoned ahead.

"Andy Branigan said he wondered what the hell was taking us so long," said Eddie.

Game time on Sunday was 2 P.M. Eddie and the three other Rovers didn't arrive until 8 P.M.

"The oddity was that they held up the game, and, as tired and angry as we were, I got a shutout and we won 5-0," said Eddie.

"Another time," said Giacomin, "we were halfway to Clinton for a game, and the windshield broke and fell off our car."

"It was a crazy life in the Eastern League," said Giacomin. "We were trainers, equipment men, and drivers, as well as players. Guys took turns sharpening each other's skates. We had to lug our own equipment around, which wasn't very good anyway, and sew up our own uniforms, which were pretty ragged and tattered. There were many times I watered and scraped the ice before I played goal."

Eddie chuckled to himself. "You had to love hockey to play in the Eastern League."

While Eddie was bouncing around in the backs of old cars and station wagons and warding off 50 shots a night, the American-League season was nearing an end and the Providence Reds were preparing for the playoffs against Springfield. Their goaltender, Bruce Gamble, had played in 71 games. He was tired. The Reds decided to give him a rest in the final regular-season game.

Coach Phil Watson suggested to general manager Terry Reardon and to club owner Lou Pieri that Giacomin be recalled from the Rovers to play the final game.

On March 27, 1960, in Providence, Eddie made his professional-goaltending debut against the Buffalo Bisons. Buffalo was coached by a former Ranger, Frankie Eddolls, and in its line-up were many players with NHL experience—Wally Hergesheimer, Danny Lewicki, Pete Conacher, Phil Maloney, Billy Dea, and Howie Glover. Opposing Giacomin as Buffalo goaltender was Roy Edwards.

It was a difficult challenge for Eddie but he proved he was equal to the task. He won the game, 5–4, and in the process made 41 saves.

"I knew we'd found ourselves a pretty good-looking young goalie," said Reardon.

Chapter 5

The Years in Providence:
Fifty Shots a Night Was Common

"EDDIE WAS OUR ITALIAN HERO."

A F T E R his successful debut in the American League on the final night of the 1959–60 season, Eddie reported to the Providence Reds' training camp the following fall fully expecting to make his team.

He worked hard during the summer at his off-season job in Sudbury with the International Copper Company and kept himself in good physical condition for the hockey season ahead. He knew Phil Watson, the Reds' fiery coach, liked the way he played in his one-game trial last season. He thought his days playing in tacky arenas and traveling from town to town in cars and station wagons in the Eastern League were over.

He was wrong.

Bruce Gamble and Don Simmons, two experienced goalies, won the goalie's job in training camp, and Giacomin was sent back to the Rovers to start the 1960–61 season.

Once again Eddie faced fifty or more shots a night for the last-place Eastern-League team from Long Island.

For once, he was lucky. The ordeal of the Eastern League did not last long. The National Hockey League Boston Bruins needed goaltending help and summoned Gamble from Providence. Simmons took over the Reds' goaltending, but when he allowed fifty-one goals in ten games, Terry Reardon, the general manager, had enough and recalled Eddie from the Rovers.

The Rovers were in last place and Giacomin's goals-against average was a sorry 4.50 in twelve games. The telegram telling Eddie to join the Providence team the next night in Buffalo came after he had just lost another game in Commack. He was glad to leave the Rovers.

Giacomin said good-by to his Rover teammates and went to a Howard Johnson's restaurant in Huntington, Long Island, to eat and kill time until his 5 A.M. flight to Buffalo. He was nervous and wondered if he would make good as he drove along the deserted Grand Central Parkway to the airport with Dick Sorkin, a sports writer who covered the Rovers' games for *Newsday*.

Eddie was so excited he forgot to find out from which airport his plane would depart and he had to rush from Kennedy International Airport to LaGuardia to make his flight.

Giacomin quickly discovered a horrifying similarity between the Eastern League Rovers and the American League Providence Reds. The defense played by the Reds was almost as bad as that played by the Rovers. But at least he earned more money.

Providence finished in last place behind Springfield, Hershey, Cleveland, Buffalo, Rochester, and Quebec during Giacomin's first full pro season of 1960–61. The Reds won only twenty-six games, lost forty-six, and the 333 goals they allowed made them the worst defensive team in the American League.

Eddie took over the Red's goaltending, and although he showed flashes of brilliance and remarkably fast reflexes, he was inconsistent and unsure of himself. His big weakness was stopping long shots. His goals-against average rose like a thermometer in the Sahara to 4.26, but he did account for all but ten of the Reds' wins. Of the forty-three games in which he played, he faced thirty or more shots in twenty-six of them. He averaged thirty-six saves a game.

Once again he felt like a sitting duck in a shooting gallery. But he realized he was getting his chance as a pro goaltender.

"Phil Watson gave me my first real break by letting me play," he said of the Providence coach.

Eddie made remarkable progress as a goaltender in 1961–62, his second full season in the American League. He made greater use of the wandering style of goaltending he was forced to develop as a matter of self-preservation in the Eastern League. The Reds had purchased Gil M₁yer from Cleveland during the off-season. He stood only 5 feet 6 inches and weighed 135 pounds but had been a pro goalie for fourteen years and played for the Toronto Maple Leafs in 1949–50. He reported to training camp with an infected hand, so Eddie started the year as first-string goaltender.

When the season ended, Providence was in third place in the league's Eastern Division, and Giacomin had a 3.60 goals-against average in forty games. He also had the first two shutouts of his professional career, which was no easy feat since the American League was an offense-oriented "shooters league."

Fern Flamen was the Reds' new player-coach that season. A hard-boiled defenseman, he spent fifteen seasons in the NHL with the Bruins and had played with or against such famous goalies as Frankie Brimsek, Bill Durnan, Harry Lumley, Chuck Rayner, Sugar Jim Henry, and Terry Sawchuk.

Giacomin's new coach was considered one of the fiercest competitors and toughest fighters in hockey.

"I never saw Fernie Flamen get licked once in a fight," said Lynn Patrick, a former Ranger associated with the NHL since 1934. Bill Chadwick, the referee who became the Rangers' television commentator, also rated Flamen one of the toughest men in the game.

"The first time I saw Giacomin play, he showed promise but his ability had a lot of limitations," said Flamen, who later became hockey coach at Northeastern University.

Flamen was not quite certain if he liked Giacomin's style of leaving his net unguarded to chase pucks. Eddie often lost sight of the puck as he returned to the goal crease, a flaw resulting in occasional easy goals being made against the Reds.

"I was upset with his roaming at first," said Flamen. "I wasn't used to seeing a goaltender do that, especially on a team such as ours, which wasn't the strongest defensive club in the league."

Flamen laughed. "Eddie gave all of us quite a few scares the way he came out of the net. But he finally sold me on it. He was so good at handling his stick that he often saved us by getting the puck out of our end. I began to realize that roaming was his style and one of his biggest strengths."

Flamen liked Eddie's attitude.

"He had to work hard for everything he ever got; things never came easily for Eddie," said the coach. "I guess that was the way it had been all his life, and I think it made him a stronger, more determined person. He had a lot of weaknesses to correct and he knew it. Some guys go through life never admitting their weaknesses and so they never improve. Not Eddie. He was always the first guy out for practice and the last to leave. I don't think I ever saw a more dedicated guy more willing to work hard to overcome his weaknesses."

Like most nongoalies, Flamen was slightly wary of goaltenders.

"Goalies are a different breed; it's because the position

they play is so specialized, so different, so difficult," said Flamen. "A lot of them are loners, very moody, sensitive people."

Giacomin was not like that. He never was and he never will be.

"He's one of the boys, a good team man, and even though he didn't have the greatest defense in front of him, I never heard him complain or blame his teammates when the other team scored on him," said Flamen.

The 1962–63 season was a memorable one, both for Eddie and for the Reds.

Providence finished first in the Eastern Division, and Giacomin chopped his goals-against average in half to 2.62 in thirty-nine games, the best goaltending average in the league. Mayer started the season as the Reds' goalie but became ill in January, missed a practice, and Giacomin took over. There was no getting Eddie out of the net once he got in.

"I'll never forget one of the games he played," said Flamen. "To me, it was the best game he ever played with Providence. He ended up with a 0-0 tie against Pittsburgh, and he was just fantastic. The puck was in our end almost the whole game and they could have had ten goals easily. Eddie must have stopped forty or fifty shots that game."

Although Giacomin had the best average in the league, averaging 34.8 saves and stopping 93 percent of his shots, he neither made the All Star team nor received formal recognition for his performance. Buffalo's Denis DeJordy made the All Star team with a 2.79 average in sixty-seven games and won the Hap Holmes Trophy as the league's best goaltender. Eddie's thirty-nine games fell three short of becoming eligible for the All Star team or the goaltending award.

"But he deserved it; he was the main reason we finished first," said Flamen.

The year 1963 was one of the most beautiful in Eddie's

life. He finally established himself as a promising young goaltender with a bright future. He and his wife Marg had something else of which to be proud: they became the parents of
their first child, a son, Mark, born May 27, 1963.

Eddie's wife was always in the stands when he played. She
was composed and quiet, but inside her heart often pounded
nervously as she watched her husband withstand 50-shot
barrages.

"I was a new bride and really knew very little about
hockey," said Mrs. Giacomin. "I always kept my eyes on
Eddie rather than watching what the other players were
doing."

Marg Giacomin still concentrates on her husband instead
of watching the overall game as most spectators do.

"After Eddie established himself with the Rangers, I began to learn more about the game from him. He would come
home and tell me what happened and what mistakes he or
the other players made that led to goals being scored against
his team," she said.

Sometimes Eddie would kid his wife by asking: "Tell me
how many mistakes I made tonight."

Did Marg Giacomin worry about her husband's hazardous
profession or that he would be injured?

"It's strange but it has never really dawned on me to
think about injuries. I have always been more concerned
about the puck being behind him in the goal," she said.

It was during the 1963–64 season that Giacomin's goaltending began to attract scouts from National Hockey
League teams. The Rangers were one of the first to express
interest and Emile Francis, the assistant general manager,
spoke several times by telephone with Flamen about
Giacomin.

Although the Reds' defensive record was poor, Giacomin
led the league with six shutouts. His average was 3.37 and

his sixty-nine games were more than any other goalie played. The Reds finished third in their division and of their thirty-two wins Giacomin was the winning goalie in thirty games. He made 2,413 saves that season.

Typical of Giacomin's play was a game on October 15, 1963, in Baltimore against the Clippers, the Rangers' farm team. Eddie stopped fifty-nine of sixty-one shots for a 2-2 tie. On November 23, 1963, he stopped fifty-six of fifty-seven shots to beat Baltimore, 2-1. The next night he made fifty-two saves but lost to Baltimore, 3-2.

"Eddie saw more rubber in Providence than they have at the Dunlop Tire factory," said Eddie Westfall, a Boston Bruin forward who was Giacomin's teammate for several games in Providence.

Two Baltimore players who would become Giacomin's teammates in New York in the years ahead were Jean Ratelle and Gilles Villemure.

"I knew the first time I played against Eddie in Baltimore that we'd see him in the National Hockey League before long," said Ratelle. "His reflexes were so quick."

"Anytime I played against Eddie when I was with Baltimore, I figured I had to be sharp because no matter how many shots we got, Eddie would stop most of them," said Villemure, Baltimore's goaltender.

Another American League player whose life would touch Giacomin's, both as a rival and teammate in the NHL, was Pete Stemkowski, then playing for Rochester.

"The first time I remember seeing Eddie I said to one of our guys, 'Look at that guy with all the gray hair. He must be at least forty.' We barraged him that night. I mean, really barraged him. He was a hard-luck guy who didn't get much help from his team. I think we beat him in overtime, but some of the saves he made amazed me. I never saw a guy work so hard or be so quick."

Giacomin averaged thirty-five saves a game. In fifty of his sixty-nine games, he faced between thirty and sixty-one shots on goal.

"A lot of times I'd have to make two or three saves on rebounds from the original shot," he said.

Ross Brooks could sympathize with Giacomin as well as anyone after Eddie was left in a weary daze following a series of 50-shot games. Brooks was one of Eddie's Providence teammates in 1964. The two goalies became close friends and shared a rented room.

"Poor Eddie. He really used to get bombed in goal," said Brooks. "It was a scorer's league and not too many guys played much defense so that made it tough for the goalies. Guys figured the only way they'd get their names in the sports pages and get known and maybe get a shot at the NHL was if they scored a lot of goals."

Eddie and Brooks used to console each other over beers in the First and Last Chance Bar, a favorite watering spot for hockey players and the sporting crowd in nearby Pawtucket, Rhode Island.

"We'd cry in each other's beer," said Brooks, laughing. "Eddie was a quiet guy, kind of reserved until you got to know him, but he was a pretty comical guy and fun to be with," he continued. "Let's face it: if you're a goalie and you don't have a sense of humor, you go crazy."

Giacomin was one of the most popular players in Providence. His roaming style and exciting and spectacular saves made him a crowd-pleaser. When he gave up a bad goal or the opposition scored on a fluke play, he seldom let it bother him. When the fans heckled or booed him for what they thought was a bad play on his part, he never reacted in anger or showed that it bothered him. He was always friendly with fans and had time to talk with them or to sign autographs.

"I used to kid Eddie by saying the only reason they liked

him was because he was Italian and there were a lot of Italians in the Providence area," said Brooks.

"I called him the 'Italian Hero' because all his Italian fans wanted to buy him spaghetti dinners. They put his picture on the wall of the First and Last Chance Bar, and it's still up there today."

One only had to skim through the Reds' line-up to see that Lou Pieri liked to have players of Italian heritage on his team. In addition to Giacomin, there was George Ranieri, Zellio Toppazzini, Danny Poliziani, Dino Mascotto, and Moe Bartoli.

Eddie was popular with his Providence teammates, especially his defensemen. A local clothing merchant offered to give Giacomin a free pair of pants for each shutout. Eddie took the first pair for himself. Then, with each successive shutout, he sent each of the Reds' five defensemen to the store to collect the free trousers for themselves.

"I couldn't have got those shutouts without my defensemen," said the goaltender. "Remember, a goalie is only as good as his defense."

The 1964–65 season was Giacomin's fifth in Providence. He knew he was being scouted by several NHL teams. He wanted to have a good season. It turned out to be his most depressing. Eddie feared he might never escape from the minor leagues.

The Reds finished last, winning only twenty of seventy-two games, and were last in offense and defense, surrendering 312 goals. Eddie was a workhorse in goal, playing in fifty-nine games, and he won all but two of the Reds' games. But he failed to record a shutout and his goals-against average was 3.84. For the second straight season he was forced to make almost 2,500 saves, an average of thirty-nine shots on goal a game.

He made fifty-seven saves on December 5, 1964 but lost in

Cleveland, 4-3. Then he lost three games by one goal, two in overtime, despite making 118 saves.

"There wasn't much Eddie, or any goalie, could do," said Al Arbour, who was playing defense for Rochester following several seasons as a defenseman in the NHL with Toronto, Chicago, and Detroit. "He didn't have much help, but he hung tough and never let down. I never heard him gripe or make alibis.

"We'd outshoot him but it was always tough to score on him and beat him. He had such a great sense of anticipation. The way he roamed out of the net was exciting to watch and really helped his own team. Eddie always seemed to have the fans on him for a while but then he'd win them over to his side because of the way he played. I knew the guy was going to be a National Hockey Leaguer before long."

Arbour is convinced all the shots Eddie faced in Providence actually helped him progress more rapidly as a goaltender.

Throughout his five years in Providence, Giacomin was closely scouted, both on and off the ice, by a diminutive French-Canadian with combed-back gray hair and horn-rimmed glasses.

He was Johnny Gagnon, a New York Ranger scout who lived in nearby Cranston, Rhode Island. They called him "the Black Cat of Chicoutimi" when he played on a line with the Montreal Canadiens' Howie Morenz and Aurel Joliat. Gagnon played in the National Hockey League from 1930 to 1940 and had seen virtually every goaltender, good and bad.

Gagnon went to every Providence game in the Rhode Island Auditorium on North Main Street. He watched Giacomin closely. He knew the Rangers were looking for a goaltender, and he soon began mailing handwritten scouting reports to Emile Francis's New York office. He constantly badgered Francis about Giacomin until the Rangers' general manager began making scouting trips to Providence to see Giacomin for himself.

"I knew Giacomin's average was not good but our defense in Providence was not very good, either," said Gagnon. "But I know talent when I see it. Eddie was a fast skater and he used his stick well to clear the puck quickly. He had his own style, not like any other goalie. He liked to roam. He had to roam to help his team because it had a bad defense."

Gagnon had not seen Eddie play until he came to Providence. But he had seen Giacomin's brother, Rollie, play goal. "His brother was a good goalie, too; I guess it ran in the family," said the Ranger scout. "Eddie learned to become a good goalie because he had to handle so many shots in Providence."

Gagnon knew the Rangers were particular about the kind of players they wanted.

"Emile did not want to bother with any player with a bad reputation off the ice," said the scout. "He didn't want troublemakers, guys with bad attitudes who didn't hustle, or players who were show-offs or chased around after the games and didn't keep themselves in good shape."

That never was a problem with Giacomin.

"But I still had to check on him," said Gagnon. "There was no problem. Eddie Giacomin was always a clean-cut guy who never got into trouble. He lived the kind of life that other players could look up to."

Gagnon became friends with Eddie. He talked with him after games, good or bad, offering encouragement and advice when things were going badly. He told Eddie the Rangers were interested in him and assured him he finally would get his chance to play in the NHL.

"Eddie was always a gentleman on and off the ice," said Gagnon. "The players would always go to the First and Last Chance Bar after games, have a few beers, talk with the fans, and relax. I would tag along and Eddie would always come over to my table and we'd drink a beer and talk about the game."

Gagnon was not the only scout who showed up at the Rhode Island Auditorium to scout Giacomin. Several NHL teams were after Giacomin, including the Detroit Red Wings. Johnny Mitchell, their assistant general manager and scout, suddenly seemed to be living in Providence.

"Montreal wanted Eddie, too," said Gagnon. "I wanted the best for Eddie but I also wanted the Rangers to get him. I was afraid I might lose him to another team."

Mitchell knew Giacomin from the Eastern League and Hamilton, Ontario. He was the Detroit scout who sent Eddie home after a tryout in Junior A Hockey. He was at Johnstown when Eddie was there for an Eastern League try-out and again he turned him down.

Mitchell walked over to Giacomin at practice one day and said hello.

"What the hell are you doing here?" Giacomin kidded him. "You had two chances to get me for nothing and now you're willing to pay to get me. You've already got two strikes on you. One more and you're out."

For Eddie, it was poetic justice.

Giacomin and Gerry Cheevers, the goalie for the Rochester Americans, were considered to be the best major league prospects in the American League and there was considerable debate about them. Cheevers played for a superior team so he had a better record than Eddie.

"Giacomin's a good stand-up goalie, and that's important with all the slap shots, screen shots, and rebounds," said Baz Bastien, general manager of the Pittsburgh Hornets and a former goaltender whose career ended when he was blinded by a puck. "I like him. He'll definitely make it in the NHL."

"Giacomin plays the angles well and uses his stick well, but he sometimes tends to be too loose and could be more consistent. But he's a darned good prospect," said Jack Riley, the American League president.

"Giacomin even hates to give up a goal in practice," said Flamen. "I like that. He's a good-living kid, too. If he has a half-decent defense in front of him, he'll make it big in the NHL."

Lou Pieri, the Providence owner, called Eddie, "a great goalie with a great future," but he said Giacomin was not for sale. "Not for anything less than $100,000 worth of players for him, and he's worth every penny of it."

Eddie had mixed emotions. He knew several NHL teams wanted him. But he was afraid Pieri's asking price might be too high and he might never get out of Providence and get the chance he wanted in the NHL. When the 1964–65 season ended, he wondered where he would be next season.

Chapter **6**

Road to the Rangers:
"The Cat" Gets His Man

"IT'S LIKE A DREAM, BEING IN THE NHL."

THE telephone on the desk rang in Emile Francis's Madison Square Garden office at eleven o'clock on a cold, dreary morning early in February, 1965.

Johnny Gagnon was calling from Providence. He was so excited he was almost out of breath as he spit out the words.

"You better get up here fast. Johnny Mitchell's in town," Gagnon told his boss.

"Oh, yeah," said Francis. "Well, you stick close to Lou Pieri and don't let that guy Mitchell out of your sight. I'll hop a plane and be up there this afternoon."

Francis called the airport and reserved a seat on the first flight he could get from New York to Providence. Then he phoned the owner of the Providence Reds.

"Lou, this is Emile. I'm coming up this afternoon. I've got to know where we stand," he said with a dramatic sense of urgency.

"O.K. Bring along the pictures of the guys you want to put in the deal and we'll talk," said Pieri.

Francis called John Halligan into his office and asked the Rangers' publicity director to bring him the best eight-by-ten-inch glossy photographs he had of goaltender Marcel Paille, defenseman Aldo Guidolin, and forwards Sandy McGregor and Jim Mikol. He slipped the pictures into his briefcase and took a cab to the airport.

The 1964–65 Rangers were going nowhere and Francis knew it. They would finish fifth out of six teams for the third straight season, would have a losing record for the sixth year in a row, and for the seventh consecutive season would rank at the bottom of the league by giving up well above two hundred goals.

Francis already was thinking about the future more than the present. He had joined the Rangers in 1962 as assistant general manager and in 1964 had replaced Muzz Patrick as general manager. He was hard at work, putting in sixteen-hour days, reorganizing the team's muddled front office, bringing in more scouts, forming an efficient farm system, and hiring new lieutenants.

The energetic little man was a master organizer with a military manner. He had lied about his age during World War II and enlisted in the Canadian army at fifteen. By sixteen he rose in rank to sergeant. He played and managed semipro baseball teams in western Canada at twenty-two.

Francis knew that if the weak, laughable Rangers ever were going to become a playoff contender, they would have to start their renovation and rebuilding where it counted most—in goal. He knew that the sensitive, injury-prone Jacques Plante and journeyman Paille were not the answer to the Rangers' goaltending future.

Goaltending was the subject Francis knew best. He had been a professional goalie for fourteen years, playing briefly in the National Hockey League with the Chicago Black Hawks and Rangers. Although he was only modestly successful and often played for defensively-weak teams, he was respected as a fierce, fiery competitor and his quick reflexes earned him the nickname "the Cat."

The Rangers' new general manager knew the demands and pressure of goaltending required a special kind of mental and physical toughness. He had definite views on what he liked and disliked in a player.

"Ability is number one to me, but desire is always 90 percent anything you do," he said.

"Laziness is the one thing I can't stand. Being lazy is a sin," he said.

Durability, dedication, and discipline also were words Francis frequently used. He would not tolerate a player who complained about injuries or said he could not play because he was hurt. He took great pride in telling a tale that reflected his attitude and the attitude he looked for in players.

"I separated my shoulder when I was playing goal for New Haven, and the doctor put my arm in a sling and told me I wouldn't be able to play for six weeks. I took the sling off, put it in my pocket, went back and played goal on Sunday, Wednesday, and the following Sunday. The doctor didn't know I was playing. He'd told me to come see him again in two weeks. When the time was up, I put my sling on and went to see the doc. He told me I was coming along fine and if I was lucky, I might be able to play in a couple of weeks."

Francis chuckled at his own little joke on the doctor.

"Hell, I'd already been playing, but I never told the doc," said Francis.

As a goaltender, Francis qualified for the Purple Heart with several oak-leaf clusters. His face was cut nineteen times by flying pucks and required 106 stitches. He dislocated his shoulders three times. Four times his nose was broken. Aside from his face, he estimated he had received at least 60 stitches from wounds in other parts of his body. "The Cat" did not believe cuts and stitches were a sufficient excuse to prevent a man from playing.

"I always told the doc to stitch me up fast so I could go back in the game," he said. "The best time to get stitched is right after you get cut. Because then the blood is still warm. Show me a goalkeeper who doesn't want to stay in the game when he's hurt, and I'll show you a guy who doesn't care if somebody else gets a chance to take his job away."

Francis thought about Eddie Giacomin.

"Eddie was brought up the same way I was brought up. He wasn't born with a silver spoon in his mouth, either," he said.

The fact that Giacomin's goals-against average while he was with the Reds was seldom very impressive did not discourage Francis. In fact, "the Cat" could relate to Eddie. He knew Giacomin's statistics did not always reflect his ability because he was playing for a losing team with a poor defensive record.

"The tip-off on a good goalkeeper is how well he reacts to adversity," said Francis. "I look for a guy who still plays hard even when he's having a bad night or his team is playing badly in front of him."

Giacomin had that quality. He would need it in his first season in the NHL.

Francis compared Giacomin's minor-league career to that of his own when he broke into the NHL with Chicago in 1946–47. The Black Hawks were a poor defensive team, and Francis's 5.47-goals-against average reflected it. He was riddled with sixty-eight shots in a 12-2 loss to Toronto on one Saturday night and then faced fifty-six shots the next night and won 2-1.

On the short flight from New York to Providence, Francis thought about Giacomin and the deal he wanted to make to get him. He had first become interested in Giacomin during the 1963–64 season. Gagnon had been sending scouting reports to Francis about Giacomin and often had phoned Francis late at night at his home in Long Beach, Long Island, to rave about how well the young goalie had played.

Emile had made a dozen trips to Providence to see Eddie play. He liked what he saw. It was not so much Giacomin's goals-against average or his shutouts. It was the way he played, win or lose: fiery, aggressive, a daring style of charging out of the net after the puck, always hustling and chattering to his teammates like a baseball catcher.

Pieri was not an easy man with whom to bargain. The owner of the Providence Reds was an old-time promoter and operator. He had been quoted as saying Giacomin was not for sale. But Francis knew that Detroit, Montreal, Toronto, and Boston were interested in Giacomin. Detroit, in particular, wanted Eddie as an immediate back-up goalie for Roger Crozier.

The Providence Reds were an independently owned team, operated by Pieri and with no affiliation to an NHL team. There was no player-draft between the NHL and AHL in which the Rangers or any other NHL could select Giacomin.

Francis understood what Pieri was doing. Knowing the great demand for promising goalies and that several NHL teams were interested in Giacomin, the Reds' owner was collecting bids and offers for Eddie. He would only part with Giacomin in return for considerable cash and quality players who could help his team. Francis had been negotiating with Pieri for several months but had made little progress. If the Giacomin deal fell through, he would try to get Denis DeJordy from the American League.

"But Giacomin was the only guy I really wanted," said Francis.

At the moment, Mitchell, Detroit's assistant general manager, was in Providence and Francis was on an airplane.

"I was afraid Mitchell and Pieri might have made a deal already and that I'd lost Giacomin," said the Rangers general manager.

When Francis arrived in Providence, he went directly to

Pieri's office in the old Rhode Island Auditorium without even checking into his hotel.

"Lou had a big office with a big icebox in it. He was a man who liked to eat a lot," said Francis.

When Francis entered the office, his heart fell; sitting in the office with the Reds' owner was Johnny Mitchell.

"I knew I couldn't make my pitch with him in the room," said Francis. "So when Lou got up to go to the bathroom, I was right behind him."

"When can we talk?" said Francis.

"In the morning," said Pieri.

"O.K., I'll be in your office tomorrow at eight o'clock sharp," said Francis.

He was greatly relieved when he sensed that Mitchell had not yet been able to make a deal for Giacomin with the Providence owner.

Francis left Pieri's office, went to his hotel, and checked in. But when he stepped into the elevator to go to his room, whom did he see?

Johnny Mitchell.

"Son-of-a-gun! There he was on the same elevator with me," said "the Cat."

The two men eyed each other suspiciously. Neither would admit to the other what they were doing in Providence. Each pretended they were looking for defensemen, not goalies. But in reality each man knew why the other was there—a goaltender named Eddie Giacomin had brought them to Providence and fittingly, put them into the same elevator at the same time in the same hotel.

"What the hell are you doing here?" asked the man from Detroit.

Francis thought to himself, "What the hell do you think I'm doing here. I'm here doing the same thing you're doing —trying to get Eddie Giacomin."

"Tell me, Emile, what do you think of this guy—what's his

name, Giacomin?—as a goalkeeper?" he asked.

"That's not for me to say; we're from different organiza-
tions," replied Francis. "The Cat" had learned from Gagnon,
his combination scout and super sleuth, that Mitchell had an
appointment to see Pieri the next afternoon and that he was
confident of completing a deal for Giacomin.

"I was afraid we might lose him. I was afraid Pieri would
ask New York for too much money or too many players and
Detroit would get him," said Gagnon.

But Francis had the upper hand. He had an appointment
to see Pieri at eight o'clock the next morning, several hours
before Mitchell would present the Providence owner with
Detroit's offer. While Mitchell was still in bed, Francis was
up at 6 A.M. and in a cab driving to Pieri's office.

The two men talked. Pieri did not want to give up Giacomin because he was a good goaltender and popular with
the Providence fans. But Francis held the trump card. All
along he had been offering Pieri a three-for-one deal: Paille,
McGregor, and Guidolin. The Providence owner liked the
deal; Paille was a goalie and Guidolin's Italian heritage
would make him popular with the area's many Italian-
American fans.

Still the crafty old owner was reluctant to give up Giacomin.

"Did you bring along the pictures of the guys you'll give
me?" he said gruffly to Francis.

"The Cat" opened his briefcase and spread the photographs of Paille, McGregor, and Guidolin on the desk in
front of Pieri. He smiled. His strategy was working. He knew
Pieri wanted good-looking young players who would appeal
to the fans, especially the women.

Then Francis made his move. He took another photograph from his briefcase.

"Lou," he said, "I'll tell you what: let's make it four-for-
one. Four New York Ranger players for one of your players,

Eddie Giacomin."

"I hadn't even brought up Jim Mikol's name until that moment," said Francis. "I could see Lou Pieri was reluctant to let Eddie go for three guys so I used Mikol as the clincher."

Pieri's eyes lit up at the thought of getting four players for one.

Then Francis put Mikol's picture in front of Pieri.

"He was a young, single, real good-looking guy," said Francis. "That's why I saved him for last."

Pieri studied Mikol's picture for a few moments. Then he said, "O.K., it's a deal. We get Paille, McGregor, Guidolin, and Mikol, and you get your goalie, Giacomin."

Pieri studied Mikol's photograph again. "Hey, you know, he's a pretty good-looking kid."

"Oh, yeah? I never really noticed that," said Francis. "The Cat" almost gagged on the words as he spoke.

He and Pieri shook hands. They agreed not to announce the trade until May. That way no one would know the Rangers had Giacomin and Francis would not have to place his new goaltender on the protected list for the June player-draft or fear that another team would claim him if the trade were announced and Giacomin were left unprotected.

Francis returned to his hotel and phoned Gagnon at his home in nearby Cranston, Rhode Island.

"Did you make the deal?" asked the scout apprehensively.

"I made the deal," said Francis.

"What did you have to give up?" asked Gagnon.

"Guidolin, McGregor, Paille, and Mikol," replied Francis.

"Four players?" Gagnon said with disbelief. "Everyone thought you'd only give up three. That's what the other teams were offering."

"I know," said Francis, pleased with himself for his shrewd wheeling and dealing.

"I sure hope Giacomin works out," said Gagnon. "If he's

a flop, I'll probably be out of a job and lose my pension."

Francis boarded a 1 P.M. flight back to New York on Saturday with the satisfaction of knowing that he had the goaltender he wanted. "The Cat" had got his man.

"Who in the hell do you suppose was on that plane?" he asked.

Johnny Mitchell.

"Can you beat that," said Francis, his face wrinkling into a smile.

"I've got to assume he saw Pieri on Friday afternoon and made his three-for-one offer," said Francis. "He looked a little down in the dumps when I spotted him on the plane. So I made darned sure I looked the same way so as not to tip my hand. I wanted him to figure I hadn't made the deal either and was just on my way home."

The Giacomin trade was announced by the Rangers on May 17, 1965. The Rangers had traded four players, worth $100,000, to Providence for a little-known goaltender with an unimpressive record and a questionable hockey background.

RANGERS HOPE FOR A NET GAIN was the headline in the *New York Post*. RANGERS TRADE FOUR FOR ACE GOALIE said the *Daily News*. WHO IS EDDIE GIACOMIN? was another newspaper headline.

"Forget his record," Francis said when newsmen asked about his new goaltender. "He's been one of the top prospects in the minor leagues for the past two years. It's no secret three other clubs have also been after him."

Francis said that, at twenty-five, Giacomin was the ideal age to break into the NHL. "It always takes a goalkeeper longer to develop than it does a forward or a defenseman. We've taken a big step in the right direction toward improving the Rangers and making the club a playoff contender by getting Eddie Giacomin."

Not everyone was as easily convinced as Francis when they

learned of Giacomin's modest minor-league record and inability to play Junior A hockey.

"Emile's word was good enough for me," said William M. Jennings, the Rangers' president. "All I heard from him all season was that he was going up to Providence again to look at some goaltender and that Eddie Giacomin was the goalie we needed to get the team out of fifth and sixth place and into the playoffs."

"The only thing wrong with Giacomin is that he hasn't had the benefit of playing for a good club in Providence, but he played just as hard when he was losing," said Francis. "I think he's going to give Plante a good run for the number-one job in training camp."

Plante had been an outstanding goalie for 11 seasons with the powerful Canadiens. He won the Vezina Trophy six times and led the league in shutouts four times. But Jake often antagonized Montreal management and was considered by some to be overly sensitive to criticism and somewhat of a hypochondriac. The Rangers traded their goaltender, Lorne "Gump" Worsley, and several other players, to Montreal for Plante in 1963. Plante immediately predicted he would win the Vezina Trophy in New York.

Not with the kind of team the Rangers had. His goals-against averages were 3.38 and 3.37 in two seasons as Ranger goaltender. He was thirty-six years old, injury prone, and occasionally temperamental and unpredictable.

"I figured Plante would play another one or two years for us and that I could work in Eddie slowly until he was ready to be number one," said Francis. "I figured a guy like Plante could teach Eddie a lot."

Francis went to Montreal for the June league meetings and player-draft in a confident mood. He would protect Plante and a young goalie named Gilles Villemure. He did not have to protect Giacomin.

"I figured I was all set in goal," he said.

Then came the phone call from Plante. Jake said he wanted to see Francis.

"I've given it a lot of thought and I've decided to retire," Plante told Francis in his suite in the Queen Elizabeth Hotel. "I'm going to pack it in because I've been away from my wife and my family too much."

Plante's retirement plans caught Francis off guard. It was totally unexpected. "The Cat" was angry. He thought Plante should have told him of his retirement plans earlier than at the last minute before the June draft meetings were about to open.

"When do you want to call a news conference to announce your retirement?" he asked Plante.

"Make it Tuesday at four o'clock," said Plante.

It was Saturday night and Francis had only until Tuesday morning in which to try to engineer a trade for an experienced goaltender. He did not feel Villemure was ready. He did not want to enter the 1965–66 season with one rookie goalie, let alone two.

"For the next forty-eight hours, I didn't eat one meal," said Francis. "I spent the whole time from Saturday night to Monday morning wheeling and dealing for another goalkeeper."

He tried to get either Johnny Bower or Terry Sawchuk, both veterans from the Toronto Maple Leafs, but the deal finally fell through when general manager George "Punch" Imlach said no at 2:30 A.M. on Sunday.

Then he phoned Sam Pollock, Montreal's clever general manager, and a trade was agreed upon at 4 A.M. The Rangers gave up Earl Ingarfield, Noel Price, Gordon Labossière, and Dave McComb for Cesare Maniago and Garry Peters. He got another experienced goaltender in the draft when he selected Don Simmons from Toronto.

Suddenly Plante's retirement seemed less significant.

Francis had two veteran goalies in Maniago and Simmons to augment the acquisition of the rookie goalie from Providence.

Giacomin was unaware of all the masterminding and sleepless nights Francis had spent in his behalf.

Eddie had known that the Rangers were among the NHL teams interested in him and that Francis often came to Providence to see him play. Gagnon told him so.

"Other scouts talked to me," said Giacomin, "but Emile didn't. All I knew was what Johnny Gagnon had told me. He'd told me Emile was scouting me and that he wanted me in New York."

Giacomin was too happy about finally getting a chance to play in the NHL to care about the strings Francis had had to pull to get him there.

"It's like a dream, me being in the National Hockey League. It's the greatest thing that's ever happened to me. Imagine, just an Italian boy from Sudbury, Ontario, and I'm going to New York to play for the Rangers," said Eddie.

Chapter 7

Dejection and Rejection
As a Rookie Goalie

"You've got to take the bad with the
good."

It had seemed as though the summer would never end. But now, finally, it was September and the leaves were turning autumn brown and gold. Outside the old arena in Kingston, Ontario, the early morning air was crisp and cool, but inside the small dressing room it was warm and crowded and the air was filled with the scent of medical ointments and coffee brewing in the trainers' room. The players hung their clothes on hooks along the wall, put on their uniforms and equipment, and methodically wound black tape around their stick blades.

Eddie Giacomin sat on the wooden bench against the wall, slipped off his shoes and socks, removed his shirt and trousers, and began to put on his uniform and bulky goaltending equipment.

As he stood up and pulled the blue-red-and-white sweater down over his head and shoulders, he felt a warm glow of pride and satisfaction swell inside him. He smiled to himself.

Suddenly the long struggle and difficult years seemed far

behind him. The legs once so painfully burned and scarred were forgotten. Gone was the terrible feeling of rejection he experienced when he tried but failed to make the team as a teen-aged goalie with the Hamilton Red Wings. Paying for the right to play hockey in the midnight industrial leagues back home in Sudbury was in the past. So were places named Clinton and Johnstown and Greensboro. Now he could joke about the countless car trips, meals eaten in highway hamburger joints, sleeping in second-rate hotels, and the harrowing 50-shot nights with Providence and the Rovers.

The hardships and heartaches he had endured finally seemed worthwhile. Eddie Giacomin was a New York Ranger. It said so in bold letters across the front of his uniform sweater. He was in the National Hockey League—at last.

If only his brothers Rollie and Jiggs, his sisters Ida and Gloria, Big Tony Giacomin, and his mother could see him now.

Marg Giacomin would have been proud of her husband, too. But she was back home in Sudbury with the couple's second child, David, born on September 13, 1965, and Mark, not yet two and a half, to care for.

Other thoughts flashed through Eddie's mind that first day of Ranger training camp for the 1965–66 season. Suddenly he had mixed emotions. He looked around the dressing room and watched the men who were his new teammates casually pulling on their uniforms. He did not know many of their names, but he sensed that most were either toughened NHL veterans or players younger than he but with greater hockey training than he had had.

Eddie was nervous.

He felt that every eye in the dressing room was trained on him. They were the insiders. He was the outsider, the new man on the job who must prove to his new teammates that he belonged in the NHL. He was twenty-six years old and his close-cropped salt-and-pepper hair made him appear older. But he knew he still was a rookie.

If the other players noticed Eddie, they didn't let on. Veteran players seldom paid much attention to rookies until the rookie proved he belonged on the team and was accepted.

Soon Eddie was on the ice, skating slowly around the rink to limber up his leg muscles. Then coach Red Sullivan appeared. He had sandy red hair and wore a blue baseball cap and Ranger jacket. The players who knew him well called him Sully. They liked him. He had a friendly Irish face and he was considered tough but fair. He had played ten years in the NHL as a clever center for the Boston Bruins, Chicago Black Hawks, and the Rangers.

Sullivan blew his whistle and shouted, "O.K., guys, let's go."

Eddie suddenly found himself skating at a furious pace around the rink with his teammates. He could hear the crunch of skate blades grinding and scraping against the ice. He could feel the breeze and hear men straining as they skated past him.

Next came a physically punishing series of calisthenics that left Giacomin and his teammates gasping for breath and soaking in sweat. The goaltending equipment Eddie wore weighed almost forty pounds and when the players did pushups or skated at top speed from one end of the rink to the other and back again, Giacomin almost wished he were a forward or defenseman instead of a goalie in heavy equipment.

By now his mind no longer was filled with delightful thoughts of the New York Ranger uniform he wore or the normal nervous tension of a rookie. He had no time for any thoughts. He was too tired to think about anything but following Sullivan's drill-sergeant orders. It was a welcome relief from skating drills and push-ups when the coach told Eddie to get in goal for shooting drills.

Pucks thumped against Giacomin's leg pads and cracked against the blade of his big stick and the blocking pad that shielded his right forearm. He was up and down, catching high shots in his glove, sprawling, kicking, diving as shooters swerved in toward him and shot their hard, black rubber missiles at him with terrific speed and impact.

Giacomin knew Sullivan was watching him closely. He knew every move he made was being studied by General Manager Emile Francis, seated in the stands with his scouting staff. He knew his teammates were testing him with their best shots. He was the new goaltender for whom the Rangers had given up four players worth $100,000. He was the new man the newspaper men had been writing about, saying he would lead the lowly Rangers out of the wilderness of defeat and into a bright, sunny new land of respectability.

Eddie was on the spot and he knew it. He wanted to look his best.

It seemed as though every teammate were shooting the puck at him and thinking to themselves: "O.K., hotshot, let's see how good you really are."

As training camp progressed, Giacomin found himself involved in a fierce fight for the job as the Rangers' number-one goaltender. Competing with Eddie for the goalie's job were Cesare Maniago, Don Simmons, Gilles Villemure, and Wayne Rutledge.

Maniago had been acquired from the Montreal Canadiens and Simmons from the Toronto Maple Leafs. Like Eddie, Maniago was of Italian descent and was coming off an outstanding 1964–65 minor-league season in which he led the Central League with six shutouts, compiled a 2.75 goals-against average, and was named the league's most valuable player and outstanding goaltender. He had the added benefit of having played in the NHL with Montreal and Toronto.

Simmons had been a pro goaltender since 1954, having

played five seasons with the Boston Bruins and three with
Toronto. The players called him "Dippy Don" because of
his habit of dropping low to the ice to make saves. Giacomin
knew Simmons from their American League days in Providence. Villemure was a product of the Ranger farm system,
had played for New York briefly in 1963–64, and he and
Eddie were old American League rivals. Like Villemure,
Rutledge was a promising young goalie.

In many ways, the odds were stacked against Giacomin.
It was not the first time. It would not be the last. But by
early October, with the opening of the season only a few
weeks away, it became apparent that Eddie was beating the
odds.

"I'm very high on Eddie Giacomin," Sullivan told sports
writers covering the Rangers' training camp one day. "He's
quick and agile and a real holler guy."

The Rangers sent Maniago to their American League farm
team, the Baltimore Clippers. They sent Villemure to Vancouver of the Western League. They assigned Rutledge to
Minnesota of the Central League.

Eddie Giacomin had made the team.

"Eddie had a great training camp," said Sullivan. "There's
no question he was the best goalie in camp. He's won the
job as our goaltender on determination, dedication, and
hard work."

Sullivan was particularly fond of the rookie's bold style of
roaming far out of the goal crease to break up enemy rushes
and clear the puck out of danger or to his teammates. It was
Eddie's trademark in the Eastern and American leagues; it
would become his trademark with the Rangers. It would also
nearly cause his downfall.

"I like his style of coming out of the net," said Sullivan.
"It helps take some of the pressure off our defenseman, and
it's sure going to give the other team trouble. Eddie's developed a style all his own. He's so good on his skates. He

gets up and down quickly and he handles his stick better than any goalie I've seen. He has strong legs and he isn't temperamental or moody, like most goaltenders. But the thing I like best about him is his attitude; Eddie works his tail off all the time."

To encourage and refine Giacomin's wandering style of goaltending, the coach designed a drill. He kept Eddie on the ice after practice to work on the routine. After the rest of the players had gone, Sullivan would get a bucket, fill it with pucks, and stand near the red line in center ice.

"O.K., Eddie, get in the net," said Sullivan.

The coach fired the puck toward the net or glanced it off the side boards or end boards and into the corner.

"Go after that puck and shoot it back out to the blue line," he yelled.

Giacomin skated far out of his crease, retrieved the puck, and fired it back toward the blue line.

Sullivan shot the puck right back into the corner.

"Let's see you get that puck and throw it back out to the red line this time," he directed.

Eddie fired the puck back out to the red line.

On October 12 the Rangers played their first preseason exhibition game in Madison Square Garden against Toronto. Ranger fans had read about Giacomin's outstanding play in training camp. They were anxious to see for themselves what the rookie goaltender could do. Simmons started the game in goal but surrendered two early goals. The crowd grew restless and began to boo.

"We want Giacomin!" fans near the Rangers' bench began to shout.

They got their wish. Giacomin played the second half of the game and held the Maple Leafs scoreless by making an assortment of acrobatic saves, and the Rangers rallied to win, 5-2. The crowd cheered Eddie. They liked the fiery way he barked loud instructions to his teammates and aggressively

skated out of his crease to trap and clear the puck. After so
many dismal losing seasons, Ranger fans had new hope. And
a new hero.

The Rangers' opening game of the season was October 24
against the Montreal Canadiens, the most powerful team in
hockey. The Canadiens had won the Stanley Cup during the
1964–65 season. They would finish first and win the Cup
again in 1965–66. The Rangers could not have asked
Giacomin to make his National Hockey League debut
against a more difficult opponent than Montreal.

Outside Madison Square Garden, on West 49th Street
and Eighth Avenue, and in the neighboring bars, the fans
gathered early. They were eager to see how the rookie goalie
would do against hockey's best team.

As the opening-night crowd of 15,024 filed into Madison
Square Garden, Giacomin was in the dressing room waiting
until it was time for the Rangers to go on the ice for pregame warm-ups. He experienced the normal jitters of any
rookie playing in his first major-league game before a critical
hometown audience, but his performance in training camp
had given him confidence.

In the Ranger line-up with Giacomin that night were defensemen Harry Howell, Arnie Brown, Jim Neilson, Wayne
Hillman, Mike McMahon, and Rod Seiling. Howell, at
thirty-two, was the oldest and most experienced; Seiling was
twenty, Neilson and Brown twenty-three, and McMahon
twenty-four. The Rangers' opening forward line had Bob
Nevin, the captain, at right wing, Phil Goyette at center,
and Don Marshall at left wing. The other forwards were
Doug Robinson, Earl Ingarfield, Rod Gilbert, Vic Hadfield,
John McKenzie, Lou Angotti, John Brenneman, Jean Ratelle,
Larry Mickey, and Garry Peters. Simmons was the back-up
goaltender.

Giacomin stood rigidly at attention for the playing of the
National Anthem. Then his teammates skated up to him

and tapped their sticks against his leg pads, the traditional pregame good-luck ritual accorded all goaltenders.

Eddie scraped up the ice in the goal crease with his skates assuring himself of better footing, rapped his stick against the ice, and crouched low in front of the net as referee Frank Udvari raised his arm to drop the puck for the opening face-off.

In a flash the slick, quick Canadiens were inside the New York blue line, mounting an attack against the Ranger goal. Eddie shifted from side to side as the play swirled around him, keeping his eyes riveted on the puck. He withstood the opening flurry and the crowd cheered.

But at 9:13 of the first period Ralph Backstrom and Claude Larose moved the puck across the blue line with a quick pass exchange, and suddenly John Ferguson had the puck only a short distance from Giacomin. He shot from ten feet away and the puck spun past Eddie and, for an instant, hung in the cord lacing in the rear of the goal cage before dropping to the ice.

Ferguson had his arms raised and his stick in the air, and the hard-boiled veteran, with the hook nose, square jaw, and piercing dark eyes, had an evil smile on his lips.

Eddie saw the red goal light flashing behind him. He heard Pat Doyle, the Madison Square Garden public-address announcer, tell the crowd, "Montreal Canadiens' goal by Number 22, John Ferguson. . . ."

Five minutes and forty-one seconds later Angotti, assisted by Hadfield and Ratelle, shot the puck past Montreal goalie Lorne "Gump" Worsley and the score was 1-1. Eddie went to the dressing room after his first period as an NHL goaltender having stopped ten of the first eleven shots he faced.

Montreal took ten more shots at the rookie goalie in the second period and the only one that eluded Giacomin was Terry Harper's twenty-foot shot at 8:22. The score was Montreal 2, Rangers 1 entering the third period.

A roar from the crowd went up when Nevin scored on assists from Goyette and Howell to tie the game, 2-2, at 9:56 of the third period. Montreal was dominating the game, but Giacomin was preventing the Canadiens from scoring with spectacular saves.

The Canadiens, however, quickly dashed Ranger hopes. Yvan Cournoyer shot the puck from thirty-five feet out. Giacomin was screened on the shot and never saw the puck until it rolled behind him into the net. Claude Provost scored from close range with a wrist shot. Within eighty-two seconds, Montreal had turned a 2-2 tie into a 4-2 game. McKenzie's goal with only thirty-two seconds remaining in the game made the final score of 4-3 seem somewhat more respectable.

Bob Waters of *Newsday* remembers the postgame Ranger dressing room.

"Giacomin had played very well in his debut, considering Montreal was so strong and had outplayed the Rangers for most of the game. But Eddie seemed very depressed by losing and didn't have much to say. I thought he would have been pleased that he had played so well in his first game."

That was the first tip-off New York sports writers received on Giacomin's character; the team takes precedence over the individual and no matter how well one man may play, it's only meaningful if his team wins.

Eddie was dissatisfied with himself for losing.

"It wasn't the hard shots that beat me. It was the tricklers," he grumbled as he peeled off his sweat-soaked uniform.

Worsley sympathized with Giacomin. "It was a tough way for Giacomin to break in," the Canadiens' goalie told reporters. "He kicked around Providence for five years before getting his chance but I figured even then he'd be a good one, if the New York fans would be patient."

Giacomin barely had time to forget losing his first game when he was confronted again by the Canadiens. New

York's second game also was against Montreal. To make matters worse, the game was in the Montreal Forum, where the Canadiens seldom lose and the Rangers seldom win.

Again Giacomin played well. Again he lost. Again the score was 4-3. Again Gump Worsley was his rival in goal. Again Eddie was beaten by a late third-period goal, Jean Beliveau, Montreal's marvelous center, scoring at 14:28 on passes from Dick Duff and Bobby Rousseau. This time Eddie faced a barrage of thirty-four shots, three more than he had had three nights ago on opening night. But although he had played well, he had allowed eight goals and lost his first two games.

"I'm not concerned," said Francis. "If he got beat 5-1 or 6-1, I wouldn't even be concerned. Montreal's a powerhouse. Eddie played well, damned well for a rookie, considering who the opposition was."

The Rangers' third game was October 30 in Boston Garden, a musty but lovable old arena that sits atop North Station and is only several slap shots from the Charles River. The pre-Bobby Orr and Phil Esposito Bruins in no way resembled the powerful Bruins of later years. The Bruins and Rangers annually engaged in a tug of war for last place in the old preexpansion league.

Boston Garden is the smallest rink in the NHL and the close proximity of spectators and players on the ice creates an intimacy which makes razzing rival players a favorite pastime among fans. When Ted Green scored early against Giacomin, the crowd began to heckle the rookie goalie.

"Giacomin, you're a bum!" a fan with a New England twang in his voice shouted down from the overhanging mezzanine seats. Eddie heard him, loud and clear.

The heckling stopped almost as quickly as it began. Robinson, Goyette, Gilbert, and Ratelle shot pucks past Bruins' goalie Eddie Johnston. Now Boston fans were calling Johnston a bum. Johnston was removed from the game and a rookie named Bob Ring took over in goal. Robinson scored again and McKenzie, Nevin, and Ingarfield added to the onslaught. The Rangers won, 8-2.

Giacomin had his first goaltending victory in the NHL. It was a nice feeling.

Then followed a stretch of games in which Eddie beat Toronto and its crafty old goalie, Johnny Bower, 4-2, and Detroit, 3-2, and tied the Maple Leafs, 2-2, the Bruins, 2-2, and the Red Wings, 3-3. He had a six-game undefeated streak in which his record was 3-0-3 and he yielded only thirteen goals. For his first eight games in the NHL, his record was 3-2-3 and his goals-against average was down to 2.63. Not bad for a rookie.

Although Giacomin's daring style of leaving his net unguarded to outrace rivals to the puck seemed risky to some NHL coaches, it caught the imagination and fancy of Ranger fans. They were ecstatic over the new goalie.

"Giacomin amused and startled the crowd in the Olympia by repeatedly leaving his net to pursue and clear the puck, sometimes ranging as far as fifteen to twenty-five feet from the crease," Gerald Eskenazi of the *New York Times* wrote of the Rangers' 3-3 tie in Detroit.

But the Rangers and Giacomin were playing on borrowed time. Their success was ephemeral. The forwards stopped scoring and the defense crumbled in front of Giacomin. He was beaten by Toronto, 5-2, and Chicago, 5-3. Then the roof fell in: On November 20 in Montreal, the Canadiens left Eddie with a severe case of shell-shock. They hammered him and the Rangers to death, 9-3, Rousseau and Backstrom each scoring three-goal hat tricks. Ordinarily, when a goaltender simply does not have it or his team is being hopelessly outclassed, it is customary and merciful for the coach to change goalies.

Sullivan chose to let Eddie face the Montreal firing squad by himself.

The roof would fall in often on the rookie goalie and his team before the ordeal that was the 1965–66 season had ended.

Afterward, the badly beaten Rangers went to the railway station in Montreal to catch a midnight train for the next night's game in Detroit. Dejected, demoralized, and torturing himself with self-recrimination and self-doubt, Giacomin drifted away from his teammates and waited on the platform by himself. Suddenly he felt a hand on his shoulder.

"Don't let it get you down," said Gump Worsley. "I know what it's like in New York."

The Canadiens also were waiting for a train. No one knew better than Worsley the pitfalls of playing goal for the Rangers in New York. The little round goaltender with the crew cut and glib sense of humor had spent 10 seasons as a Ranger in which his teammates often left him defenseless and New York fans booed and barraged Gump with garbage.

Eddie appreciated Gump's kind words. But sympathy could not save him from what was yet to come. He played goal on November 24 when the Rangers defeated Boston, 4-1, but he would not win another game until after Christmas and by then the Rangers would be hopelessly in last place, Sullivan no longer would be coach, and Giacomin would have a personal nine-game winless streak in which he had been bombed for thirty-six goals.

The rest of the league had caught up to the Rangers and their rookie goalie who had started off so impressively. The Ranger defense, for the most part, was young, inexperienced, mistake-prone and made a habit of backing-in toward its own goal when opponents' attacks were forming. Many of the forwards lacked great goal-scoring skill and the qualities of forechecking and backchecking so vital to the team's defense. The Rangers did not have enough physical size to outmuscle opponents, nor were they noted for having much fiery aggressiveness or enthusiasm.

A team can either make or break a goaltender. The Rangers were not doing much as a team to make it easy for Eddie to break in the NHL.

Eddie himself was not totally blameless. His habit of wandering from the crease to clear the puck was proving more of a hindrance than a help. It was not normal procedure for a goaltender; certainly not as frequently as Eddie vacated his net. It was new to his teammates, often causing confusion and missed assignments in the Rangers' end of the ice. It was new to Giacomin's opponents and, for a time, it worked. But opponents adjusted to Eddie's roaming goaltending more quickly than the Rangers themselves. They took advantage of Giacomin's leaving his goal cage unguarded, often embarrassing him by scoring uncontested goals into the empty net.

"His wandering gave us heart failure; we just weren't used to it," said Hadfield.

As Ranger losses mounted and Giacomin's goals-against average increased, many of New York's fickle fans became infuriated and turned on the rookie goaltender, blaming him for Ranger defeats.

In addition to leaving the net unprotected too often, Giacomin frequently was guilty of breaking too quickly from the goal post, allowing opponents to score on the short side. Sometimes he neglected to keep the blade of his stick pressed flat to the ice, letting low shots skim under it and slide between his legs into the goal. He played some shots with his leg pads when he should have used his catching glove to prevent rebounds.

Giacomin's reflexes were sharp and he made spectacular saves that made the crowd gasp, but often the saves were more spectacular than they had to be; had he been in the right position, covering the angles correctly, many saves might have been easier. But he was only a rookie, new to the league, and he did not yet know the moves and tricks of rival shooters.

Many New York fans did not understand Eddie's problems. Or if they did, they did not care. He was booed and jeered. He was not playing well and he knew it. But he did not deserve to be singled out by the crowd as being totally responsible for losing. He had plenty of help in that from his teammates.

"Goaltending is the toughest position in hockey for a player to break in at," Francis said in defense of Giacomin. "The mistakes a forward or a defenseman make don't show up that much. But every mistake a goalie makes ends up as a goal for the other team. Everybody sees what the goalie does wrong and everybody blames the goalie. This is not all Eddie's fault; the team in front of him isn't that strong."

Still the criticism continued. The fans blamed Giacomin for the Rangers' defeats when, in reality, it was the fault of an entire team, not just one player. The boos grew louder and Eddie was severely criticized in print.

"Stay in the damned net, Giacomin!" fans screamed when Eddie roamed in search of the puck only to give up a goal.

"I roam away from the net because it's my style and it helps my defensemen," Giacomin explained. "I once went into the corner to get a puck and after I shot it up ice, my defensemen thanked me. I do it especially on penalties when we're short-handed; it enables the defensemen to watch the forwards coming down the ice and helps them avoid hard bodychecks in the corners."

Sullivan was asked if he felt Giacomin would be better off staying at the net instead of skating out so far after the puck.

"I'm not going to tell him he has to change his style," said Red. "Eddie knows what he's doing. He's like a careful drinker; he knows just how far he can go."

Eddie's roving goaltending provided a source of amusement for Jerry Mitchell, the whimsical sports humorist of the *New York Post.*

"In Edward Giacomin, the Go-Go Goalie, the Rangers obviously have the greatest explorer on ice since Admiral Richard E. Byrd. Giacomin makes more fall and winter cruises than the Holland-American steamship line," Mitchell wrote in a column headlined FREE-STYLE GOALIE.

After the 4-1 victory against Boston, the Rangers and Giacomin self-destructed together. They failed to win in six games and the offense and defense collapsed together: eleven goals scored, twenty-three goals against them in five losses and a tie. The Rangers were in last place with a 5-10-5 record for their first twenty games.

Then on December 5 they lost to the Black Hawks, 6-2. Stan Mikita scored three goals against Giacomin. Bobby Hull scored twice. A crescendo of boos virtually shook Madison Square Garden.

Francis decided it was time for a change, behind the bench and in goal. At a press conference the next day, he announced Sullivan had been dismissed and that he was taking over as coach.

"I think our problem is psychological more than anything else," said Francis. "We've forgotten how to hang on to a lead."

Sullivan took losing his job as coach philosophically. "It didn't come as a shock. I wasn't winning but I feel I gave the job my best. I don't know what I could have done that I didn't do. I'm going out with my head held high," he said.

Giacomin was saddened that Sullivan had been fired. Red gave him the chance he needed in training camp. He encouraged and worked with him. He stuck with him through the first twenty games. Eddie felt he had let down Red Sullivan.

"Not at all," said Sullivan. "There's no tougher job than breaking in as a goaltender. Sure, Eddie's made some mistakes. But he's young and inexperienced; he's still learning the game. Don't blame Eddie for what's happened. He had all this thrust on him at once and he's handled a tough situation well. He works as hard as any man on the clubs. There's no way it's his fault. Give Eddie time and he'll become one of the best goaltenders in the business."

Francis also refused to blame Giacomin for the Rangers' poor showing but said he didn't think benching the rookie for a few games would destroy his confidence.

Giacomin sat on the bench and Simmons played goal for the first time on December 8 when the Rangers tied the Black Hawks, 2-2, in Chicago in Francis' first game as coach. Eddie was on the bench the next night when Simmons was beaten by Toronto, 7-3. Francis restored Giacomin to goal on December 11 but he lost to Detroit, 4-2.

Eddie would have been much better off on the bench in Maple Leaf Gardens on December 18. Bob Pulford and Dave Keon each scored three goals and Giacomin was beaten, 8-4.

Francis found it as difficult to win as Sullivan did, failing to win in his first five games as coach. New York slid deeper into last place, winning only once in fifteen games and failing to win in eleven. Giacomin was back on the bench. The Rangers finally presented Francis with his first victory on December 19 against Montreal, 3-2, with Simmons in goal. But the Rangers reverted to their losing form and Giacomin played only once in the next seven games.

On January 2 in Madison Square Garden the Canadiens raced to a 3-0 first-period lead against Simmons. Francis sent Giacomin into goal in the second period. The crowd booed. Eddie allowed two soft goals and the boos grew louder. The Rangers rallied for three goals but again the rookie goalie faltered; he fanned on a third-period shot, killing any hopes of a Ranger comeback. Montreal won the game, 6-3.

Two days later Francis called Giacomin into his office after practice.

"We're going to send you down to Baltimore for a little while," the general manager and coach told Eddie.

Being demoted to the Rangers' American League farm team hurt Eddie's pride. But he accepted it and did not sulk. Francis softened the blow. He told Eddie he was going to the minor leagues for his own good, assuring him that he would be back.

Many fans and members of the press assumed that after only a half-season Francis had given up on Giacomin and that the demotion to the minor leagues was an admission the Rangers had lost faith in Eddie and were blaming him for the team's poor record.

"Not on your life," bristled Francis. "No way I've lost faith in Eddie Giacomin. He'll be with the New York Rangers for a long time, and what's more, I'm telling you he's going to be a hell of a goaltender. You wait and see. He understands why he's going to Baltimore, and you can bet he'll be back."

Francis then explained why the goalie he had brought from Providence to New York needed to go to Baltimore.

"He was getting a bad time from the fans and in the press. We were blowing leads and Eddie was getting caught out of position and the crowd was on him. I could see he was fighting himself, as well as the puck. That's why I decided he needed to go to Baltimore, get away from all the pressure, play some games down there, and build his confidence back up. I don't want to see his career ruined or his confidence destroyed because of all the abuse he's been taking."

Criticism of Giacomin's goaltending was not limited only to fans and sports writers. Even some of his own teammates had turned against him.

"We were losing games we should have won because the other team had better goaltending," one Ranger veteran told the *New York Journal-American*'s Stan Fischler. "There was a game in Toronto when we were tied and should have come out with a tie, but a little dribbler got by Eddie near the end of the game, and that was that. That stuff happens too often."

Three days after Giacomin was sent to the Baltimore minor-league team and Maniago was recalled as his replacement, the Rangers sold Angotti to the Chicago Black Hawks. Angotti had scored only two goals and four points and was used sparingly in twenty-one games. He was angry at being traded and because he had not played more.

"You work like hell and the guy in the net gives it away," Angotti said in his farewell blast at the Rangers. He didn't mention Giacomin by name. He did not have to. Everyone knew to whom he referred.

Adding to Eddie's misery was a quote attributed to George "Punch" Imlach, successful coach and general manager of the Toronto Maple Leafs. Imlach was asked about the sad plight of the Rangers. He said Giacomin was "no goalie," noting that Eddie once lacked the ability to play Junior A hockey.

But for all those who ridiculed, booed, and unjustly placed the blame for the Rangers' shortcomings on Giacomin, voices were heard that rallied to Eddie's defense.

Rod Gilbert was one of the first to speak up.

"I predict Eddie Giacomin is going to be a great goalie," the player destined to become the highest scorer in Ranger history told a luncheon meeting of the New York Hockey Writers Association.

Not many of the writers believed Rod. They thought he was just being kind to Giacomin, trying to lift his spirit in troubled times. Like most fans, many sports writers were convinced Giacomin was not a major-league goaltender.

Gilbert continued to crusade in Eddie's behalf in an interview with Red Fisher of the *Montreal Star*.

"I'm disappointed with the way our season is going,"

Gilbert told Fisher. "I knew we had some weaknesses but I didn't think they were that bad. I'll tell you something else, and maybe you won't believe me, but I feel we'll do a lot better next season. For one thing, our goalkeeper is much better than anyone thinks he is. I watched him in training camp and I played against him and I couldn't beat him. It's not Eddie Giacomin's fault alone that we're losing. No one on the team works or tries harder in games or practice than Eddie. I was surprised when they sent him down. They should have been more patient with him. The team was playing poorly and the fans blamed it all on Eddie. They made it seem that he, rather than the whole team, was the cause of our problems."

Jean Ratelle also spoke up.

"Eddie's in a tough spot. He came in with a losing team and he's getting all the blame because he's the goalie and people always blame the goalie. A goalie can only be as good as the team in front of him. Give Eddie credit; he's the hardest worker and best team player I ever saw. He stays late at practice and works on correcting his mistakes. He never once has blamed us. I can see great potential in Eddie. Once he gets more experience and learns the teams and shooters in the league, he's going to become great."

Looking back at Giacomin's disastrous first season, Hadfield and Seiling tried to put things in proper perspective.

"Let's face it; we weren't a very good team. In fact, we were pretty bad," said Hadfield. "We had a losing situation for a long while and Eddie was the unlucky guy who walked right into the middle of it. It was a bad situation. We took defeats in stride. We had some guys who weren't playing as well as they could and a lot of young, inexperienced guys, but when Emile took over you could see things start to change. He got rid of the guys who didn't fit into his system, brought in more scouts, reorganized the farm system, and made some key trades. Eddie's big problem his first year was that his style of goaltending was new to us and we weren't used to him."

"It was very difficult for Eddie at first," said Seiling, another Ranger often maligned by New York fans. "First of all, he was new. There was a lot of pressure on him. He got so much publicity at the start of the season that the fans and the press expected him to be an immediate sensation and to be our savior. But it doesn't work that way. It takes more than one player to turn a team around. The fans and press got on Eddie and he took all the blame. It wasn't fair. It was cruel and uncalled for. I don't know how he put up with it."

Giacomin's demotion to Baltimore did not last long. Maniago bruised his ribs on January 19 against Toronto. Eddie was recalled to share the goaltending with Simmons until Maniago recovered from his injury and could play.

Things had not changed with the Rangers while Eddie was in Baltimore. They still were losing and going nowhere. Eddie lost to Detroit, 5-1, two days after rejoining the team. Then he beat the Red Wings, 4-3, on January 26 for only his second victory since November. He lost to Montreal, 6-2, on January 29 but was in goal again the following night when the Rangers caught Toronto off guard and won, 8-4.

It was Eddie's last winning fame of the season. He lost four straight games, surrendering sixteen goals, and after a 5-2 loss to Chicago on February 16, he was through for the season.

"He was a disappointment—a major disappointment," Francis reluctantly admitted. But the coach insisted he still had not lost faith in Eddie's ability.

It did not seem that way. Maniago played the final 18 games of the season. Although the Rangers didn't win that often, Maniago played well and became popular among Madison Square Garden spectators.

Francis saw to it that Giacomin did not waste time sitting on the bench. He told him to study the goaltending techniques of such veterans as Glenn Hall and Terry Sawchuk. He devised a series of practice drills for his struggling rookie goaltender. Long after other players had gone home or out for beers, Francis and Giacomin would still be on the ice together.

"He was constantly after me," said Giacomin. "Pushing, pushing, pushing, all the time. Making me demand more of myself than I usually did myself. He chided me. He bugged me. He lectured me. He kept on me. Over and over and over again."

Francis paid special attention to Eddie at practice. He told him to go after each practice shot as though it were a real game. He had teammates line up rows of pucks on the ice and machine gun Giacomin with shot after shot. Sometimes he told Eddie to drop his stick and stop the rapid-fire shots with his arms, legs, and chest.

"If I did something wrong at practice, he'd stop everything and point out my mistake," said Eddie. "If I did it again, he'd stop practice again and correct me. We'd sit down together and have long talks about goaltending. I learned things from Emile about goaltending that I never knew before."

Francis's decision not to play Giacomin in the final two months of a losing season was simple: He wanted to protect the rookie from the anger and abuse of the fans. He did not want Eddie to lose his confidence. Emile Francis was thinking of next season.

"Even though Eddie wasn't playing, he kept working hard in practice and made every effort he could to improve and overcome his weaknesses," said Francis. "We had a lot of long talks, going over shooters in the league, and discussing goaltending."

"For the first time in my life I had a goaltender coaching me," said Eddie. "In the past I always played for coaches who had been forwards or defensemen, and they didn't know much about goaltending."

Despite the confidence-building pep talks and practices, Eddie could not erase from his mind the memory of a depressing season.

The season ended on April 3 in Madison Square Garden as it had started on October 24. The Rangers played Montreal and lost. Only the score was 4-1 not 4-3, and Maniago, not Giacomin, was the goaltender. Eddie had not played in almost eight weeks and there was little reason for him to feel proud of his first season as an NHL goaltender: only seven winning games out of 36, not one shutout, and a goals-against average of 3.66. Those numbers might have looked fine as Ted Williams's batting average, but for a goaltender they were as depressing as a baseball player who batted .220.

As for the Rangers as a team, they had even less to be proud of. They finished last, failing to qualify for the playoffs for the fourth consecutive year. They won only eighteen of seventy games and for the eighth season in a row had a losing record. Forty-seven points represented their lowest total since 1948–49, and the 261 goals scored against them were the most since 1943–44. They scored only 195 goals as a team. Only the Bruins had a more inept offense and defense than the Rangers.

Now it was spring and the sun was warm in New York. Eddie put away his skates and went back to his summer job in Sudbury driving an ice cream truck for Silverwood Dairies.

There were those critics who believed after the 1965–66 season that Giacomin had a far better future selling ice cream than he did as a goaltender. There were games that first season in which even Eddie himself may have wished he were driving an ice cream truck instead of being the sitting duck behind the team with the worst defense in hockey.

"I've been a pro six years and I've been with a lot of losers," said Giacomin. "I guess I know you've got to take the bad with the good."

The first season had been almost all bad.

"Everything went just about as bad as it could go," said Eddie, looking back at the ordeal of his first season in the NHL. "But," he vowed, "it's going to be different next season."

Chapter 8

The Night They Threw Garbage at a Goalie in the Garden

"IT WAS A WICKED THING TO DO."

THE ugly noise started in the seats high above the Madison Square Garden ice. At first it was muffled and distant. But then the rumbling of hostile, angry boos from the crowd grew louder and louder, until it reached a deafening roar. It seemed as though every voice in the old arena was booing in collective rage and disapproval.

Suddenly, without warning, the first missile came hurtling down from the gallery at the Ninth Avenue end of the building. A beer container hit the ice and splattered its foamy liquid near the Ranger goal.

It was the beginning of one of the most vile and cruel demonstrations of spectator abuse against an athlete in New York sports history.

It was November 9, 1966, a night that will live in infamy for Eddie Giacomin for the rest of his life.

Apple cores. Orange peels. Half-eaten sandwiches. Paper cups. Popcorn boxes. Eggs. Coins. Shredded programs. Rolled-up newspapers. All were among the debris raining down toward the forlorn figure standing in front of the Ranger goal.

There was no place for Eddie to hide. As the litter the fans threw at him fell around him, he could only stand alone and humiliated and use his stick to slowly sweep the garbage inside the goal cage.

Marg Giacomin sat with the other players' wives and watched as her husband was pelted with garbage thrown by the fans.

"I must have been very naïve as a hockey player's wife at the time," said Mrs. Giacomin. "It didn't upset me that much at first because I thought the fans were angry because the team was very poor that season. It didn't dawn on me until later that people were making Eddie the victim. That made me angry. It was a terrible experience for him."

Catcalls, jeers, and boos echoed through the arena. A banana peel and other assorted fruit and missiles hit the ice. The fans cursed Giacomin and shouted obscenities at him.

The Bruins had scored twice in the final 89 seconds of the game to tie the Rangers, 3-3, in a game New York should have won. For the third straight game Giacomin had been unable to protect a third-period lead. The team was playing poorly. Clearly Giacomin was struggling and not playing well.

It seemed like his rookie year all over again. Only worse. New York fans took out their anger and frustration against Eddie. They blamed him for the tie that should have been a win.

And now they were throwing garbage at him.

The Rangers were in last place with a 2-5-2 record and it was all Eddie's fault.

He was not even supposed to be playing against Boston. He had come off the bench early in the second period to replace Cesare Maniago. New York's starting goaltender had stopped John McKenzie's shot with his chin and had to leave the game for stitches. New York led, 2-1, at the time on goals by Reggie Fleming and Bob Nevin, and when Harry Howell scored to make New York's lead 3-1, it appeared the Rangers would win easily.

The fans thought so. So did Giacomin. He was performing well in relief, turning aside every Boston thrust, including several long slap shots by a crew-cut eighteen-year-old Boston rookie defenseman named Bobby Orr.

The Rangers thought they had the game won. They must have. The forwards stopped checking. The defensemen became careless. The Rangers quit but the Bruins did not. Suddenly the game was tied and the fans were booing and throwing garbage down at Eddie.

He didn't really deserve it.

The Bruins' second goal came with 1:29 left in the game. Some of the crowd already had moved toward the exits, assuming there was no way New York could lose. Wayne Connelly swept behind the Ranger net with the puck and met indifferent resistance from the Ranger defense. Giacomin had the goal post blocked against a possible shot by Connelly. Instead the Bruins' forward rifled a shot pass in front of the net.

Ron Murphy was unchecked. Before Eddie had time to turn toward the new threat, the puck was past him.

The crowd booed.

Question: Do you blame the goalie when an enemy is permitted to stand unmolested in front of the net?

With forty-five seconds to play in the game, Emile Francis sent his best men—Don Marshall, Phil Goyette, Wayne Hillman, Nevin, and Howell—out to protect the one-goal lead.

Boston coach Harry Sinden removed goaltender Gerry Cheevers and sent out Connelly as an extra skater. The stocky forward took a pass-out from Ron Stewart from behind the net. Connelly's point-blank shot whizzed past Eddie and, with only thirty-four seconds left, the score was 3-3.

That's when the booing reached its peak and the deluge of garbage came down from the fans.

"I'm glad Connelly happens to be a right-hand shot because he was in perfect position for the pass and the shot. A left-hand shot couldn't have received the pass or shot," said Sinden.

Question: Is it Giacomin's fault that Connelly isn't left-handed?

The boos and garbage directed at Eddie were only the beginning of the criticism of the Ranger goaltender. Most of the next day's newspapers blamed Eddie for costing New York a victory.

One hockey writer, however, who knew that Giacomin was not totally responsible for the Rangers' dreadful collapse was Mel Woody of the *Newark News*.

PUT THE BLAME ON GIACOMIN, RIGHT?... WRONG! was the eight-column banner headline above his story.

"The unfortunate part of being a goalie is that no one really cares whether a goal is his fault or not. If he stops the puck, he's great. If he doesn't he's a bum," wrote Woody.

Clearly Eddie was a bum in the eyes of the fans who booed, cursed, and pelted him with garbage.

"Giacomin took a bum rap," he continued.

In the dressing room after the game, it was obvious that Giacomin was badly shaken, both by his failure to hold the lead and by the wrath of the crowd. But unlike many athletes following defeat, Eddie did not hide from the reporters nor vent his anger upon them.

"Ed Giacomin looked like a man who had just awakened from a nightmare," Tim Moriarty wrote in *Newsday*. "The Ranger goalie sat in front of his locker, head bowed. When he raised his head, he looked as if he was ready to cry, but he didn't. He merely shook his head."

"It's hard to believe. We looked like easy winners," he said, his voice barely audible and thick with emotion. "It's my fault. I allowed them to tie it."

Did he ever think of throwing back the garbage at the fans?

"You bet I did. Many times—but you can't. It's happened before, but never like this," he said.

Eddie's teammates were angry at themselves for having allowed victory to elude them and they were angry at the crowd for having treated their goaltender so poorly.

"Fans can be brutal and they were to poor Eddie," said Rod Gilbert. "It was a disgraceful sight. They should be ashamed of themselves for what they did to Eddie."

Rod Seiling looked at Eddie and shook his head. "Eddie's not one to show his emotions outwardly, but I'm sure he was hurt deep down. He'll always bear scars inwardly for what they did to him. It would be easy for Eddie to say who needs this and quit. But Eddie's not that kind of man."

Even the Bruins were disgusted by what New York fans had done to Eddie.

"My god," said Eddie Westfall, "what an awful thing for people to do to another human being. Poor Eddie. When all that junk was coming down on him, he had to stand there and just take it. I thought he'd have to hide in the net."

No one was more enraged by what some fans had done than Francis.

"I thought it was wicked of them to throw things," said the energetic little coach, his eyes flashing. "It was one of the worst things I've seen in hockey. Holy geez, everything but the seats came down. I felt so sorry to see him have to stand there with all that crap falling around him."

Francis also was displeased with Maniago.

After Cesare was hit in the chin by the puck and Giacomin replaced him in goal, he went into the medical room for stitches. Then he returned to the Ranger bench.

"O.K., Cesare, get out there and get back in goal," ordered Francis.

Maniago walked past Francis and headed for a seat at the end of the bench. Francis assumed the goalie had not heard him.

"O.K., Cesare, let's go," he shouted.

Maniago looked at Francis with a pained expression on his face. "I don't think I can play anymore tonight. It's hurting me too much," he said.

Francis narrowed his eyes. As a goalie, "the Cat" never refused to play even if he were hurt. He had done so with a broken shoulder and a face full of stitches. He knew Giacomin never would refuse to play, no matter how badly hurt. Maniago had committed an unpardonable sin in the eyes of his coach.

"Get back down at the end of the bench," snapped Francis.

Up until that moment Francis had been undecided as to who would be the Rangers' number-one goaltender. Giacomin had not played well and Francis had been alternating Eddie with the injury-prone Maniago. He did not like alternating goaltenders. He planned to alternate them for about 10 or more games before one or the other played himself in or out of the job.

Maniago had just played himself out of a job.

"Right then and there that settled it; that convinced me that Eddie Giacomin was my goalkeeper," said Francis. "I don't mean to say it was a lack of intestinal fortitude on Maniago's part, but I knew then that Eddie was the man I wanted."

Francis may have been the only man in New York who wanted Eddie at that moment.

Giacomin feared he was probably done for as Ranger goalie. He expected to be told he was being sent to the minor leagues—again. He felt his career was a disaster and might be over. He was playing poorly and the fans and the press were on him.

Four nights before the Boston disaster he had blown a 1-1 tie in the third period in Toronto and lost, 3-1. He turned the wrong way on one goal, wandered out of the net and allowed the Maple Leafs to dribble the puck across the red goal line for an embarrassing winning goal. Ranger fans had watched him self-destruct on television.

The following night in Madison Square Garden he was booed when he appeared on the ice. He was booed during and after the game, too. The Rangers led, 3-1, late in the third period. He fanned on an easy shot by Brian Conacher. Then Tim Horton shot from the blue line. The puck was going wide of the net. Something inside Eddie impelled him to reach for the puck.

Suddenly he realized his mistake.

He had deflected the shot he should not have touched in the first place, and now he was trapped too far outside the crease. The puck bounced directly to Dave Keon, who pushed it into the unguarded net with 3:17 remaining to play. Eddie tried vainly to get back to the net, stumbled, sprawled on his rear end, and watched Toronto gain a 3-3 tie because of the error he had made.

"Giacomin, stay in the damned net, will you?" bellowed fans behind the end boards as the boos and jeers started.

"Why, if he knows Francis frowns on it, does Giacomin persist in wandering," Stan Fischler wrote in the *Hockey News*. "Is it something psychological? Is he masochistic? Or is it simply a mere aberration born of inexperience that will be eliminated in time. Most likely it is the latter."

Eddie was wary of coming to practice the next morning at Madison Square Garden. He did not know what to expect.

"We were dead last and I knew damned well this was a crucial time," said Francis. "Either we'd get going now or get nowhere."

Francis ordered the players into Room 28 next to the dressing room at ten o'clock.

"O.K., get the film ready," he told John Halligan, the Rangers' publicity director. Francis intended to put on his own horror show: movies of last night's Boston game.

"I wanted to make damn sure every guy on the team saw all the mistakes they made that cost us the win," he said. "I didn't want any of them using the goaltending for a crutch and blaming the goalkeeper."

The lights were turned out and the film began to flicker on the screen when there was a pop and smoke suddenly filled the small room.

"Can you beat that," said Francis. "Things are already going badly enough for us and now the film projector blows up."

The coach thought fast. "O.K., into the dressing room," he told his players.

For the next thirty minutes Francis talked . . . and talked . . . and talked. He went over the Boston game and all the mental and physical mistakes the Rangers had made. He explained what had to be done—and what would be done—to see that those mistakes never happened again.

"I was hot," said Francis.

He wasn't talking about the unseasonably warm weather.

Giacomin sat stiffly in the dressing room, staring blankly ahead, the boos and curses from the fans the night before still ringing in his ears. He felt self-conscious. He waited for the words he feared were coming from the coach.

"From here on in, Giacomin, you're my goalie," said Francis.

Eddie could hardly believe his ears.

"I wanted to be sure every other guy on the club heard me," said Francis. "I didn't want anybody thinking badly about Eddie.

Afterward, Francis took Eddie aside. He had not talked to

him after the dreadful experience of the Boston game. He did not try to console him then and, although he felt sorry for what Eddie had gone through, he would not console him now.

"You're my goalie and you'll be in goal Saturday in Montreal and you'll be in goal the rest of this season," he said. "Let them yell their damned heads off," Francis told Eddie. "No fans are ever going to chase a player of mine out of the line-up—not as long as I'm here. If they ever throw garbage at you again, you make sure you pick it up and throw it right back at them."

Bolstered by Francis's faith in him and the coach's unwillingness to knuckle under to popular opinion, Giacomin played goal in Montreal on November 12.

He won the game, 6-3.

He played and won many games thereafter.

From that night of humiliation, self-doubt, boos, and insults, with the garbage falling around him, he compiled a 7-1-2 record with a 1.70 goals-against average. He went through a 12-2-2 streak with a 1.75 average. He increased it to 15-3-2 with a 1.60 average.

He was the goaltender on December 11 when the Rangers overpowered Montreal, 6-3, and found themselves in first place for the first time in five years.

There were no more boos. No more garbage. They cheered Eddie's every save that night. Outside in the streets after the games, the fans were waiting. They wanted his autograph.

Eddie could have said, "Go to hell." Perhaps he should have. But he didn't. Other men might have walked away. Giacomin signed autographs.

The 1966–67 season became gloriously delightful for Eddie and for the Rangers. Giacomin went from zero to hero in executing his remarkable turnaround.

He played thirty-eight consecutive games, beginning on November 12 and continuing until March 12. His record during the span was 23-12-3 with five shutouts. Four of his losses were by only one goal. He received a bonus of $750 from the league for leading the Vezina Trophy competition for the season's first thirty-five games and he was chosen to play in his first All Star game.

The Rangers, who had been picked to finish in last place, were either in first place or challenging for the lead for most of the second half of the season.

The terribly humiliating experience in the game against Boston and the unexpected chance for redemption given him by Francis in the following game against Montreal were Giacomin's turning points.

"I would never have made it unless Emile had faith in me," said Eddie. "The next game in Montreal, that was the key to it all; that was the turning point for me. I expected Emile would switch to Maniago but he stuck with me, and every guy on the club played his best and we won."

"I always had confidence in Eddie's ability and I never lost faith in him, even though things were going badly for him," said Francis. "He never quit on himself and he never gave up or let it get him down. He's a fighter, and that's what I liked about him."

The special practices the coach devised for his goaltender as a rookie continued on the road and at the team's practice rink at Skateland in New Hyde Park, Long Island. Teammates bombarded Eddie with shots for thirty-five minutes without interruption. Francis worked with Giacomin on his style of roaming out of the net. He told Eddie not to abandon his style of wandering but to curtail it and use it as a tactical weapon or as an element of surprise, much the way a baseball player might suddenly lay down a bunt or a football quarterback might catch the opposition off guard with an end-around or double-reverse.

Rivals as well as teammates could hardly believe the sudden transition of Giacomin from a goaltender with immense potential but a propensity for inconsistency and making glaring mistakes into a consistently steady goalie.

"All of a sudden he turned it around and became the best in the league," said the Bruins' Westfall.

"He became great almost overnight," said the Canadiens' Jean Beliveau. "Eddie was always at his best as a stand-up goalie, but he had fallen into a habit of flopping to the ice too often. Now he only went down when he had to."

There were a profusion of memorable moments for Giacomin during the 1966–67 season.

He was confronted with hockey's most rare and dramatic play on December 26 against Boston—a penalty shot—and he handled the goaltender's most dreaded shot perfectly.

Referee Bill Friday called the penalty shot when Howell fouled Dallas Smith from behind in the act of shooting on a breakaway.

"Come out a little on this guy," teammate Bernie Geoffrion whispered to Eddie before players from both sides cleared the ice and Smith prepared to take the puck in center ice and attack Giacomin.

The Madison Square Garden crowd was tense as Smith moved slowly in crisscrossing motions toward Giacomin, gradually increasing speed. Giacomin skated out of his crease in a low crouch to challenge the Boston defenseman. Smith had virtually no shooting angle. He shot from point-blank range and Eddie smothered the puck.

The crowd roared its approval. Geoffrion and other teammates raced to the Ranger net and hugged Eddie. Geoffrion, the former Montreal star whom Francis had coaxed out of retirement, scored two goals and the Rangers won, 5-1.

"We're Number One!" the crowd chanted. They were right. The Rangers were in first place.

On December 4 Giacomin played one of his finest games

of the season. Although he was beaten by Montreal, 3-1, he faced constant pressure and forty-three shots. He stopped forty of them.

On November 26 he shut out Toronto, 5-0, and in his next start on November 30 he made thirty-two saves and shut out Chicago, 5-0. Now he was seeking his third consecutive shutout on December 3 against Boston. The game ended in a 2-2 tie but when Eddie's streak of 175 minutes, 24 seconds of shutout goaltending finally ended, the crowd rose to its feet to cheer and applaud him.

On Christmas night he shut out the Black Hawks again, 1-0, on Geoffrion's goal, stopping six of Bobby Hull's blazing shots.

But there was nothing so delightful as the first shutout of his NHL career on October 23 in Madison Square Garden against Toronto. The teams were locked in a suspenseful, scoreless tie in the third period and Eddie and the Maple Leafs' Johnny Bower were matching one another with outstanding saves. The second period was particularly scary for Giacomin; he was forced to make sixteen saves. Something had to give. Someone had to score a goal.

At 7:15 of the final period, Red Berenson's shot deflected off Wayne Hillman's skate and into the Toronto goal cage. Eddie went on to protect his insecure lead and won, 1-0, stopping twenty-nine shots.

As the final seconds ticked off and the Maple Leafs swarmed around Giacomin, the crowd stood and stamped its feet and when the game was over the fans cheered Eddie. Francis and every Ranger rushed to Eddie and embraced him.

The shutout had added significance for Eddie. George "Punch" Imlach, Toronto's coach, had criticized Giacomin as a rookie.

"Anytime I play Punch Imlach's team, I try that much harder," Eddie said in the dressing room. He was clutching the souvenir puck of his first NHL shutout. "Anytime it's against him, I want to win that much more. Anytime I can beat his team, I get that much more satisfaction."

"I've got a good memory; I haven't forgotten what he said about me. He called me a lousy goaltender. He said I was nothing more than a Junior B goalie and that I'd never be anything else but that. He said I'd never make it as a goalie. I guess I always have to keep proving myself to the man, eh?" Eddie said with a wink and a smile.

Imlach agreed that Giacomin had, indeed, played a fine game and that, yes, he had developed into a fine goaltender.

But if Punch still needed more convincing, Eddie took care of that. He shut out Imlach's team three times that season.

"You can't get away from it," Giacomin told Bob Gockley of the *Long Island Press* after shutting out Toronto, 5-0, on November 27. "The guys out in front of me are doing a terrific job. The defensemen have been great, particularly Arnie Brown and Al MacNeil."

When the defense had let him down as a rookie and later in the 1966–67 season, Eddie never blamed his teammates. Now when he was playing so well and shutting out opponents, he was giving credit to his teammates.

It was typical of Eddie Giacomin.

Another of the goaltender's brilliantly played games was his 1-0 conquest of high-scoring Detroit on February 22. He had not played well in the previous game against Toronto, and Maniago had come off the bench to relieve him in the 6-0 defeat. Eddie had been flopping on the ice, instead of playing his stand-up acrobatic style.

"Right then and there I decided to stop sprawling, stay on my feet, cut down the angles, and see what happened," said Giacomin.

Bob Nevin scored the only goal Eddie needed to win after the game was only seventy seconds old. Two former Rangers,

Andy Bathgate and Dean Prentice, tested Giacomin with difficult shots late in the game but Eddie gloved them both. Once the clever Bathgate tried to jab the puck between Eddie's legs in a goal-mouth scramble for a loose puck, but Giacomin's fast reflexes blocked the scoring attempt.

The most dangerous of the twenty-six shots the Red Wings' propelled at him came in the first period when Gordie Howe had Giacomin at his mercy. Seldom did the highest scorer in hockey history miss in such situations. But Eddie made the save.

"That was the most crucial play of the game," said Francis. "Howe had plenty of time to crank up but Giacomin timed his move perfectly, came out just far enough to cut down the angle, and got Gordie to fire into his pads. It was a great play on Eddie's part."

The Red Wings' star was muttering and cursing to himself for having been stopped by Giacomin. He had tried to fake Eddie into believing he would shoot high but instead he kept his shot low. The move did not fool Giacomin.

"Eddie's improved quite a bit," observed Bathgate. "He doesn't give up those cheap goals anymore."

Eddie never told anybody but he played the game with a painfully swollen finger on his stick hand.

Giacomin still wandered from his net to clear pucks, but he did not overuse the maneuver as he had as a rookie. He remembered what Francis told him: "When a goalie comes out too far and then has to go back, he loses sight of the puck."

"I'm more or less restricted by Emile from coming out of the net too often," he said. Then he chuckled to himself.

"There was one game where I fell back into my old habit of getting caught out of the net too much. Emile came into the dressing room and gave us all a little talk," said Eddie.

"The Cat" never mentioned any names but he said: "A goaltender's place is in the net, not playing defense, and a goaltender isn't being a goaltender or helping the team when he's always over in the corner of the rink."

Eddie got the message.

One of the reasons Francis admired Eddie was that his goaltender reacted so well to adversity and had a high-pain threshold.

The Rangers were playing in Toronto on January 4 when a shot by Frank Mahovlich, one of hockey's hardest shooters, smashed into Eddie's jaw, and he fell back into the net, knocked unconscious by the terrific impact of the shot.

Francis and trainer Frank Paice rushed across the ice to where Eddie lay sprawled in front of the net, his jaw cut open, and blood spilling down the front of his uniform and forming a crimson pool on the white surface of the ice. All his teammates stood by and watched.

Everyone thought Eddie's jaw was broken.

"O.K., Eddie, you're comin' out," said Francis as Paice bent over Eddie and revived him with smelling salts.

"He wouldn't come out. He wouldn't leave the game," said Francis.

"I don't care if my jaw is broken. I want to stay in the game," Eddie told his coach.

Eddie stayed in the net and made many outstanding saves to help the Rangers gain a 1-1 tie. His jaw was cut and swollen and he could hardly move his mouth, much less talk. Later it was disclosed that he had a severe bruise.

"Certainly Giacomin has courage and was in obvious pain and yet he continued to play," Stan Fischler wrote in the *Hockey News.*

Other hockey writers now were telling their readers of Giacomin's rise to success.

"Goaltending in hockey is as important as quarterbacking is in football and pitching in baseball. If you haven't got an ace to handle the chores, you're as good as dead," Red Burnett, the dean of Canadian hockey writers, wrote in the

Toronto Star. "That's why Eddie Giacomin deserves so much credit in the New York Rangers' drive to the top of the National Hockey League. A year ago experts rated the wandering rookie the Achilles heel in the Rangers' line-up. Now Giacomin is the reason why the Rangers are where they are."

And in the *Montreal Star*, Red Fisher wrote: "The Rangers may not finish in first place this season, but even if they do not, their rags-to-riches progress is the achievement of the year where professional hockey is played. It may well be the story where any game is played and the man who has contributed the most exciting chapters is Giacomin, a goaltender who was flayed unmercifully by the people in the gallery as recently as the opening weeks of the current schedule."

The respected Montreal writer concluded by saying: "Now Giacomin is the man who should be named to the league's first All Star team for the first half of the schedule. He has my vote for the first All Star team."

Tony Marenghi of the Newark *Star-Ledger* wrote: "A goalie can only be as good as the rest of his club and now the rest of the Rangers are getting to be as good as their goaltender."

"I don't think I've ever seen a player work so hard in practice or try to correct his weaknesses and want to succeed as much as Giacomin," said Wayne Hillman.

Suddenly everyone seemed to have become an Eddie Giacomin fan, even most of the fickle New York fans who had booed and hurled garbage at him. After Eddie was hit in the face by Mahovlich's shot, many fans wrote to Eddie and the Rangers and implored that, for his safety, the goaltender wear a protective mask.

Giacomin refused.

"No, a mask isn't for me," he said. "Not in games, anyway. I'm not concerned about anything but my eyes. Cuts? I haven't had that many and I really don't worry about them.

No matter what the design of your mask, your eyes must be exposed. And if a puck hits you there, it doesn't matter whether you're wearing a mask or not. In fact, a goalie might be better off without a mask."

The prematurely gray-haired goaltender recalled an incident he had witnessed in the American League when goaltender Claude Dufour of Hershey was hit in the face with a shot. He was wearing a mask.

"The force of the puck drove the edge of the mask into his eye and he lost it. If the puck had hit skin, it might have given, and Dufour might not be blind in one eye," explained Giacomin.

The risk of injuries was just part of the danger of the most hazardous job in sports.

Reporters continued to ask Eddie about the reasons for his sudden success. His answers were almost always the same. He credited Francis for having faith in him when things went badly. He credited the improvement of the Rangers as a team for his success. His rise from obscurity to the NHL was compared to that of Johnny Unitas, the quarterback for the Baltimore Colts who was discovered as a sandlot football player for a semipro team in a small Pennsylvania town and rose to stardom in the National Football League.

The Rangers did not finish in first place. They slumped late in the season, winning only three of sixteen games and suffering through a nine-game losing streak. The season ended on April 2 with an 8-0 loss to Chicago. Giacomin had a chance to win the Vezina Trophy, but it ended when he gave up six goals and was replaced in the second period by Maniago.

"Why should Eddie stand there and take all that abuse?" Francis answered rhetorically after the game. "The reason we finished as high as we did is all because of that guy. I'm not going to let him take the blame for this one game."

Chicago finished the season in first place with a 41-17-12

record and was one of the league's highest-scoring teams. Giacomin accounted for five of the Black Hawks' defeats and twice shut them out.

Montreal finished second and Eddie beat them five times and held them to an average of 2.38 goals per game.

Giacomin's record against third-place Toronto included five wins, three shutouts, and a 2.06 goals-against average.

The Rangers, meanwhile, still had much to celebrate. They finished in fourth place and qualified for the playoffs for the first time since 1962. They compiled their first winning record since 1958. They won thirty games and Giacomin was the winning goaltender in all of them.

It was a remarkable season for Giacomin.

He led the league's goaltenders in games played (sixty-eight of seventy), minutes played (3,981), shutouts (nine), and the 173 goals he surrendered were only 2 more than Chicago, whose goaltenders Glenn Hall and Denis DeJordy won the Vezina Trophy.

He was selected to the first All Star team, was named the Rangers' most valuable player, and his 2.61 goals-against average was the second best in the league.

He finished second behind Chicago's Stan Mikita in voting for the Hart Trophy as National Hockey League MVP.

Many of his teammates, as well as New York fans and hockey writers, believed Giacomin deserved to win the MVP award more than Mikita.

"I know all about Mikita," Francis told Red Foley of the *New York Daily News.* "But I also know the Black Hawks would have finished first whether or not they had Mikita or Bobby Hull. I also know that without Giacomin we wouldn't even be in the playoffs. I don't know where we'd have finished. As far as I'm concerned, Eddie should have been the MVP."

A season-and-a-half of self-doubt had been erased for Giacomin. But as fate would have it, the Rangers were matched against Montreal in the first round of the Stanley Cup play-offs.

It was an overmatch. The powerful Canadiens, with far greater depth and more playoff experience, eliminated New York in four straight games.

Eddie's first playoff game was April 6, in the Montreal Forum. He was tense before the game but once play started the normal nervousness of his first playoff game vanished and he played with cool confidence.

Geoffrion scored for a 1-0 Ranger lead. It was a special moment for "the Boomer," who had starred for fourteen years in a Canadiens' crimson-and-blue uniform. Ralph Backstrom's goal created a 1-1 tie. But the Rangers and Giacomin were outplaying the favored Canadiens. Rod Gilbert scored twice and Vic Hadfield scored at 5:18 of the third period.

There was 14:42 to play in the game and the Rangers led, 4-1. How could they lose?

They found a way. Claude Provost scored on a shot Eddie should have stopped at 9:12. J. C. Tremblay scored at 9:34; John Ferguson scored at 11:00; Backstrom scored at 14:55; Jean Beliveau scored at 18:07.

Montreal won, 6-4. The Canadiens had scored five goals with 10:48 left in the game, overcoming a 4-1 deficit to win in one of the most remarkable comebacks in Stanley Cup playoff history.

For the Rangers, victory had seemed so certain with a three-goal lead that the entire team relaxed. Montreal, however, refused to quit.

"From the minute they got their second goal to the end of the game, we hardly seemed to touch the puck," lamented Francis.

"I felt sorry for Eddie," said Gump Worsley. "It was his playoff debut and he was coasting along with a 4-1 lead. Then he collapsed."

Gump did not play goal for Montreal. He had been hit in

the head by an egg thrown by one of Madison Square Garden's hostile spectators during the season and suffered a mild concussion. His replacement was a short, chunky rookie named Rogie Vachon.

Unlike Worsley, Beliveau believed the Ranger collapse was more the fault of the team rather than its goaltender.

"The Rangers became too overconfident and thought they had the game won; they let up," said the Montreal center. "It's wrong to place all the blame on Giacomin. It wasn't the goalie who allowed us to get into position so close to take so many shots."

The Rangers had neither the speed nor size to match Montreal in the second game, and when their forwards did get scoring opportunities, Vachon stopped them with brilliant saves. It was 1-1 with 12:14 remaining in the game when the Canadiens won, 3-1, on goals by John Ferguson and Backstrom.

New York lost the third game in Madison Square Garden, 3-2, when Montreal scored twice in the first three minutes and Vachon held off the Rangers' late threats. Now the Canadiens were only one victory from eliminating the Rangers.

They did it on April 13, winning, 2-1, on Ferguson's goal after 6:28 of a sudden-death overtime period. The weather outside was unseasonably hot in Manhattan; inside Madison Square Garden, the temperature was also warm and the ice soft.

Tremblay broke a scoreless tie midway through the first period when his rising 60-foot slap shot from the blue line eluded Giacomin. Goyette, with help from Nevin and Marshall, tied it for the Rangers with 2:04 left in the second period. After that, Giacomin and Vachon kept the crowd on the edge of its seats with spectacular goaltending. The Canadiens could not put the puck past Eddie and Vachon rejected every shot the Rangers fired at him.

"We should have won. In fact, I was sure we had," said Gilbert.

Rod was talking about Red Berenson's shot at the five-minute mark of the overtime period. Berenson broke across the Canadiens' blue line with the puck and whipped a 50-foot shot toward Vachon. The Montreal goalie reacted late, kicked out a leg, and the puck flew past him.

The crowd rose in excitement. Berenson raised his stick in goal-scoring tradition. The Rangers were ready to leap off the bench in jubilation. This was it. They had won.

"I couldn't believe it. I just couldn't believe the puck did not go in," moaned Gilbert.

The puck hit the goal post. It was a bad break for the Rangers, a good break for the Canadiens. Just the break they needed. Less than two minutes later they won the game, 2-1, and wiped out the Rangers in four games.

Again it was Ferguson who scored the game-winning goal. Claude Larose shot and Giacomin caught the puck. Then it slipped out of the webbing of his glove and dropped at his feet in front of the net. Ferguson bullied his way past defenseman Arnie Brown, skated past the net, swiped at the puck with his stick, and missed it. The puck still sat inches from the red goal line, but before Giacomin could recover it, Ferguson reached backward, took a second poke with the tip of the blade of his stick, and nudged the puck into the net for the winning goal.

Eddie blamed himself for the Rangers losing the playoff series in four games.

"I blew two of those games myself," he said. "There were a couple of goals I should have got in the first game, and I made the wrong move in the third game on a shot by Beliveau. I'm not satisfied with the way I played."

Giacomin's teammates tried to console their goaltender.

"Eddie's goaltending is the reason we made the playoffs for the first time," said Ratelle. "He had nothing to be ashamed of. We finished in last place the year before and he led us into the playoffs this season."

Geoffrion said: "The Canadiens thought it was going to be a cinch. Even though they beat us, it was no cinch."

Then "the Boomer" nudged a reporter's arm in the dressing room and drew him aside.

"Hey, this is just the beginning. We'll be back. We got ourselves a goalie who is great. This you can believe. 'The Boomer' is telling you this and you can believe him."

Chapter **9**

Second Season in New York:
A Star Is Born

> "EDDIE HAS MADE A PLACE FOR HIMSELF
> AS ONE OF THE BEST GOALIES IN THE NHL."

"OF all the goaltenders in hockey, Eddie Giacomin has the brightest future," said Jacques Plante.

Eddie felt a great sense of pride and accomplishment when he learned what Plante said about him. "Jake the Snake," as the players and sports writers called Plante, had not played since his retirement from hockey following the 1964–65 season. But he kept a close eye on hockey from his home in Montreal and often watched Giacomin play against the Canadiens in the Forum.

Plante was highly opinionated and quick to criticize. He gave praise grudgingly and used superlatives judiciously. Even though he was retired from hockey he still was considered the master craftsman of the goaltending trade, an astute student of goaltending and one of the best ever to play the position. Giacomin studied Plante's techniques closely and adopted some of his goaltending nuances.

As the 1967–68 season approached, Eddie knew he could not afford to lull himself into a state of false security. He knew, as any man must know, that life is a series of challenges and one success does not guarantee another success.

"I have to prove last season wasn't any fluke," said Eddie.

The 1967–68 season would be different in many ways, for Giacomin and every other player. It would mean more games, more opponents, more travel, and more pressure.

The National Hockey League was expanding from six to twelve teams, the most ambitious expansion program in professional sports history, and the regular season schedule was being increased from seventy to seventy-four games. The season would start earlier, end later, and for the first time there would be coast-to-coast travel.

Entering the league were the Philadelphia Flyers, St. Louis Blues, Los Angeles Kings, Minnesota North Stars, Pittsburgh Penguins, and the Oakland or California Golden Seals, the city name depending upon the whim of the team's various owners. The expansion teams were each stocked with twenty players from the established six teams and the NHL was divided into East and West divisions; expansion teams in the West, Boston, Chicago, Detroit, Montreal, Toronto, and the Rangers in the East.

Enthusiasm among Ranger followers was high when the season opened. The Rangers had finished fourth last season and with Giacomin, now an all-star goalie, and a potentially stronger team, they could finish higher. Still the teams to beat in the East were Chicago, Montreal, and Toronto, the Stanley Cup champion.

"We've got to get off to a fast start if we're going to be in the race," said Eddie, a look a determination in his eyes.

The Rangers did. They compiled a 6-1-3 record in their first ten games, garnished by an eight-game undefeated streak, and moved into first place. It was the team's best start in almost fifteen years. Eddie was in the net in each game and his goals-against average was 2.10. He recorded his first shutout on November 1 in Oakland and the Rangers' defense and checking was so efficient that he was required to make only sixteen saves.

It was a far cry from his fifty-shot nights in the minor leagues and his troubled rookie season in the NHL.

Giacomin's practice routine never varied from the day he joined the Rangers. Only now he had a new drill. Vic Hadfield would line up on the left, Rod Gilbert on the right, both fifteen or twenty feet from the net. They would alternate shooting 10 pucks at Giacomin in skeet-shoot fashion, firing pucks almost simultaneously. Eddie would toss his stick aside and bat the barrage of pucks away with his hands, legs, arms, and feet.

"I like to kid around as much as the next guy," said Eddie, "but not at practice. You fool around at practice and it's going to hurt you in a game."

Giacomin then disclosed that for the first time in his career he was experimenting with wearing a mask in practice, but he continued to refuse to wear a mask in games.

"I'm not the nervous type and I don't worry about getting hurt by the puck," he told *New York Post* columnist Milton Gross. "But the lighting is so much poorer in practice rinks that I might as well reduce the odds against getting hurt. Besides, you can't tell where the puck is going these days with everybody using these new sticks with the curved blades. A goalie used to know what the puck was going to do when it was shot with a straight-bladed stick. With the curved blades, you never know. The puck is as unpredictable as a knuckle ball in baseball."

Of all the shooters in the league, no one shot the puck harder than Bobby Hull. The Golden Jet had the most feared slapshot in hockey. Goalies disliked playing against the powerfully built Chicago left wing. His shot traveled as fast as 120 miles per hour. And now, to make him even less appealing to goaltenders, he was using one of the new "banana-blade"-curved stick blades.

Hull set an NHL record during the 1965–66 season with fifty-four goals. Thirteen of them came at the expense of the Rangers. He scored eleven of his fifty-two goals in 1966–67 against Giacomin.

There were some Ranger-watchers who claimed Hull "owned" the Rangers. They claimed Giacomin choked when he played against the Golden Jet.

On November 22 Hull brought his curved blade to Madison Square Garden to play the Rangers. Bobby had scored fifteen goals in the previous seventeen games and Chicago had lost only once in eleven games. Giacomin was in a mild slump: two wins in six games after his fast start.

"If I told you Bobby Hull doesn't bother me, I'd be lying," Eddie said one afternoon between bites on a meatball sandwich in an Italian restaurant.

"He has the hardest shot I've ever seen. But I've got to try not to let him bother me too much. When I play Chicago, I play a little game inside my head. If I can stop Hull on the first couple of shots he takes, I figure maybe I've got him. It builds up my confidence, and I like to think maybe it breaks his confidence down a little."

Eddie's game plan did not stop Hull. The Golden Jet scored three times against Giacomin and the Black Hawks won, 7-1. Emile Francis sent Gilles Villemure into the game for the third period.

By now more people were convinced it must be true: Giacomin could not handle Hull's rifle shots. He was "gun-shy."

Giacomin was angry at the accusation.

"I'm not 'gun-shy.' They keep talking about how bad I play against Chicago. Stan Mikita and Bobby Hull are the two best and hardest shooters in the league. I don't know any goalie who really enjoys standing up to them."

Eddie often was asked by reporters if the terrific speed with which pucks are propelled toward his unprotected face bothered him. They wanted to know if the constant sixty minutes of goaltending pressure and responsibility to his team concerned him.

"If it did, I'd never admit it," he said, annoyed at the suggestion. "Too many goalies have, and once they did they were labeled as guys who will crack under pressure."

Eddie's eyes narrowed and his voice rose. "The day my nerves ever get the best of me, I'll never go back in goal again," he said.

The Rangers and Black Hawks played four more games in December and January. Each time Giacomin was on the bench and Don Simmons was in goal. It seemed as if Coach Emile Francis were admitting Hull's shot was too much for Giacomin to handle by keeping Eddie on the bench against Chicago.

The next meeting between Hull and the Rangers was March 3 in Madison Square Garden. Giacomin had shut out Philadelphia, 4-0, the day before. Would he play against the Black Hawks? Or would Francis keep him on the bench?

Eddie wanted to play. He wanted to prove the skeptics were wrong. He wanted to show them he could stop Hull and the Black Hawks.

Stop the Golden Jet he did. Giacomin scored his second straight shutout, 4-0, and Hadfield scored his second straight winning goal. The Rangers checked so persistently that the high-scoring Black Hawks were able to take only thirteen shots. Eddie stopped them all, including three by Hull. He made his point.

Now Giacomin was working on his third consecutive shutout on March 6 against Detroit. He won, 6-1, but when the Red Wings scored to end his shutout streak, a strange thing happened. The crowd at Madison Square Garden gave Eddie a standing ovation.

"It was the first time I ever got cheered for allowing a goal. It was quite a thrill," he said.

Often they had booed him. Once they had thrown garbage at him and cursed his name. Now they wanted to let him know how much they appreciated him.

Giacomin went on to lead the league with eight shutouts, joining a select group of goaltenders who have led the NHL in shutouts in successive seasons. He disclosed after one of the shutouts that it was worth more than the personal satisfaction of not having allowed the opposition to score a goal.

"I get $100 every time I get a shutout," said Eddie, a twinkle in his eyes.

He explained that it was part of a system of incentive or performance bonuses devised by Francis. Forwards receive bonuses for twenty- or thirty-goal seasons. So why not a shutout bonus for goalies?

Once Giacomin had a shutout late in the game, but one of his defensemen, Rod Seiling, inadvertently shot the puck past his own goaltender while attempting to rebound the puck off the end boards.

"Shouldn't Eddie get $100, anyway?" a reporter asked Francis.

"Hell, no. The puck went into the net, didn't it?" Francis said with a sly look.

The Rangers feasted upon the weaker expansion teams throughout the season and their 17-4-3 record against West Division foes helped them stay close to first-place Montreal.

From February 1 until the final game of the season on March 31, Giacomin played in all twenty-seven games without relief. He was superb and so were his teammates: seventeen wins, four ties, only six losses, four shutouts, and a goals-against average of 2.11. The Rangers lost three straight games during the second week of March. If they had not slumped, they might have finished first in the East. They won the last four games of the season and six of their last seven.

Montreal was first with ninety-four points. The Rangers finished with ninety points in second place, their highest level since 1957–58.

"New York gave us quite a scare," said Jean Beliveau, the Canadiens' captain. "Giacomin was the reason they finished second, so close to us. There is no doubt in my mind that Eddie has made a place for himself as one of the best goalies in the NHL."

Figures don't lie. The Rangers set a team record with thirty-nine victories and Eddie had a hand and a stick in thirty-six of them. He led the league in shutouts and wins and played in sixty-six games, twelve more than his closest rival, Les Binkley of Pittsburgh, whose occasional habit of smiling after he made a save caused him to earn the sobriquet of "the Smiling Goalie."

Giacomin also had much to smile about. His goals-against average was 2.44 and he was voted to the second All Star team. Montreal's Gump Worsley, playing in only forty games, was chosen for the first team on the basis of his remarkable 1.98 average.

Now it was time for the playoffs.

Eddie would face his old nemesis—Bobby Hull and the Black Hawks in the opening round.

Chicago had struggled to edge Toronto for fourth place and the last playoff position in the East. The Black Hawks had more scoring power than the Rangers: Stan Mikita led the league with 87 points and scored 40 goals; Bobby Hull led the league with 44 goals. The Hawks had other dangerous scorers in Kenny Wharram and Doug Mohns. But their defense was suspect; it had allowed 222 goals, compared to the Rangers' 183.

Clearly it was up to Giacomin to stop the high-scoring Black Hawks' forwards.

Because the Rangers had finished higher in the standings,

they received the home ice advantage; the first two games would be in New York's new Madison Square Garden, which had been opened earlier in the season.

Giacomin was sharp in the opening game on April 4 and so was Denis DeJordy, Chicago's goaltender. But Eddie was sharper. Orland Kurtenbach, Harry Howell, and Rod Gilbert scored the Ranger goals in Giacomin's first playoff victory, 3-1.

Now the Rangers, who had been picked to win the best-of-seven series, had momentum on their side. They could hardly wait for the second game on April 7.

National tragedy struck. Dr. Martin Luther King was assassinated in Memphis, Tennessee. President Lyndon B. Johnson declared April 7 as a day of mourning. The second play-off game was rescheduled for April 9.

It seemed insignificant at the time. What difference did two days make? It made a difference to the Rangers and to the Black Hawks. It took some of the edge off the intangible momentum that the Rangers had gained by winning the first game. It gave several of the Black Hawks' injured players more time to heal. Adding to Ranger problems was the disclosure that Bernie "Boom Boom" Geoffrion had a bleeding ulcer and would miss the remainder of the playoffs.

Despite the delay between games, the Rangers won the second game, 2-1. Gilbert scored the first goal. Then Giacomin's old friend, the Golden Jet, tied the score with a mighty shot. Eddie and DeJordy kept the crowd boiling with excitement by making breathtaking saves. The score remained tied until Don Marshall's third-period goal gave New York its winning margin.

New York fans were delighted. The Rangers had won the first two games of the series and looked as though they could sweep Hull and the Black Hawks off the ice in four games.

Or at least it seemed that way.

Game three was played in Chicago Stadium, a stark gray edifice that rises out of the jungle of concrete, blacktop, cyclone fences, and boarded-up bars in one of the city's dreary South Side neighborhoods. The Rangers led, 3-2, in the second period and were in full command of the tempo and of the game.

Then the roof fell in. Some say the Rangers sabotaged themselves by easing up, relaxing, forming a defensive shell too soon.

Pit Martin caught Giacomin off guard with a shot at 2:36 of the third period. The game was tied. The unpredictable pendulum of momentum had swung toward Chicago. The Black Hawks were fired up and their supporters in the crowd were urging them on. Mikita scored and it was 4-3, Chicago. Bobby Hull's brother, Dennis, scored and it was 5-3.

Francis paced nervously behind the Ranger bench. His players on ice were rattled and disorganized. Now Chicago was in complete control and every move the Rangers made, or didn't make, seemed to be an act of futility or a mistake on which the Black Hawks capitalized.

Seiling's goal narrowed the Ranger deficit to 5-4 and, for an instant, New York fans watching the game on television nurtured hopes of a comeback.

Mohns and Gilles Marotte scored. The Black Hawks had won, 7-4. They won the fourth game, 3-1, the winning goal by Marotte deflecting off Orland Kurtenbach and past Giacomin. Now the series was tied, 2-2.

The series was resumed in New York and, in a brilliantly played game, the score was 1-1 with 3:14 remaining in the third period. Sudden-death overtime seemed imminent.

The Black Hawks were executing a line change during play in center ice. Bobby Schmautz, a rookie forward who had scored only three goals all season, fired the puck blindly from near the red line toward the Ranger end zone, then turned away and skated toward the bench.

Suddenly the crowd gasped. The puck was behind Giacomin and inside the net and the red goal light was glowing. Chicago had scored the winning goal in its 2-1 victory and led in the series, 3-2.

How?

The puck Schmautz shot from center ice hit the stick of Ranger defenseman Jim Neilson, changed course in its ninety-foot flight, and flew over Giacomin's left arm and into the net.

"It was a freak goal," Seiling said softly in the dressing room. "I never saw a goal like that in my life. I doubt that I ever will again."

Seiling was Neilson's defense partner on ice and had the best view of the bizarre play.

"Schmautz just slapped wildly at the puck in center ice. He was just trying to shoot the puck down ice into our zone so his team could make a line change. 'The Chief' (the Rangers' nickname for Neilson, who is half Danish-Canadian, half Cree Indian) just happened to be in the way. As he was turning to go back after the puck, it hit the blade of his stick, changed direction, traveled in the air only about twenty feet, and went in the net."

Giacomin could not believe what had happened. No one could. Least of all Schmautz.

"It was strictly a fluke, the luckiest goal I ever scored. I couldn't believe it happened," Schmautz still says of his ninety-foot, game-winning goal.

"Eddie had the puck lined up," said Seiling. "Until it hit Neilson's stick and changed direction. There was nothing Eddie could do then; it happened so fast. It was just a bad break for Eddie. A bad break for all of us."

For all intents and purposes, the series was over for the Rangers when Schmautz golfed his billiard shot off Neilson's stick and past Giacomin. They were eliminated from the playoffs two days later in Chicago, 4-1.

The Rangers, who had led in the series, 2-0, had lost four straight games and their season was over.

New York outshot Chicago but its leading scorers failed to threaten DeJordy. Ratelle, a 32-goal scorer, did not score a goal in the six games. Neither did Bob Nevin, a 28-goal scorer during the season. Goyette also failed to score. Hadfield scored only once, Marshall only twice. The lone Ranger who was an effective scorer was Gilbert with five goals. The third period was the Rangers' downfall; they were outscored, 10-3.

People began to wonder how the Rangers could have lost. People began to wonder when they would ever survive the first round of the playoffs. People began to wonder if Giacomin was jinxed in the playoffs.

Eddie wondered about that himself.

"We played so well all season and then this happens to us," he said. "People don't remember what you did during the season. They only remember what you do in the playoffs. If you have a good playoff, you're a hero. If you have a bad playoff, they say you're a bum."

They weren't calling Eddie or any of his teammates heroes after they folded and blew a two-game lead and were beaten by the Black Hawks.

Schmautz' freakish goal that won the fiffh game was the turning point of the series.

"You could never blame Eddie, or any goalie, for a crazy goal like that one," said Hadfield.

Not everyone was as sympathetic toward the Ranger goaltender after New York's astonishing collapse against Chicago. Punch Imlach, who had criticized Giacomin as a rookie, still was not convinced.

"Eddie is usually very good, but he will sometimes give you the bad game when you least expect it," said the Toronto coach.

Chapter **10**

The Goalie Almost Scores a Goal

"I'M GOING TO KEEP TRYING; ONE OF THESE
DAYS I'LL DO IT."

THE Rangers led Montreal, 3-2, with less than 1 minute
to play. Ron Stewart's goal had put them in front. Madison
Square Garden fans were shouting the rhythmic "We're
No. 1! . . . We're No. 1! . . . We're No. 1!" Victory would
catapult the Rangers into first place in the East Division.

But the sixteenth game of the Rangers' 1968–69 season
was far from over. The Canadiens had the puck in New
York ice and were bombarding Eddie Giacomin with shots.
They had removed goalie Gump Worsley from the net,
dispatching a sixth forward into the game in an effort to gain
a tie. Additionally, the Rangers were short-handed; tough
guy Reggie Fleming had hooked Jean Beliveau and was in
the penalty box.

"When the Canadiens have a power play, watch out,"
warned Bernie "Boom Boom" Geoffrion. "The Boomer"
knew that better than anyone. He had starred for fourteen
years as a member of Montreal's mighty power play. Now he

was nervously pacing behind the bench in his first season as Ranger coach.

Beliveau, one of the best stickhandlers and shooters in the league, carried the puck across the New York blue line, and braked to a halt forty feet from Giacomin. He might have shot but instead he elected to leave a drop pass for Yvan Cournoyer, who had trailed him into the Ranger zone. Cournoyer drilled a rising shot, face high, at Giacomin.

Eddie reached up with his catching glove and the puck made a slapping noise as it smacked deep into the pocket of the trapper's mitt on the goalie's left hand.

Most goalies would have done one of two things: toss the puck aside to a teammate or hold it for a face-off. But Giacomin does not always do the expected. He often does the unexpected.

He dropped the puck at his feet, looked up ice, and caught a glimpse of Montreal's empty goal cage. He resembled a quarterback stepping up into a pocket of blockers before passing as he took a running start from his goal crease and shot the puck up ice through a maze of players.

The puck flew out of the Ranger zone, danced along center ice, and skipped across the Montreal blue line. It had plenty of momentum. And it was heading directly toward the open net.

The puck suddenly lost momentum and speed, veered to one side and slid past the goal post. The crowd gasped. The puck had traveled the length of the ice and only missed by a matter of inches going into the net.

Giacomin had come close to making hockey history. He had almost become the first goalie in history to score a goal in a regularly scheduled NHL game.

Chuck Rayner, a former New York goalie, and Clint Benedict had scored goals in exhibition games but until Michel Plasse scored in a minor-league game in Kansas City in 1971, no goalie ever had scored in a pro game.

Giacomin would come close to making hockey history again several times in years to come.

"If any goaltender ever scores a goal in the NHL, it will probably be Eddie," said Emile Francis. "He's not afraid to come out of his net and he shoots the puck so well."

Eddie never has concealed the fact that he wants to score a goal. Although the odds are certainly against him, or any goalie, doing so.

"I'm going to keep trying and one of these days I'll do it," he said with a cheerful smile. "I'd like to be the first goaltender to do something that has never been done before."

Giacomin explained that the chances of a goaltender are somewhere between slim and none.

"First of all, it has to be the perfect situation; we have to be short-handed so icing the puck can't be called and, of course, the other team must have pulled its goalie and be trying for a tie. The time left in the game and the situation we're in have to be just right, too, or it could backfire. I'd never take the chance of trying to score if it was too risky."

Eddie received a lot of good-natured kidding from his teammates after almost scoring a goal. He enjoys showing off his stickhandling and shooting ability in front of his teammates during frivolous moments in practice and often likes to challenge his teammates in one-on-one drills for beers or dollar bets.

"Hey, Eddie, quit trying to show the rest of us forwards up, will you?" Vic Hadfield often teased the popular goaltender.

After Giacomin almost scored against Montreal, Herb Goren of CBS Sports asked Worsley about it.

"He was taking a chance," said Gump, puffing on his usual postgame cigarette in the dressing room. "Somebody could have grabbed the puck he shot and fired it right back at

Eddie. And if that happened, Eddie would have been out of position."

The 1968–69 season was another successful one in which Giacomin continued to establish himself as the most durable goaltender in the league. He tied an NHL record by playing in 70 of 76 games and now, in the last three seasons, was an iron man who had played in 204 of his team's 220 games.

New York set a team record with forty-one victories and the gray-haired goalie with the gaunt, expressive face who constantly shouted instructions and warnings to keep his teammates alert in games, won 38 of those games to lead the league. His goals-against average was 2.55. His 7 shutouts fell one short of Glenn Hall's league-leading eight. Fourteen times he held opponents to only one goal in a game. He was named to the second All Star team and New York's West Side Association voted him the Rangers' most valuable player.

"Eddie is something special," Geoffrion said one day in his thick French-Canadian accent. "He has not played one bad game. He wants to win very badly and he is the spirit of this hockey club."

This was the season in which Eddie revealed for the first time that he was keeping a secret black book.

No. It wasn't the kind of little black books bachelors keep with them or husbands hide from wives.

"I keep a black book on all the shooters in the league," said Giacomin. "Everytime a guy scores against me, I write down a description of how the goal was scored in my black book. I don't want it to be a guessing game when a guy comes in on me with the puck. I like to know what to expect."

Eddie found his little black book useful during the season. After each game in New York, he jotted down how the goals were scored against him, where he felt he made a mistake, and the various moves of the shooters. He recorded his entries as soon as he and his wife Marg returned home from the game. On the road he scribbled notations into his little black book on the team bus, in his hotel room, or on the flight home. Before each game he opened his little black book and reviewed his notes on the shooters he would play against.

"Goaltending takes 100 percent concentration, especially since there are more teams now and we don't see each team as often anymore," Eddie said of his hazardous profession. "If I can get any little edge on the shooters that helps me beat them, I'll sure take it."

Eddie displayed some samples from his little black book about Detroit's top line.

Alex Delvecchio: "Always tries to fake me on the glove side. . . . Always around the net."

Frank Mahovlich: "Always be ready . . . he's a threat from the blue line in . . . tries to beat you with speed."

Gordie Howe: "Expect a shot almost anytime . . . might be looking somewhere else but be ready because right at that moment he could be in the act of shooting, even if he isn't looking at you . . . when he's got the puck, be ready . . . watch his backhand, he uses it a lot."

Sometimes there are surprises that even keeping a black book can't solve.

"Take Ralph Backstrom of Montreal," said Eddie. "He has always shot low on me since I've been in the league. So I had him pegged that way in my book. Then this season he comes in on me and I get set for the low shot and he puts a high one in past me."

Giacomin laughed.

"You know, I think that guy must keep a book on goalies," he said.

Eddie started the season auspiciously. He played the first thirty-one games and on December 4 New York was in first place with a 16-7-0 record. Then Eddie and his teammates went into a tailspin: an eight-game winless streak in which the offense produced only thirteen goals and Eddie was strafed for thirty goals.

It seemed like his rookie year all over again.

The Rangers were in Oakland on January 17. They had won only six of their last twenty-one games and had fallen from first-place contention. Their record was 22-18-3 after beating the Seals, 3-1, but although they had won they had not played well.

Geoffrion collapsed in the dressing room after the game. He had undergone stomach surgery one year ago and his midsection was a criss cross of surgical scar tissue. He suffered from nervous tension and bleeding ulcers. Because of his health, he was finished as Ranger coach.

Emile Francis was back in the demanding dual role of general manager and coach.

"The Cat" was angry with his players. He was disgusted with their poor record. The Rangers flew from San Francisco to St. Louis for a game the next night and arrived well after midnight.

The players assumed Francis would allow them to sleep late and then go to the rink for the normal noon meeting and pregame optional skate.

"Practice at nine o'clock sharp. Everybody on ice in uniform," Francis snapped at his travel-weary players on the team bus. He put the Rangers through a grueling practice. It was skate, skate, skate. He didn't even allow them to use pucks, an insult to a major-league team.

The Rangers were angry. Francis was happy. He wanted them angry.

That night they tied St. Louis, 2-2. It was a turning point. The defense tightened up and cohesion returned among the forward lines. Giacomin and the Rangers won six straight games, allowing only seven goals.

Francis had infused a new spirit within the team. Under

his direction, New York completed the season with a 19-8-6 record and finished in third place. Giacomin was brilliant down the stretch, losing only twice and allowing just fourteen goals in the final twelve games of the season.

"Giacomin is the best in the league and the figures back him up," proclaimed Francis.

But might it not be better if Eddie received more games off to prepare himself for the playoffs? Because of the increased schedule and travel, most teams had adopted the two-goalie system and alternated their goaltenders. Francis, however, refused to change. He believed in playing his best goaltender in virtually every game.

"You always go with your best," he snarled at reporters. "Eddie is the best. The only way I'd alternate goalkeepers is if I had two Giacomins. If the other clubs had anyone like Eddie, they wouldn't be fooling around using two or three goalies."

One game in particular stuck in Francis' mind as he extolled Giacomin's performance. It was on March 6 in Detroit. New York was coming off an 8-5 loss to Boston and a 4-4 tie with Chicago and with three weeks left in the season was in fourth place, two points ahead of Toronto and one point behind the third-place Red Wings.

Eddie played magnificently and the Rangers won, 4-1, starting a six-game undefeated streak. He robbed the Red Wings of numerous goals with his saves and when Detroit's power play was on, he destroyed it almost single-handedly, coming out of the net to shoot pucks back out that the Red Wings had shot into the Ranger end zone.

Standing outside the visiting-team dressing room in the Olympia and dragging on his Lucky Strike, Francis called it "the finest job of pressure goaltending I've seen. It was the biggest win of the season for us. We knew when we came in here that if we could get a win, it would go a heck of a long way toward getting us into the playoffs."

Giacomin minimized his performance. He praised the way his teammates had played in front of him.

"The funny thing about the game is that I really didn't feel the pressure," he said, toweling himself dry from his postgame shower. "I was surprised. When we got to the arena, I didn't feel anything. Maybe I should have, but I didn't."

Jean Ratelle, who scored the winning goal, said: "Eddie never lets the pressure bother him. It would not be good for a team before a big game if the players looked at their goaltender and saw he was nervous or had the jitters. If we see the goalie is relaxed and confident, it helps the rest of us feel the same way."

Ratelle shook his head: "I don't know how Eddie can be so relaxed. I don't know how any goalie can ever be relaxed. A goalie has to be on the ice for sixty minutes while the forwards and defensemen do not. There is pressure on a goalie all the time. It's the worst job in hockey."

Giacomin finished the season by playing more games than any goaltender in the league, and his goals-against average was a smart 2.55. But for the third straight season he was denied the Vezina Trophy, the symbol of league goaltending supremacy.

Glenn Hall and Denis Dejordy of Chicago won the Vezina in 1966–67. Gump Worsley and Rogie Vachon of Montreal won it in 1967–68. Hall, who had joined St. Louis in the expansion draft, and Jacques Plante, who had come out of retirement, won the trophy in 1968–69 with a combined goals-against average of 2.07.

Francis was angry. He insisted Giacomin deserved the Vezina Trophy.

"Eddie played seventy games and St. Louis goalies each played about half as many. I think the Vezina Trophy rules are wrong; to get the trophy a goalie should have to play at least fifty games," said Giacomin's strongest supporter.

The former goaltender had a point: Hall played forty-one games and had a 2.17 average and Plante played thirty-seven games and had a 1.96 average for the Blues.

"I'm not knocking what Hall or Plante did," said Francis, "but they probably wouldn't have maintained those averages if either of them had played as many games as Giacomin. It's just not fair."

Giacomin had other thoughts on his mind—the Stanley Cup playoffs. New York would face Montreal in the first round. The Canadiens had lost only nineteen games all season in edging Boston for first place. They had swept the Rangers out in four games in Eddie's first playoff in 1967. They had won the cup in 1968 and in three of the last four seasons.

Giacomin, however, was optimistic and confident. He had a score to settle. He had a point to prove. He wanted to show he could win in the playoffs. He wanted to end the criticism among fans and in the press of his goaltending failures the previous two seasons.

"We're a better team. We proved it this year by winning the season's series from them and we'll prove it again in the playoffs," he told Hal Bock of the Associated Press.

Then he smiled. He knew his remarks would be read by the Canadiens and he did not want to give them added incentive by sounding as though he were overconfident.

"But I'm no Joe Namath," he said, alluding to Broadway Joe's bold but correct prediction that the New York Jets would upset the Baltimore Colts in football's Super Bowl. "I'm not predicting anything—until the final round."

The Ranger goalie went on to assess the playoff series between New York and Montreal. "We're stronger this year than we were before and the experience of those other playoffs will help us. We've got new young guys like Brad Park and Walter Tkaczuk with us this time and they're going to make us tougher to beat."

And Giacomin himself?

"This is the third time around for me. I know what to expect. I know what I have to do. I know the Montreal players better. I know I have to play better than I did before."

But what about playoff pressure?

"It's there, of course. The playoffs are where the extra pressure is. You can't afford to make a mistake. You can't give up a cheap goal. During the season, if you give up a bad goal, it's not the end of the world but now . . ."

Eddie didn't finish the sentence. He didn't need to.

"I'll start feeling the extra tension the night before the first game," he said. "I'll sleep O.K., but maybe it will be a little harder to fall asleep because it's a playoff game. I'll feel the tension in the dressing room; we all will. If you don't get the butterflies, there's something wrong with you. Feeling the pressure is part of being an athlete. Once you're on the ice, and after I make that first save, it becomes a little easier."

The Canadiens won the first game, 3-1, and Eddie did not look sharp on the winning goal scored by John Ferguson. He was angry at losing and because Ferguson had deposited the winner into the net. There had been little affection between Eddie and Ferguson since the tough Montreal forward allegedly shot the puck at Giacomin after a stoppage of play earlier in the season. Giacomin claimed Ferguson had done it to him when the two played in the American League.

Montreal won the second game, 5-2, and again neither Giacomin nor the Rangers played especially well. New York led, 2-1, but frittered away its advantage. As a team, the Rangers lacked intensity and seemed incapable of coping with the Canadiens.

The third game was over almost before it began and now the Rangers were one game from being eliminated in four straight games. Montreal scored only thirty seconds following the opening face-off. Dick Duff was unchecked behind the

Ranger goal cage and set up Mickey Redmond's point-blank shot. The Rangers were completely caught off guard.

"Nobody seemed to be moving," said Redmond. "Eddie Giacomin just stood there, like it was a dream."

But before the Canadiens had completed their 4-1 conquest, the game was enlivened by one of the wildest fight scenes in Madison Square Garden. It also provided comic relief.

Ferguson and Jim Neilson got into a fight. Ferguson was considered the best fist-fighter in the league; Neilson was a far better defenseman than fighter. "The Chief" was taking a pounding so Park came to his aid and entered the fight.

That prompted Gump Worsley, the Montreal goalie who earlier in the season had suffered a nervous breakdown caused by goaltending pressure, to leave his net and join the fracas.

Out of his net at the other end of the rink came Giacomin, skating full speed in his cumbersome goaltending equipment into the thick of the hostilities.

Now players from both benches were scrambling over the dasher boards and fights erupted all over the ice. Don Simmons, New York's back-up goalie, and Rogie Vachon, Montreal's spare goalie, climbed over the boards and raced to the scene. Simmons took a pratfall and slid across the ice. The crowd roared gleefully.

Giacomin, meanwhile, had jumped on and had a headlock on Gump Worsley's back. The Canadiens' goalie gave his account of the bizarre scene to Tim Moriarty of *Newsday*.

"Hey, Eddie, stop choking me, will you? I didn't start this thing," pleaded Gump.

"Yeah, I know, but when you butted in I had to butt in, too. Why don't you go back where you belong," replied Eddie.

"I will if you let me. I'm no fighter," answered Gump.

"You can say that again. Besides, I don't want to hurt an

old man," said Eddie.

By now Gump, who would be forty in less than a month, and Eddie were laughing at the ludicrous situation in which they found themselves.

Worsley had the last laugh. He limited the Rangers to only four goals in the four-game series.

Francis was not laughing. Nor was Giacomin. In a desperate move for playoff survival, the coach placed a telephone call to Buffalo and told Gilles Villemure to pack his clothes and fly to New York. He would be leaving the Rangers' minor-league farm team and play goal in the fourth playoff game against the Canadiens.

Giacomin would be on the bench.

"Maybe the team will play better with a different goalkeeper," said Francis, not sounding overly convincing.

It was a difficult situation for Villemure. He was playing in his first playoff game. He did his best but it wasn't good enough. A new goalie was not the answer. Montreal moved to an early 4-1 lead, then withstood a late Ranger flourish and won, 4-3.

The Rangers were dead—again. They had lost in four games to the team destined to win still another Stanley Cup.

The Rangers outshot Montreal, 114-104, but they certainly did not outscore the Canadiens. Montreal scored sixteen goals, the Rangers only seven.

Seven goals in 114 shots is either the result of unbelievably poor shooting or spectacular goaltending. In the case of the Rangers it was mostly poor shooting. For example, first-period goals are considered vital, especially in the playoffs. New York outshot Montreal in the first periods of four games, 41-29, but was outscored, 8-2.

"We ran into all that Montreal depth," said Francis, chin up and head high. "We wore ourselves out. We did not have enough size or stamina. Harry Howell played with a bad back. Phil Goyette isn't big. Donnie Marshall only weighs

162 pounds soaking wet."

It was more than that.

The Ranger forwards, to be exact. They produced six goals. The offense was impotent, especially at right wing. Bob Nevin scored thirty-one goals during the season but none in the playoffs. Rod Gilbert scored twenty-eight goals during the season but only one in the playoffs.

Nevin might have turned the first game around. The soft-spoken captain missed several close scoring chances, including a short-handed breakaway. In the second game he skated in alone on Worsley only to lose control of the puck. He had Gump at his mercy in the third game. The Canadiens' goalie was flat on his back in front of the net and had lost his stick. All Nevin needed to do was lift the puck over the fallen goaltender.

He shot the puck directly at Gump.

Gilbert had fewer scoring opportunities. Ferguson saw to that. Mean John stymied Rod with pestiferous and intimidating checking from one end of the ice to the other.

Gilbert had an opportunity to prolong the series in the fourth game. Breaking free from Ferguson's clutches, he reduced the Rangers' third-period deficit to 4-2 with a goal. He was in alone an instant later, but instead of wrist-shooting or faking the goalie, he wound up for a slap shot. The delay gave Vachon the time he needed to react and make the save.

Many fans and hockey writers placed the blame for defeat on Giacomin.

"It burns me up the way everybody is always pinpointing him," said Francis, his voice rising in anger and his face turning red. "If it weren't for Eddie Giacomin, we wouldn't even be in the playoffs. He's the one who got us here the last three years."

"You can't blame it all on the goaltender," said Rod Seiling.

True. But it was becoming a familiar April refrain.

"We had to fight so hard just to make the playoffs. Maybe we were a worn-out team, emotionally and physically, when we got to the playoff. I just don't know," said the introverted defenseman.

Montreal's Beliveau gave his opinion.

"It seems that when Giacomin has a bad game or makes a mistake, it always hurts him more and shows up more than with other goalies. They just come at the wrong time for Eddie. Maybe he's just unlucky. Maybe he's tired, mentally and physically, from playing all those games in the season. But remember: you can't just blame the goalie. When a forward makes a mistake, the defensemen are there to help. When a defenseman makes a mistake, the goalie is there to help. But when a goalie makes a mistake, there is no one who can help him."

The Canadiens' captain suggested that people stop looking for flaws in the Ranger goaltender and give Montreal some credit. "After all," he said, "we are a pretty good team, and I would like to believe we were just better than the Rangers."

Still, like many fans, Beliveau agreed that he was puzzled about Giacomin. "Eddie is one of the finest goalies in the game and when he plays as well as he does all season, there is no reason why he can't win in the playoffs. There must be something wrong, but I don't know the answer."

Giacomin insisted he was not tired from playing so many regular-season games. Francis also insisted the number of games his goalie played was not a factor.

Eddie had played more games in the last three seasons than any other goaltender in the league. He had made the All Star teams and had led the Rangers into three consecutive playoffs.

Yet there was a flaw. In each first-round playoff series he had faltered and the Rangers had collapsed around him. He had lost seven consecutive playoff games and eleven of thirteen in three years.

The executioner struck swiftly in the 1969 playoffs. The Rangers were in on April 2 and out on April 6.

Two days later, on April 8, Giacomin became the father of his third child and first daughter, Nancy, born in North Shore Hospital, Manhasset, Long Island.

It was the only nice thing that happened to Eddie in April.

Eddie as a rookie with the minor-league Providence Reds.

Thanks for the memory. Eddie chats with Bob Hope at NHL All-Star awards banquet.

Eddie exults in response to Madison Square Garden fans' cheers after playoff victory against Montreal.

How sweet it is! Bruce MacGregor (right) and Eddie, heroes of Rangers' 1974 playoff conquest of Montreal, celebrate in the dressing room after the game.

Eddie explains his feelings after defeating the Rangers in his first game as a Redwing. (PHOTOGRAPH BY BOB GLASS)

We're Number One! Eddie and Gilles Villemure (right) display victory smiles after winning the Vezina Trophy in 1971.

Rod Gilbert (right) consoles Eddie, who sits on the bench dazed
from being hit in the face by a puck shot at him during a training camp
scrimmage.

Eddie fights unsuccessfully to keep back the tears upon his emotional
return to Madison Square Garden after being traded to Detroit.
(PHOTOGRAPH BY BOB GLASS)

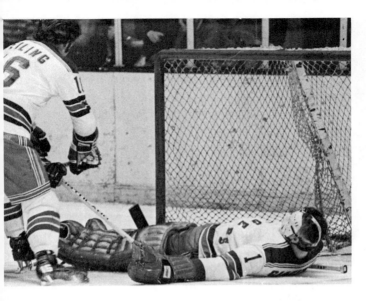

Down but not out. Eddie was knocked unconscious when a shot by Chicago's Dennis Hull struck him in the mask on February 9, 1972. He recovered, refused to leave the game, and the Rangers won. Rod Seiling (left) checks opponent trying to pry puck loose from Giacomin's leg pads.

Save. Eddie dives across the goal crease and uses his stick and blocking pad to stop breakaway shot by Ted Hampson during a 1963 American League game between the Providence Reds and Pittsburgh Hornets.

Eddie receives the New York West Side Association Trophy as Rangers' most valuable player for the 1970–71 season.

Eddie awaits his turn to take the ice in St. Louis for the 1970 NHL All-Star Game.

Madison Square Garden Center president Mike Burke (right) chats with Eddie during a sports celebrity luncheon in New York.

It's a girl. Eddie and Marg Giacomin gaze fondly at new daughter Nancy, born in Long Island's North Shore Hospital.

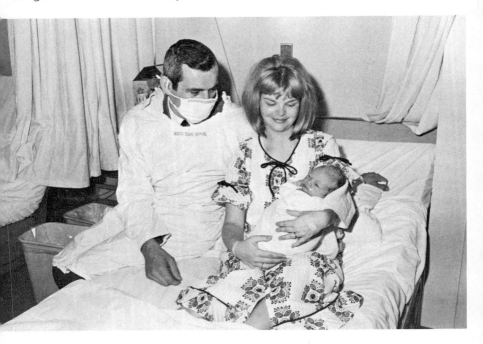

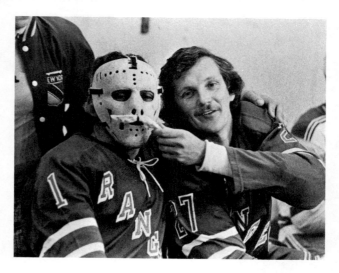

The new look. When conservative Ranger management finally allowed its players to grow mustaches in 1974, Ted Irvine (right) glued a fake mustache on Eddie's mask as a training-camp gag.

The wandering goalie. Eddie uses his speed and daring to roam far out of his goal crease to beat Montreal's Bob Gainey to a loose puck near the corner of the rink.

Chapter 11

Battle with the Bruins
and a Warning for Derek

"You better keep your head up."

Crowds began to gather on the sidewalks outside Madison Square Garden three hours before the third game of the Stanley Cup playoffs between the Boston Bruins and the Rangers on Saturday night, April 11, 1970. Hockey fans poured off the Long Island Railroad and Penn Central trains. They were loud and boisterous and added to the weekend congestion in Pennsylvania Station. Tickets were being scalped for as much as $75 to $100. Mounted police encircled the building to maintain order and disperse groups of unruly fans.

In a small office next to the Ranger dressing room, Emile Francis talked with Eddie Giacomin.

"You're a great competitor and a great goaltender—the best goalie in the business," the coach told Eddie. "But when things don't go the way you want, you worry and blame yourself. Relax. Just be yourself. And forget about the losing streak or what happened in Boston. The only guy you have to worry about putting the blame on you is me. And I'm not going to."

The Bruins were the most dynamic and physically intimidating team in hockey. They had overwhelmed the Rangers, 8-2, in the first playoff game, scoring five of their goals within a period of 10:21, four within 6:12, and three in 3:23. They drove Eddie to the bench when the score reached 7-1, and Francis replaced him with Terry Sawchuk as an act of mercy. He benched Eddie for the second game but the forty-year-old Sawchuk was shaky and lost, 5-3, and Boston held a 2-0 lead in the series.

Francis was asked if he felt Eddie was to blame for the Bruins' crushing 8-2 victory.

"No," said the coach, annoyed at the question. "What could he do? They were swarming all around him. He didn't get the support he needed from the rest of the team."

Why then did Francis bench Eddie and play Sawchuk in the second game?

"Switching goalkeepers has been known to pick up a team and change things around," was the coach's answer.

At least one Bruin was surprised to see Eddie on the bench.

"I was surprised they didn't start Eddie," said Ken Hodge. "It looks like they're trying to pin all the blame on him again. Hell, we just played a great game and the rest of the club was pitiful in front of Giacomin. Sawchuk was great in his prime, but . . ."

The third game was the pivotal one for Eddie and the Rangers—they had the advantage of playing in New York. If they could win, they would remain alive in the playoffs; if not, the Bruins would need only one victory to eliminate them.

"I felt that the pressure hadn't been bothering me, but maybe it had and I just didn't realize it," said Eddie.

"After what Emile told me, I decided to say the hell with it and play like it was just a regular-season game."

Ranger loyalists were in an ugly mood when the Bruins skated out on to the ice in their black-and-gold uniforms. The fans booed and cursed them. Many younger fans leaned over the side boards, shaking their fists at Boston players, spitting, shouting obscenities, and making vulgar gestures.

Several Bruin players reacted by waving their sticks at the fans, and at least two players gave the crowd the finger. The fans' chief target of abuse was Derek Sanderson, the controversial center who had ridiculed the Rangers as a team and gave Bill Fairbairn the choke sign in Boston.

Kill Derek . . . Deck Derek . . . Derek the Derelict . . . Derek: Wanted Dead or Alive . . . Derek Bites the Turd . . . Derek Eats Shit . . . Derek is a Dreg . . . Sanderson is Schizo . . . Sanderson is a Hairy Fairy were among the signs on display that reflected both the lack of intelligence or class and hatred for Sanderson among some New York fans. Eddie Layton, the Madison Square Garden organist, helped work the crowd up to an emotional frenzy by playing "Talk to the Animals."

A young man whose face was tear-stained and whose eyes reflected violent hatred raced down through the seats behind the Bruins' goal and called Gerry Cheevers vulgar names. He shook his fist and challenged the Boston goaltender to "come up here so I can kill you." Some of the men and women seated near the youth cheered and applauded.

Cheevers had to cover his unprotected head as eggs, coins, and rubber balls were flung at him by spectators.

Boston sent out its high-scoring line of Phil Esposito, Ken Hodge, and Wayne Cashman to start the game. The Rangers countered with the line of Jean Ratelle, Rod Gilbert, and rookie Jack Egers, a replacement for injured Vic Hadfield. Esposito shot from point-blank range and Giacomin made the save and froze the puck. The clocks on the twin-message boards at either end of the arena showed that 18:40 remained in the first period.

The Esposito line left the ice and Harry Sinden, the Boston coach, replaced it with the line of Sanderson, Ed Westfall, and Don Marcotte. The crowd booed when the long-haired Sanderson skated into view. The Rangers sent out a new line of Walt Tkaczuk, Dave Balon, and Fairbairn.

As Referee John Ashley was about to drop the puck for the face-off to the right of the New York goal, Eddie skated from his goal crease to the face-off circle and said something to Sanderson. The two players glared at each other for an instant as the crowd roared. Security police had to form a barricade behind the Boston bench to protect the players.

Sanderson faced off with Tkaczuk and the puck was shot into the left corner. Derek went after it and was immediately smashed into the end boards by Tkaczuk and Arnie Brown. Then he collided with Balon. Sanderson dropped his stick and gloves, whirled around and started pounding the Ranger in the head with his fists.

Brad Park and Fairbairn joined the fight. So did Marcotte. Suddenly the game erupted into a series of fights. Sanderson resembled an enraged animal. He threw punches at anyone near him. The violence-minded crowd loved it. Eggs splattered on the ice. Apple cores flew from the stands. An aerosol can filled with shaving cream was thrown by a spectator and nearly hit a Ranger on the head. By now Sanderson was locked in combat with Arnie Brown.

When linesman John D'Amico finally restored order and maintenance men cleared debris from the ice, Sanderson was ejected from the game. Derek charged the referee and screamed in his face. When he reluctantly skated off the ice, he gave the hostile crowd a defiant V-for-victory sign with his hands.

More eggs and litter were hurled by fans. So was a rubber chicken. Police guarding the players on the Bruins' bench were grappling with spectators who wanted to attack the enemy players. A Boston player stood up and swung his stick toward a fan who menaced him. Then he made an obscene gesture to the crowd with one finger.

The game erupted into more fights and brawls on the ice and the crowd threw eggs, nails, coins, and garbage. It took 19 minutes to play the first 91 seconds of the game. When the most violent, penalty-ridden game in play-off history finally was over, the teams had set a record of 38 penalties totaling 174 minutes.

Giacomin played brilliantly and the Rangers won, 4-3, on goals by Ratelle, Tkaczuk, Gilbert, and Ted Irvine. But the outcome of the game almost seemed secondary.

What had Eddie said to Sanderson that set off the violent game?

"We're getting paid to get you tonight" is what Sanderson said Giacomin had told him.

The Bruins' forward was in an angry dither as he sat in the dressing room, puffing on a cigarette. He was resplendent in a double-breasted pin-stripe Edwardian suit with a purple scarf and tie.

"Giacomin told me the Rangers were out to get me and that they were getting a bonus to get me. He said they were getting paid to get me. They put a bounty on my head. Can you believe that? They put a price on my head. I thought Emile Francis had class. I thought the Rangers had class. They don't. They're just as bad as New York fans. They're the animals, not us."

Sanderson was furious at Giacomin and at the Rangers.

"I hate Giacomin's guts," he told newsmen. "Look at him, will you? Look at the way he wears his hair. Giacomin's nothing but a short-haired jerk. He and Francis, they're both short-haired jerks. They're not together. You wear your hair as short as they do and that doesn't show me you're a together person."

What had Sanderson said in reply to Giacomin.

Derek laughed. "I said, 'Groovy. That's cool, man,'" he said, laughing.

At first, Eddie did not want to talk about the incident. But when the reporters told him what Sanderson had said, he exploded in anger.

"I never told Sanderson we were getting paid to get him," said Eddie. "I told him he better keep his head up or 'you'll get it.' That's standard advice for any hockey player. I just wanted to get his goat because he's always popping off."

Eddie and Derek were always opposite types. Eddie is conservative in dress and life style and avoids controversy. Derek is mod, flamboyant, outspoken and built his image by being a colorful and controversial character.

"I don't like the guy but I respect him as a hockey player," said Giacomin.

Sanderson called Eddie a liar when told that Giacomin said he had not told him the Rangers had put a price on his head.

"I know what he said," said Sanderson, "but who cares? I really got nothing against Giacomin. He could be a together guy, although he wears his hair so short you'd never know it."

Now Sanderson was more interested in bad-mouthing Dave Balon, a 33-goal scorer for the Rangers.

"If I had to be kicked out of a game, at least I'd like to be able to take a high-caliber player with me," he said. "Someone like Tkaczuk or Ratelle. Not some ordinary guy like Balon. Did he really score thirty-three goals? I don't believe it. He's still an ordinary player to me. He's a jerk, a short-haired jerk like Giacomin. He's not together. And he sure can't fight. New York's only got four fighters on the team—Orland Kurtenbach, Tim Horton, Ted Irvine, and Brad Park. Balon's gutless; he don't scare anybody."

The mild-mannered Balon kicked a towel across the dressing-room floor when told of Sanderson's remarks.

"As far as Sanderson is concerned, I think he's an idiot. He's not as great as he thinks he is. He just likes publicity," said Balon.

Meanwhile, back in the Boston dressing room, Sanderson was still holding court.

"They say our Boston fans are bad. Sure, they get pretty rowdy. But they only throw paper and peanuts on the ice, and you don't see filthy signs all over Boston Garden, do you? New York fans have to be the worst in the league. They threw oranges, eggs, and marbles on the ice. They threw bottles at our team bus. They're berserk. They put up all those signs with filthy words. Hey, it's great to bring your wife and kids to see a game in New York, right? The New York fans are jerks. They have no class."

Most of the Rangers were forced to agree with Sanderson about some of the New York fans.

"I was hit by an orange someone threw," said defenseman Arnie Brown. "It felt like a brick. As an athlete, you hate to see people act this way, especially when some of the ones who do the damage are your own fans. It was a disgrace."

What made Giacomin skate out to Sanderson and antagonize the Bruin player in the first place? Was it a subtle move on Eddie's part to rattle Derek and to perk up his own team?

"Definitely," said Boston's Ed Westfall.

Giacomin said no.

"I honestly don't know why I did it. It was a spontaneous thing; it just happened. I know I didn't do it to show off or to try to get our team worked up. I wasn't trying to start trouble."

Eddie's remark to Derek that started the riotous game may

have been prompted by what he said had happened to him in previous games between the arch rivals.

"A lot of the Boston players kept telling me they were going to cut my head off," said Eddie. "Sanderson was one of them. He's been yelling things at me all season. He'd skate by me and say, 'We're going to shoot for your eyes tonight, Giacomin. You're going to get the puck shoved down your throat.' Things like that. I knew what he was trying to do: shake me up, get me to take my mind off the game."

As far as Eddie was concerned, the case was closed. The Rangers won the game and he wanted to forget about Sanderson.

Derek, however, enjoyed the controversy. He insisted Giacomin told him the Rangers had put a price on his head and were out to get him. He said he was shocked that the Rangers would do such a thing and get away with it. Boston newspapers played the story prominently. Wire services and television gave the incident wide coverage. National magazines quoted Sanderson. Soon he was a guest on Johnny Carson's "Tonight Show."

Eddie was disturbed by the controversy in which he found himself. He wrote a letter to National Hockey League President Clarence Campbell and expressed his regrets at what had happened. He explained that he had not made his remark to Sanderson with the idea of stirring up trouble.

"I just wanted to set the record straight," said Eddie. "I always had a clean record and I wanted to try and keep it that way."

Eddie was able to laugh about the Sanderson caper.

"In a way, what I did made him the big shot he thinks he is today," said Giacomin, smiling. "His picture's been in *Time* and *Life* magazines. They wrote a book about him. And he's got his own TV show in Boston."

"Sanderson made so much of what I said to him that I decided to write Mr. Campbell and apologize for anything I might have done that was wrong," said Giacomin.

Eddie heard a rumor that Derek was anxious to have him as a guest on his TV show.

"Sure," said the Ranger goalie, "if he asks me to go on his show, I will."

What would Eddie say to Derek?

"I don't know," he said with an impish grin. "I might tell him, 'Hey, keep your head up tonight or you'll get it.'"

Touché!

The Rangers beat the Bruins the following night in New York, 4-2. Gilbert scored two goals and the series was tied, 2-2. Eddie played brilliantly and among the saves he made was a spectacular stop of Sanderson's short-handed breakaway.

Eddie could not conceal his emotions as he skated off the ice at the end of the game after being selected the game's number-one star. He had a smile on his face. He was still smiling inside the dressing room, but he became serious when he talked about the torture he had endured after past playoff games.

"It was unbelievable," he said. "All that talk. All the things I read. I was so tired of hearing the word 'choke . . . choke . . . choke.' Nobody wants to play badly, especially in the playoffs. I sure didn't, but all that talk I heard about choking in the playoffs was pretty hard for me to take."

Giacomin entered the playoffs against the Bruins with a seven-game losing streak in previous playoffs. He had won only twice in fourteen playoff games.

"I'd have to say that these two wins probably were the most satisfying I ever had," he said, mopping the sweat from his face. "I hope they proved to some people that I can win in the playoffs."

Eddie said he almost disliked going home to Sudbury in the summer off-season because people constantly asked him: "What happened to you in the playoffs?"

"People started saying 'choke-up' and some writers said I couldn't stand the pressure in the playoffs. It was very unpleasant for me. I was beginning to think about all that talk myself. That's why it's so satisfying to do well in the last two games. I never gave up. I never lost confidence in myself. But I guess a lot of people gave up and lost confidence in me."

Meanwhile, Sanderson was telling people in Boston: "Wait until we get back to Boston. We'll get 'em."

They did. The Bruins won the fifth game, 3-2. Esposito put two shots between Eddie's legs within five minutes in the third period to wipe out a 2-1 Ranger lead. Bobby Orr stole a Ranger pass in center ice to set up the winning goal when New York foolishly was caught in a line change.

"We can win it now," Esposito proclaimed in the dressing room after the game.

He was right. The Bruins simply had too much intimidating muscle for the Rangers to cope with and won the series in six games, 4-1, in New York. Madison Square Garden again was the scene of crowd violence and misbehavior. Some fans threw eggs and ball bearings at the players on the ice. They tried to attack the Bruins' players and, when the outcome no longer was in doubt, they set fires in the mezzanine.

They also booed and cursed the Rangers, who failed to protect a 1-0 lead and were forced into numerous mental and physical errors by Boston. Ron Stewart lost the puck in Ranger ice and Orr drove a 50-foot slap shot under Giacomin's right leg. Tim Horton lost the puck behind the Ranger net and Wayne Cashman caught Eddie off guard with a short-side shot. Orr's 55-foot slap shot deflected off a stick and glanced off Eddie's chest and into the net after Esposito won a face-off from Ratelle in the Ranger end zone. Sanderson scored the final goal.

"I didn't see the puck that well," Eddie said of Cashman's

unassisted goal. "I didn't see that one well, either," he said of Orr's winning goal.

The game might have been more one-sided if it were not for Giacomin. Twice he stopped Hodge on breakaways. He made a darting lunge to stop Fred Stanfield on a two-on-one. Early in the game he stopped Don Awrey, John Bucyk, and John McKenzie on a tricky sequence of close-range shots.

For the fourth straight season, the Rangers had failed to survive in the first round of the playoffs.

"We knew we could take the Rangers if we hit them," said Esposito. Sanderson smiled and nodded in agreement. "They overwork Giacomin. They kill the guy during the season and then in the playoffs he hasn't got it anymore," said Derek.

There was logic behind that reasoning. Eddie played in 70 of the Rangers' 76 games during the 1969–70 season. In the last four seasons he had played in 274 of 296 games, and in each of those years the Rangers had been eliminated in the playoffs' opening round. Certainly he had to be exhausted.

Perhaps Gump Worsley, the old Ranger goalie, had the answer.

"You show me a goalie who plays every game and I'll show you a guy who'll be swinging from a tree by the time the season is over and the playoffs start," philosophized Gump.

Francis had acquired the aging Sawchuk as back-up goaltender, but Terry was forty years old and his best years were behind him. The Rangers spent more than three months of the regular season struggling to stay in first place and so Giacomin played in all but six games.

"The season took a lot out of Eddie and all of us were pretty tired for the playoffs," said Rod Seiling.

Milt Dunnell summed up Giacomin's heavy workload during the season this way in the *Toronto Star*: "He never has been in fewer than sixty-six games during a regular season. If the Rangers did that to a horse, they'd be arrested."

The Rangers might have brought New York its first hockey championship since 1942 by finishing in first place during the 1969–70 season. They led the NHL with a 22-7-9 record as the season reached the midpoint. But in the end it was fatigue and injuries that contributed to the collapse in which they won only four of their final eighteen games from February 25 to the end of the season and barely qualified for the playoffs.

Eddie enjoyed another successful season and his 2.36 goals-against average was the best of his professional career. He was the goaltender in every game when Emile Francis's team achieved a 14-game undefeated streak that started on November 7 in Oakland and lasted until December 11. The Rangers won ten and tied four and Eddie's average was 1.86.

One of the two shutouts he recorded during the long undefeated streak was on November 22 in St. Louis. He beat the Blues and their goalie, Jacques Plante, 5-0. Oddly, it was one of the few times in his career that he was reprimanded after the game by Francis.

Plante, always a showman, had a habit of raising his arms in an exaggerated victory salute and skating around the rink after a shutout. Eddie imitated Plante's victory sign after the game as he skated off the ice.

"I've got nothing to say about that," he said with a slight trace of a smile afterward.

Francis took Eddie aside after the game and suggested that he refrain from any more victory salutes to the crowd after a shutout. "The Cat" doesn't like his players to clown around on the ice, no matter how pleased they are about winning.

Giacomin's six shutouts fell short of the league lead, but he didn't seem to mind.

"Our job is to win and finish first. Shutouts are always nice but how can I be disappointed if I give up a goal or two and we still win?" he said.

One of Eddie's shutouts carried special significance. He beat Pittsburgh, 2-0, on March 18 and preserved the perfect game by stopping Keith McCreary's penalty shot.

"It was one hell of a save," said McCreary. "What made it so good was that I made Giacomin make the first move and had him beaten. But the guy's reflexes are so fantastic he was able to recover and just get his toe on the puck as it was going over the goal line."

Eddie again came within inches of making goaltending history by scoring a goal. It happened on April 2 in Toronto in a game in which he made thirty-one saves and beat the Maple Leafs, 2-1, to keep New York's playoff hopes alive.

With one minute to play in the game, Toronto Coach John McLellan removed goalie Bruce Gamble. Five seconds later, Giacomin banked a clearing shot off the protective glass above the side boards. The puck was gliding directly toward the center of the empty net when it suddenly struck a rough patch of ice, changed direction, and slid three inches outside the goal post.

"It kept getting closer and closer, and I was sure it was going in," said Eddie. "Oh, well, maybe next time."

The Rangers were a physically crippled team in the second half of the season. Their defense was decimated. Jim Neilson tore knee ligaments on February 13 in Oakland when he was boarded from behind by Earl Ingarfield. Brad Park broke his right ankle on February 19 in Detroit when his skate caught between the ice and the side boards as he was attempting to clear the puck. He missed 16 games and the Rangers won only three of them. Don Marshall separated his shoulder on February 25. Hadfield, Arnie Brown, and Seiling also were sidelined with injuries. Desperate for help, Francis acquired veteran defenseman Tim Horton and had to rely heavily on rookie defensemen Ab DeMarco, Larry Brown, and Mike Robitaille.

The Rangers' collapse in the second half of the season was so bad that they barely qualified for the playoffs. They seemed virtually eliminated when they lost in Detroit, 6-2, in the next-to-the-last game of the season.

"It doesn't look too good for them," said Gordie Howe. "They look tired. They've been hit with so many injuries. It looks like they've just run out of gas."

New York's final game of the season was nationally televised the following afternoon in Madison Square Garden. Having clinched a playoff position by beating the Rangers on Saturday night, the Red Wings celebrated with champagne on their flight to New York, and Sid Abel, the general manager and coach, rested many of his regulars in the final game.

The Rangers' only hope was to beat Detroit and hope that Montreal lost that night to Chicago. Even so that was no guarantee the Rangers would qualify for the fourth and final playoff position. New York had ninety points. Montreal already had ninety-two. If the Rangers won and the Canadiens lost, the teams would be tied for the final playoff position, each with ninety-two points and thirty-eight wins. To break the tie, the team that scored the most goals during the season would be the one to make the playoffs.

The Rangers had 237 goals. The Canadiens had 242. In addition to winning and hoping Montreal lost, the Rangers had to make up at least 5 goals to assure themselves of fourth place.

Francis devised a desperate scheme. He instructed his team to do nothing but shoot and concentrate on scoring goals. It did not matter how many goals the Rangers gave up. Only that they won and scored as many goals as possible. To do so, he would remove Giacomin from goal as often as he could during the game in order to put a sixth attacker on the ice.

All the odds were against the Rangers making the play-offs, but in the dressing room Eddie started a little game.

"C'mon, guys, we can do it," he said. "We've got to score a lot of goals, that's all. We got to go get 'em early."

Soon the rest of the players picked up Eddie's spirit. They began to kid each other. "O.K., put me down for three goals . . . I'll take four . . . you go for two."

As the players left the dressing room to go out on to the ice, Tom "The Bomb" Barnwell, an equipment man known for his corny jokes, quipped: "O.K., guys, let's show Gordie how."

They did. They kept the puck in the Detroit zone for almost the entire game, taking a record sixty-five shots at Red Wings' goalie Roger Crozier. They won, 9-5, against an indifferent Detroit team. It was a remarkable effort by the Rangers.

Now they had tied Montreal for the fourth playoff position. Each team had an identical ninety-two points and thirty-eight wins. The team that ended the season with the most goals would qualify for the playoffs. New York had 246 goals. Montreal had 242 but would be playing Chicago in a few hours. If the Canadiens won or tied, they would make the playoffs. If they lost but scored five goals, they still would make the playoffs.

The Rangers returned to their homes on Long Island to listen to the radio broadcast of the Canadiens-Black Hawks game that would determine who would be in the playoffs.

Chicago beat Montreal, 10-2, and the Rangers were in the playoffs.

"It was one of the most unbelievable days and nights in my life," said Giacomin.

"I'll never forget the date April 5, 1970," said Francis.

"It was the longest day of my life—and one of the proudest. But then you never stop fighting until the last soldier is dead."

Claude Ruel, the chunky Montreal coach, was infuriated at the way his team had been prevented from playing in the playoffs for the first time in twenty-two seasons. He accused Detroit of allowing the Rangers to win their game and called the indifferent performance by the Red Wings "a disgrace to hockey and to all sports." He said the Rangers did not deserve to be in the playoffs.

"If I see that guy Ruel, I'll punch him in the mouth," said Vic Hadfield.

It was true that the Red Wings gave little visible effort of trying or caring if they won. Detroit kept many of its best players out of the game and allowed the Rangers to control the puck and shoot almost at will. The Red Wings already had clinched a playoff position and so the game was meaningless to them.

Few people could believe that the Rangers were in the playoffs. Especially after their horrible slump late in the season had prompted Sanderson to declare on national television: "The Rangers are dead."

But now the playoffs for the Rangers were over and once again the critics were at work. As usual they blamed Eddie Giacomin. They claimed that four first-round playoff failures were sufficient proof that he was a poor playoff goaltender.

The word they used most to describe Eddie was the most detested in an athlete's vocabulary.

The word was "choke."

Red Fisher of the *Montreal Star* was among those who disagreed. He did not believe Eddie was the reason the Rangers had again failed in the playoffs.

"When a team falls back into a defensive shell, how can anyone blame the goalie when the opposition scores goals?" he wrote. "The Rangers almost did it, largely because of

Giacomin's work. But they lost it because of injuries and even while a lot of people were talking in terms of a Boston sweep, the Rangers surged back for 4-3 and 4-2 victories in New York, winning the first one because Giacomin managed to needle Derek Sanderson into a match misconduct."

The Montreal hockey columnist concluded by saying: "Plante, Sawchuk, and Hall were the best goalies. From what I've seen in recent seasons, Giacomin is in an area right with them, and that's a high-class area. I say this: It's a fact that the Rangers have not progressed beyond the quarter-finals of the Stanley Cup playoffs for the last four seasons. It is also a fact that they got into the playoffs BECAUSE of Giacomin, not in spite of him."

Chapter 12

The Goalie Gets a Mask, More Help, and a Trophy

"It's a great feeling to win the Vezina Trophy."

EMILE Francis arrived at LaGuardia Airport almost three hours before the Rangers' flight to St. Louis was scheduled to depart on October 9, 1970.

Outside the sun was bright and the sky was blue. It was a perfect afternoon. But the general manager and coach of the Rangers was glum the day before his team would open the 1970–71 season.

He sat at the counter of an airport restaurant and drank coffee and smoked a Lucky Strike. He repeatedly glanced at his wrist watch and excused himself several times to walk to a nearby telephone booth and call his office in New York.

Finally he returned to his half-filled coffee cup with a disgusted expression on his face. He took two airline tickets from the breast pocket of his blue business suit and stuffed them into his briefcase.

"Well, we won't be needing these today," he said.

Park and Tkaczuk were contract holdouts. They would not play in the Rangers' opening game in St. Louis on October

10. Francis was angry. He thought surely they would have agreed to contract terms and shown up at the airport to accompany the team to St. Louis.

Francis changed the subject when Eddie Giacomin walked into the restaurant and sat down across the counter with Trainer Frank Paice.

"You'll have a new story to write about Eddie," said "the Cat." "I think he's going to put on the mask."

Eddie had resisted wearing a protective mask until this season and was one of the few barefaced goaltenders in hockey.

There was another story about Giacomin that Francis was not ready to disclose. Eddie's days as the indestructible goalie were over. No longer would he play sixty to seventy games a season. Francis had decided during the summer that the lengthened schedule and constant travel added to the mental strain and pressure of goaltending. He finally had become convinced that Eddie would be a better goalie in the playoffs if he played fewer games during the season.

The man who would share the goaltending with Eddie was Gilles Villemure, the easygoing, sandy-haired harness-racing driver and trainer who had spent most of his career in the Rangers' minor-league system.

"After all those years in the minor leagues, I'm just glad to be here," Villemure said one day in training camp as he twirled a toothpick between his teeth. "I won't mind not playing much. I know Eddie's a great goalie so I don't have much chance to take his job. If I can give him some rest, good. I'll be content to sit on the bench and maybe get to play fifteen or twenty games."

Giacomin played with a mask for the first time in the opening game of the season. The Rangers lost, 3-1, and Eddie was in a sour mood in the dressing room after the game. He wanted to avoid questions about his new mask. He thought that some of the sports writers might blame defeat on his having switched to a mask.

"The mask had nothing to do with winning or losing," he said in a low voice. Then he walked to the shower room.

On the bus ride back to the hotel, Eddie was more cordial and willing to talk about his new mask.

"I just reached the point where I felt a mask had become part of a goalie's equipment," he said. "I still have to get used to wearing it."

He was asked if his wife Marg would worry less about her husband's being injured now that his face was protected by a mask.

"When I told her I was going to wear a mask, she asked what I wanted to do a thing like that for. She said nobody would know who I was or who was playing goal," said Eddie, laughing.

Giacomin had one of goaltending's most expressive faces as a maskless goalie, and it made him appealing to fans and news photographers alike. Now the emotions of triumph and tragedy reflected in his face would be hidden from view.

After losing the opening game of the season, the Rangers moved into first place. Park and Tkaczuk signed their contracts and rejoined the team. Eddie went through a five-game streak in which he won four games, tied one, and stopped 121 of 126 shots. The only bad experience during the first month of the season was on Halloween night in Boston. The Bruins bombarded the Rangers' new masked man with 46 shots and won, 6-0.

But by now it was evident that Francis fully intended to rotate his goaltenders. One night it would be Giacomin. The next night it would be Villemure. Sometimes one goalie would play several games in succession. There was no discernible pattern as to how Francis selected his goalie and the fans and sports writers tried to guess which goalie would play.

Francis enjoyed the guessing game immensely. He refused

to disclose the identity of his goaltender until the day of the game. He liked being coy with the press and he knew that by playing musical chairs with his goaltenders he was keeping opponents guessing, as well as the sports writers.

"Who's the number-one goalie—Giacomin or Villemure?" Francis was asked countless times.

"We don't have a number-one goalie and we don't have a number-two goalie," he said. "They're both number one." He became annoyed throughout the season when he heard or read of anyone referring to either Giacomin or Villemure as a spare or back-up goalie.

"Just call them goalies—period!" he demanded.

Actually, most insiders knew that Eddie still was number one and, in the long run, would play the most games and be used against stronger opponents. Francis, however, would never admit that. At first he was uncertain if Villemure could be depended upon to alternate in the net with Eddie.

The phlegmatic French-Canadian removed all doubt when he compiled a 14-1-3 record, allowing only thirty goals in his first eighteen games.

"I'm glad for Gilly," Giacomin said one day. "He spent a long time in the minor leagues like I did, and now he's finally getting his chance and making the most of it."

Some sports writers tried to build a rivalry between the two goaltenders. Giacomin quickly squelched that.

"There's no rivalry between us," said Eddie. "We're like business partners; we're just working together for the same firm. When I'm in goal, Gilly is the one on the bench rooting for me."

Villemure shared the same feeling.

"When I'm in the game and Eddie's on the bench, I can hear him rooting for me," he said.

"I knew in training camp that Eddie and Gilles could be the best one-two goaltending punch in hockey," said Francis. "The league has gone from six to fourteen teams and the schedule is up from seventy to seventy-eight games. You travel coast-to-coast, more than 80,000 miles a year, and play as many as seven games in twelve nights. One man can't handle all the goaltending by himself anymore."

Giacomin agreed. "I know one thing: the Rangers won't have a tired goaltender in the playoffs this season."

Essentially, Giacomin understood what Francis was doing by alternating goaltenders and in principal he agreed. But at first he disliked sharing his job with another goaltender.

"It's no fun sitting on the bench. In fact, I hate it," said Eddie. "I'd still like to play every game. But I guess I have to admit that's just not possible any longer. The one-goalie system is dead. But if sharing the job helps the team, then I'm all for it."

As the regular season neared completion, it was obvious that Francis's decision to use two goaltenders had helped the Rangers tremendously. New York finished in second place and established a team record with forty-nine wins and 109 points.

"I guess Emile knew what he was doing, eh?" said Eddie. "He told me the occasional rest would lengthen my career and make me become a better goalie, especially in the play-offs. For this late in the year I do feel more relaxed and stronger mentally and physically."

Opponents also found the Rangers more difficult to contend with. They never knew until game time whether it would be Eddie or Gilles in goal and could not adjust their game plan accordingly. Giacomin was a right-hander who held the stick in his right hand and caught with his left. Villemure was the direct opposite. That made it more difficult for shooters because until game time they did not know which goalie they would be facing.

There also was a slight difference in style. Eddie was a combination stand-up and acrobatic goaltender who frequently roamed from the net to clear the puck. Villemure also played stand-up goal and was skillful in judging and anticipating shots, as well as blocking the angles. Unlike Giacomin, he seldom flopped to the ice to make a save.

Still, stories occasionally appeared in which Eddie was rumored to be unhappy and that he and his partner supposedly were jealous of each other.

"That's bull," Vic Hadfield said on the team bus one night in Vancouver.

"Hey, who's making all that noise?" Park shouted from the rear of the dimly lighted bus.

Giacomin and Villemure, seated in adjacent seats in the middle of the bus, had been talking incessantly.

"The goalies are at it again," said Rod Gilbert.

"Yeah, just like a couple of old ladies who can't stop talking over the fence," said Hadfield.

That ended rumors about animosity between the two goaltenders.

"The day of one regular goalie is over," said Eddie. "The pressures of travel and a longer schedule demand a team has two guys of comparable ability. Physically and mentally I am an entirely different man this year. The change is due entirely to sharing the load with Gilles Villemure instead of carrying the brunt of the burden myself."

The season went into its final weekend, Eddie and Gilles leading in the race for the Vezina Trophy as hockey's best goaltending team by a slight margin over Chicago's Tony Esposito and Gerry Desjardins.

Villemure played goal on April 3 in Montreal and lost, 7-2, while Chicago was defeating Detroit, 4-1. Entering the last day of the season on April 4, Eddie and Gilles had only a 177–181 goals-against advantage over the Black Hawks' goalies.

"Don't talk about winning the Vezina Trophy. You'll jinx us," joked Eddie. "I remember a few years ago when I went into the last game of the season with a six-goal lead over Chicago. They got eight goals on me and there went the Vezina Trophy."

There was no keeping the Vezina Trophy from Giacomin this time. He made 33 saves and shut out Detroit, 6-0, on the final day of the season. The Black Hawks lost to Toronto, 3-2. The Vezina Trophy was the Rangers' for the first time since Dave Kerr won it in 1940. Giacomin and Villemure allowed 177 goals for a combined goals-against average of 2.26. Chicago surrendered 184 goals for a 2.35 average.

As the final seconds ticked off, the crowd in Madison Square Garden rose to its feet and cheered Giacomin for the shutout that was only a few seconds from completion. Villemure was standing on the bench cheering, too. So were all the Rangers.

When the game ended, Villemure led the parade of Rangers out on the ice to embrace Eddie. Eddie and Gilles raised their arms together in triumph and the crowd roared its approval.

Winning the Vezina Trophy was worth $1,500. Eddie and Gilles split the money. They decided to treat their team-mates and wives to a team dinner in a Manhattan restaurant.

"It's the least we can do," said Eddie. "It's a great feeling to win the Vezina Trophy but the big thing about the award is that goalies can't win it unless their defensemen and their forwards help them. That's why Gilly and I have decided to treat all the guys and their wives to dinner after the game. We got the idea ourselves, but we kept it quiet until the game was over and we had won. Then we told the guys we were taking them out to dinner."

Eddie played forty-five games and surrendered only ninety-five goals. His goals-against average of 2.15 was the best of his career. He led the league with eight shutouts for the third time in five years and his record was 27-10-7.

Villemure compiled a 2.29 goals-against average in thirty-four games and yielded only seventy-eight goals. He had four shutouts and a 22-8-4 record.

There was little time for Eddie and Gilles to celebrate. The playoffs started in three days against the Toronto Maple Leafs. Once again Eddie would hear the whispers and innuendos from his critics about his inability to win in the playoffs.

This time he reacted with anger when asked about his playoff record. "I'm sick and tired of hearing the same stuff every year about what a lousy goalie I am in the playoffs," he said. "I'm always getting the rap for not being a good money goaltender. I know I've had bad playoff games but I don't think I've been the reason we've lost. I know they say a team goes as far as its goaltending takes it in the playoffs. O.K., that's true. A team needs good goaltending. The thing is, I answer to one man—Emile Francis—and he hasn't faulted my goaltending."

Giacomin was only warming up.

"When I go home to Sudbury, it's the same old thing. People always asking how come the Rangers do so badly in the playoffs. They might as well come out and say it's me. Right? That's what they mean, don't they?"

New York had not survived in the first round of the playoffs since 1950 and, with Giacomin as goaltender, they had been eliminated in the first round in four consecutive seasons.

Deep down inside, Eddie knew he had something to prove.

The first playoff game was in New York and before the game John McLellan, the Maple Leafs' coach, was asked about Giacomin's poor playoff record.

"That's bull," said McLellan. "It's a dirty knock, a bum rap. Eddie Giacomin has always been a great competitor and he's taken a lot of abuse he didn't deserve just because his team hasn't won in the playoffs. He's the best goalie I ever saw when it comes to handling the puck. He passes better than some forwards I know. Most goalies don't have the guts to come out of the net to clear the puck. They're afraid they'll get hit."

It was obvious that McLellan was in Giacomin's corner. Or was it just typical preplayoff talk in which no one will criticize a rival for fear of creating extra incentive?

"No," said the Toronto coach. "Eddie's my kind of goaltender. He hasn't had the greatest luck in the playoffs, and I'm just afraid that this might be the year he finally comes through. If we're going to beat the New York Rangers, we have to get to Giacomin."

The Maple Leafs appeared to be doing just that when they led, 4-2, with 6:47 remaining in the second period. Then the Rangers struck. Bob Nevin, Hadfield, and Tkaczuk scored within less than seven minutes, Giacomin withstood a late flurry of shots, and the Rangers won, 5-4.

Neither Eddie nor his teammates had played well in the second game. The Maple Leafs won, 4-1, and by the time they led, 3-0, some of Madison Square Garden's fickle fans were booing Giacomin. They mocked him with false cheers when he made routine saves.

They soon had something else on which to vent their hostile emotions. With 4:42 left to play in the game, Hadfield brought the puck down the left side boards and was slammed hard against the boards by Jim Harrison. Hadfield retaliated with a flurry of punches at Harrison. One of the most bizarre fight scenes in playoff history was about to unfold.

Bernie Parent, the Maple Leafs' goalie, went to Harrison's aid. That brought Giacomin out of his net at the other end of the rink. He skated up the ice as fast as he could and cut down Parent with a football lineman's shoulder block.

While the linesman tried to restore order, fans hurled boxes of popcorn and containers of beer on the ice. Parent took off his mask to wipe the sweat from his face after the fighting had subsided. Hadfield, standing beside him, grabbed the mask from Parent's hand and threw it into the crowd of spectators. The fans passed Parent's mask up through the stands. Bernie was grief-stricken and pleaded with them to return his mask.

"Will the person who has the goalie's mask please return it," public-address announcer Pat Doyle asked the crowd.

"Don't Give It Back!...Don't Give It Back!...Don't Give It Back!" chanted the crowd. Parent threw up his arms in anger and stalked off toward the bench. He did not know what to do. Darryl Sittler, Bob Baun, and Harrison were all trying to get revenge by attacking Hadfield so Brad Park had joined the fracas. Parent refused to play without his mask.

"Since he didn't bring an extra one along, we had to put Jacques Plante in goal," said McLellan.

Plante was in the game only thirty-four seconds when Jim Dorey and Ted Irvine started trading punches behind the Toronto goal cage. Plante skated into the fight to try to help his teammate. Giacomin again came skating up the ice and made a beeline for Plante. He threw an overhand right that grazed the rival goalie on his mask.

The final 4:42 of the game took twenty-five minutes to play because of the delay caused by Hadfield's throwing Parent's mask into the crowd and the ensuing fights and bench-clearing brawls.

Francis was asked why Giacomin became involved.

"It's the code of the hills," said the coach. "Anytime a goalie from the other team sticks his nose in where it doesn't belong, I damned well better not see my goalie still in his course."

Then "the Cat" took a shot at Plante, the goalie who had deserted the Rangers without advance warning in 1965.

"Compared to Eddie Giacomin, that guy Plante handles his stick like a washerwoman with a mop in her hand," he said, laughing.

The extracurricular activities between the teams, which resulted in heavy fines and a feud between Toronto and New York over payment for Parent's missing mask, did not change the outcome of the game. Toronto had tied the series and in two games had scored eight goals against Giacomin.

Francis chose Villemure as goaltender in the third game in Maple Leaf Gardens. Eddie's business partner lost, 3-1, and Toronto held a 2-1 advantage in the series.

Francis turned to Eddie in the fourth game. He played brilliantly and the Rangers won, 4-2. Ron Stewart, killing a penalty, took a pass from Glen Sather and scored the decisive fourth goal at 18:10 of the second period, breaking in alone and drawing Parent to his knees for a graceful goal. Bernie was wearing a new mask but it didn't help him.

"I've never been so nervous before a game," Giacomin said afterward in the dressing room. "This was a big one—one we had to win. My one big aim is to get past the first round of the playoffs."

"Eddie was mad," said Rod Gilbert. "All that talk about how he always folded in the playoffs had started again and it had him burned. He showed them a thing or two tonight."

The Rangers won the fifth game, 3-1, and led in the series, 3-2. Eddie stopped fifteen third-period shots and frustrated Toronto by skating out of his crease to retrieve the Maple Leafs' long-lead passes into the corners and shooting the puck back outside the blue line.

"He's like a third defenseman out there," complained McLellan.

The Rangers and Giacomin ended their first-round playoff jinx by beating Toronto, 2-1, to win the series in six games. Bob Nevin's goal at 9:07 of sudden-death overtime provided the winning margin. Eddie played superbly under great pressure. Twice he stopped breakaways in the third period by Ron Ellis and Brian Spencer. He made a seemingly impossible off-balance save on a point-blank shot from the slot by Dave Keon. He kick saved on Dorey's bullet shot. He stopped Norm Ullman's lift shot with his chest following a wild scramble for a loose puck in front of the net.

Finally Eddie and the Rangers had made it through the playoff's opening round.

It was a double triumph for Eddie and for Nevin. Like Giacomin, the right wing, whose goal won the game, was often booed by New York fans. Nevin, the Ranger captain, led New York with 5 goals in the Toronto series.

Francis came out of the dressing room in Maple Leaf Gardens to greet the horde of newsmen waiting in the corridor.

"O.K., now let's hear from all you guys who said Eddie Giacomin was a lousy playoff goalie," he said in a voice hoarse with emotion. "Eddie Giacomin just showed everybody what I've always said he was—a great goalie. I don't want to hear anymore of the crap about him."

Inside the Rangers' dressing room, Eddie marched from one teammate to another, shouting, "Way to Go Gang! . . . Way to Go!" He was so excited at finally having proved to his critics that he could win under playoff pressure that he still wore all of his heavy goaltending equipment.

Anger flashed in his eyes when reporters clustered around him.

"Eddie Giacomin, the goalie who always chokes in the playoffs. That's me," he said sarcastically. Eddie could not continue the charade. He was too pleased to be angry. He could not keep from smiling.

"I think this is my proudest moment," he said. "Now they can't say Eddie Giacomin chokes in the playoffs every year."

His brothers, Jiggs and Rollie, were among the dressing room well-wishers. They had come down from Sudbury to see Eddie in his moment of triumph.

William M. Jennings, the Rangers' team president, was there, too. "I think I'll always recall this game when I think of Eddie Giacomin," he said.

Someone asked Eddie about the Rangers' next opponent in the playoffs, the Chicago Black Hawks.

"How do I know?" he said with a smile. "I've never been in a next series. Remember?"

Everybody laughed. So did Eddie.

"But I know this much," he said, raising his voice so he could be heard over the noise his teammates were making. "We've set our goals high. We haven't come this far to lose."

John McLellan, the Toronto coach, sat on a medical table in a room next to his team's dressing room.

"Eddie Giacomin was the reason they won and we lost," he said softly. "He was our stumbling block. I told you all that talk about his being a bad playoff goalie was a lot of bull."

Plante brushed reporters aside. "How can I stop what I don't see," he said of Nevin's overtime goal. "Go talk to Eddie Giacomin. He's the story of this game. Not me."

The Rangers did not win the semifinal playoff series against Chicago. They lost in a dramatic seven-game series in which three games were decided in sudden-death overtime. But in the process they shed themselves of their reputation as a poor playoff team, and, even in defeat, Eddie emerged as a hero and man of courage.

Bobby Hull inadvertently skated over Eddie's left hand in the second period of the first game. Although he was in severe pain and needed five stitches to close the bloody wound, Giacomin refused to leave the game and the Rangers won, 2-1, on Stemkowski's overtime goal.

"I've never seen Eddie so sharp," said Jean Ratelle. "How can we lose with a goaltender like him who plays even when he is badly hurt?"

The Black Hawks threw every shot imaginable at Giacomin in the beginning of the game. He made eight spectacular saves in the first period, two on blistering shots by Bobby Hull.

With the bandage on his injured hand soaked with blood, he stopped Cliff Koroll's breakaway in the third period, kicked out Pat Stapleton's slap shot, and regained his footing to block Jim Pappin's ensuing rebound. Then, near the buzzer, with the score 1-1, he executed a split save to prevent Pappin's shot from catching the far corner of the net.

Tony Esposito made thirty-two saves and shut out the Rangers, 3-0, in the second game, but Vic Hadfield's three-goal hat trick and tight Ranger checking that allowed Chicago to take only 17 shots made it easy for Eddie in the third game, 4-1.

The deep gash on Giacomin's hand, inflicted by Bobby Hull's skate, became infected between the third and fourth games. Eddie had only himself to blame.

"It got infected because I soaked it in hot water to relieve the swelling," he said. By soaking his injured hand in water, the stitches absorbed moisture and provided a wonderful spawning ground for infection.

The Rangers collapsed in front of Giacomin in the fourth game and lost, 7-1. Chicago capitalized on four two-one-one rushes and two breakaways and four of its goals against Eddie followed Ranger giveaways. The wound on Giacomin's hand started to bleed and Eddie left the game to have the stitches removed because of the infection.

"He'd had enough," said Francis. "He was hurt and he'd been left alone back there enough for one game."

Villemure took over in goal but it made little difference to the Black Hawks. They continued to pierce the Rangers' disorganized, error-prone defense and tied the series, 2-2.

"This was one of those nights when I couldn't stop anything," said Eddie. "None of us played well. We were all lousy."

Bobby Hull's rifle shot eluded Giacomin at 6:45 in over-time to win the fifth game, 3-2. Hull was set up for his winning goal when Pit Martin won a face-off from Tkaczuk in the Ranger zone. Now Chicago had won three of five games and the Rangers were one game from playoff elimination.

The sixth game, played on April 29 in Madison Square Garden, was a classic. It ended one minute before midnight when Stemkowski scored after eighty-nine seconds of the third overtime period in a triple-overtime game that took four hours and 29 minutes to play and was the longest in New York hockey history.

After Chico Maki scored at 1:54 of the second regulation period for a 2-0 Chicago lead, Eddie shut the door on the Black Hawks. He did not allow another goal and the Rangers fought back to tie the score.

"Eddie kept us in the game," said Stemkowski. "I don't know how in the hell he did it. The pressure on him must have been terrific."

Both teams were so fatigued that the players needed oxygen between periods and shifts on the ice. Eddie saved the Rangers from almost certain defeat in the third period by sliding out of his crease to stop Dennis Hull's breakaway. In the nineteenth minute of the second overtime period, he was knocked over backward when Stan Mikita's rising shot struck him in the mask.

The Rangers flew to Chicago for the seventh game. They took an early 2-1 lead, but Chicago scored three goals to win, 4-2, and captured the playoff series. Again it was Gia-comin's old nemesis, Bobby Hull, who scored the winning goal with a slap shot following a face-off won in New York ice by Lou Angotti. The Golden Jet's shot flew through a crowd of players in front of the Ranger goal. Eddie never saw or touched the puck until it was too late.

Eddie blamed himself for not stopping Bobby Hull's shot,

a shot so fast few goaltenders could have stopped it. He sat alone and stared out of the window on the chartered flight home to New York following the afternoon game in which the Rangers had been eliminated from the playoffs.

Then he realized that he must accept the defeat and that neither he nor the Rangers needed to feel ashamed. He had won the Vezina Trophy with Villemure during the regular season and he and the Rangers had proved they no longer were pushovers in the playoffs.

He poured himself a glass of wine after dinner and walked to the front of the plane where several sports writers were seated. He thanked them for many of the stories written about him during the season.

"I guess you have to look positively at the season as a whole, not just dwell on the one game we lost today," he said. "We've come a long way in just a few years. I think we proved a lot about ourselves as a team to quite a few people."

The Rangers were surprised and gratified to find a crowd of almost 3,000 of their fans waiting for them when they landed in New York. Even though they had lost in the playoffs to Chicago, the manner in which they played had brought them new respect and admiration from many of their followers.

The crowd, gathered in the waiting room, cheered loudly when the Rangers stepped off the plane.

When Giacomin appeared, the fans shouted, "Eddie! . . . Eddie! . . . Eddie!"

Chapter 13

A Memorable Moment
on the Montreal Ice

"I WAS JUST SO HAPPY MY EMOTIONS TOOK
OVER."

O N March 19, 1972, in Madison Square Garden, Eddie Giacomin did something no other goaltender had done in the history of the National Hockey League.

He set a record by becoming the first goalie to receive two assists in one game. He did it in a 5-3 conquest of the Toronto Maple Leafs, boldly dashing out of his crease and setting up two teammates' goals with long clearing passes. One of his assists was on Rod Seiling's winning goal.

"Hey, Eddie. Now you're only 95 points behind Esposito," Pete Stemkowski, the Rangers' resident dressing-room wit, quipped.

"Yeah. Phil better watch out. I'm making my move to win the scoring championship," said Eddie.

"That was a classic example of why it's so important for a goalkeeper to know how to come out of the net and clear the puck up ice to his teammates," said Emile Francis. "Eddie's the best in the business when it comes to passing the puck. Hell, he's not only a third defenseman back there for us, he's an extra forward, the way he passes that puck."

The odds are stacked against a goaltender being credited with an assist. Most goalies play an entire career without ever collecting an assist. Giacomin had the first two assists of his NHL career during the 1969–70 season. He assisted on a goal in a 9-1 win against St. Louis on January 5, and when the 1971–72 season ended he had tied an NHL goaltender's record with three assists in one season.

"Maybe I'll become a forward," he said with a grin one day at practice.

The Rangers started the season as though they were un-stoppable. They compiled a 12-1-4 record, garnished by a 14-game unbeaten streak, and were in first place from October 10 until January 22. They experienced their annual dry spell (Francis never likes to use the word slump) in the second half of the season and were relegated to second place behind Boston.

The Bruins were the most awesome team in hockey. They placed first with a remarkable 54-13-11 record, 119 points and 330 goals. New York finished second with 48-17-13 record and was second in offense with 317 goals. If it had not been for that 14-game undefeated streak, in which Giacomin played ten of the games, the Rangers might not have finished in second place, one point ahead of Montreal.

Giacomin and Villemure again formed the best goaltending tandem in the league. Eddie had a 6-1-2 record in his first nine games. Villemure was 7-0-2 with only eleven goals scored against him in his first nine games. His record was 15-2-2, and he led the league with a marvelous 1.72 goals-against average at midseason.

Eddie, however, was not satisfied with his play when he arrived at Kennedy International Airport on December 7 for a flight to Chicago.

"My goals-against average is too high," he said. Although his record was 8-3-2, he had surrendered forty goals and his average was 3.07. "I guess some people think I'm playing poorly. That's the price you pay for a 2.15 goals-against average. We're winning and that's the main thing. But I'd like to get my average down under three goals, say around 2.50."

Eddie allowed only eleven goals in his next six games, and his average began to drop. He finished the season at 2.70 in forty-four games. Villemure's goals-against average was 2.08 in thirty-seven games. The two goaltenders each were twenty-four-game winners.

For Eddie, the season was not without its usual depressing or scary moments.

On February 5 in St. Louis, Larry Hornung flipped a weak, back-handed shot from the blue line. Somehow the puck slithered through the maze of legs in front of the net, and Giacomin missed the easy shot. It was the winning goal in the Blues' 6-5 victory. Francis was angry after the game and did not conceal his feeling from his players.

"After giving up a fluke goal and losing a game like that, I thought Eddie would be throwing things around the dressing room because he was mad at himself," said Stemkowski. "But he was calm. I know he was angry, but he didn't let it get to him. Most goalies would have gone crazy. But then most goalies are a little weird, anyway. The job makes them that way. Eddie? He's always calm and relaxed. He's the only goalie I can remember who doesn't smoke or act nervous."

The comical Stemkowski illustrated Giacomin's proper attitude by telling of a prank he pulled on Eddie at practice the next day.

"I decided to bug him about Hornung's goal," said the husky center whom teammates called Stemmer. "I stood out at the blue line in shooting practice in just the same position where Hornung had been. Then I yelled, 'Hey, Eddie, try this shot.'"

Stemkowski flipped the puck at Eddie in the same manner Hornung had done the night before.

"I figured I'd stop if Eddie seemed touchy about it or got mad," said Stemkowski. "But when he finally saw what I was doing, it got his spirits up and he laughed about it."

Eddie was not laughing in the next game on February 9 in Madison Square Garden against Chicago. Dennis Hull broke free from his check and slipped behind the Rangers' defense. He skated in from the left side to an angle only ten feet from Giacomin. Eddie skated out in a crouch to meet the one-on-one challenge. Hull's point-blank shot hit the Ranger goaltender squarely in the middle of his mask, directly between the eye slits above his nose.

Eddie flung out both arms and fell over backward to the ice in a daze as if he had been gunned down gangland style. He was out cold.

"He could have been killed without the mask," said Jimmy Young. The Rangers' assistant trainer looked at Eddie's fibo-glass mask. There was a deep dent in it where Hull's power-ful shot had struck.

When Eddie was revived he refused to leave the game. Young hammered out the dent in the mask, and Eddie con-tinued playing. He made a profusion of difficult saves and the Rangers won, 4-1.

No one who knew Eddie's background should have been surprised.

"When the puck hit me in the mask, it was lights out," he said. "I don't remember a thing until I came to." He wore a bandage across the bridge of his nose because the mask had caved in and gouged his face.

Francis was asked if he considered taking the injured goalie out of the game.

"Are you kidding?" he replied. "I didn't even bother. I would have been wasting my time. I knew Eddie wouldn't come out of the game, no matter how badly he was hurt."

In 1972, both Eddie and the Rangers reached hockey's promised land. They made it to the Stanley Cup playoffs' final, New York's furthest playoff advancement since 1950.

They swept the Black Hawks out of the playoffs in four games in the semifinal round. They fooled the experts who had picked the team to lose by beating Montreal in a six-game opening-round series. That put Eddie and his teammates in the Cup final against the Bruins.

There was not much personal satisfaction for Giacomin beating Chicago. He injured his left knee in the Rangers' 3-2 victory in the first game and was unable to play in the next three games.

"What a lousy break," said Eddie. "But we're in good shape. We can win it. Gilly can do the job." Villemure did the job and the Rangers clinched the series with 5-3, 3-2, and 6-2 victories.

Only 1:25 remained in the first game in Chicago when Giacomin was injured. He was guarding the corner of the cage when Christian Bordeleau shot from close range. Eddie made the save to protect New York's 1-goal lead. But in the ensuing scramble for the loose puck, Jerry Korab rammed Ron Stewart from behind. The two 200-pound players fell on top of Giacomin, crunching him backward to the ice.

Eddie's left leg was twisted underneath him. He tried to get up but he could not. Francis and Trainer Frank Paice rushed to his side and it was feared at first that he might have broken his leg. He lay on his side with his injured leg still twisted beneath him.

"I thought I snapped something when I went down," said Eddie. "But I knew I could get up. I knew I wasn't going to take myself out of the game."

Eddie insisted upon staying in the game. Despite his sore knee, he made tricky stops on shots by Pit Martin and Bordeleau in the final minute of play to preserve New York's victory.

Afterward, he sat in the same place in the dressing room where he sat one year ago after Bobby Hull's skate blade ripped open his left hand. The scene was almost identical. The invading gray hairs atop his head were continuing to win their war with the retreating black hairs. There was the lumpy trace of the old wound inflicted by Dennis Hull's shot across the bridge of his nose. He pressed an icebag to his injured left knee and the hand holding the cooling pouch bore the remnants of the jagged scar from Bobby Hull's skate.

"My hand, my face, and now my knee," he said wearily. "History repeats itself, eh? They haven't missed much, have they? Maybe the Black Hawks don't like me, eh?"

Beating Montreal was one of Eddie's greatest personal triumphs. The Canadiens still were the most respected name in hockey and twice they had overpowered Giacomin and the Rangers in the playoffs.

Eddie played all six games and allowed the high-scoring Canadiens only fourteen goals. He stopped their breakaways. He stopped their two-on-one and three-on-one thrusts. He personally pulled the plug on their power plays, darting out of his net and into the corners to steal Montreal passes and ice the puck. New York won the first two games, 3-2 and 5-2. Montreal won the third game, 2-1, but the Rangers won the fourth game, 6-4. Although he played brilliantly, Giacomin was beaten in the fifth game, 2-1.

The sixth game was one of Eddie's most glorious and memorable playoff games. He won it, 3-2, and the Rangers won the playoff series.

The Canadiens appeared to have the edge in momentum at the outset from their victory in the fifth game. They swarmed around Giacomin for most of the first period. They tested Eddie with good shots but he stopped them. He was getting excellent support from his teammates. Brad Park and Dale Rolfe starred on defense. So did Rod Seiling and Jim Neilson. A rookie with long blond hair, Gene Carr, contained the Canadiens' dangerous Yvan Cournoyer with impeccable checking. Eddie's roommate, Walt Tkaczuk, scored the winning goal and with Bill Fairbairn played superb two-way hockey.

But the night belonged to Eddie.

In the third period, he made a save so unbelievable that even the most imperturbable spectators in the partisan crowd in the Montreal Forum were moved to cheer and applaud.

Frank Mahovlich skated full speed from the blue line to the top of the crease, took a crossing pass from the right corner, and shot without breaking stride from only three feet out. Eddie had been hugging his left goal post to guard against a shot from the short side. The puck reached Mahovlich so fast that there seemed to be no way Giacomin had time to move to his right and cover the open side of the net.

Somehow he found a way. The puck shot by Mahovlich was in midair for a split second, virtually inside the goal cage. But in a flash, Eddie lunged across the crease and stopped the shot from entering the net with his body.

It was an incredible twisting lunge and save by the goaltender with the gray hair and astonishingly fast reflexes.

Mahovlich stood there and stared dumbfounded at the net even though play continued to swirl around him after Giacomin knocked aside the shot.

The Canadiens' forward could not believe Eddie had stopped the shot that would have tied the game.

"Damn it," he said. "How could he make that save? There was absolutely no way he should have stopped that shot."

Ken Dryden, the Montreal goaltender, called Giacomin's spectacular save one of the best he ever saw a goalie make.

"Giacomin produced some of the best goaltending ever seen in the playoffs," said Scotty Bowman, the Canadiens' coach.

Montreal removed Dryden from goal in the final minute of play and fired shot after shot at Giacomin. He stopped them all. When the game ended, Eddie was so happy and so emotionally charged up that instead of skating off the ice, he flung himself down on the ice in front of the net and lay there on his back kicking his legs in the air and whooping with joy.

Eddie's display of emotional joy at winning the playoff series was viewed by thousands of fans in the New York area who watched the game on WOR-TV. They had never witnessed such a bizarre demonstration of happiness by a victorious athlete. Some viewers telephoned the television station or newspapers and asked if anything were wrong with the Ranger goaltender.

Dan Decher, an ardent Ranger follower since 1950, was watching on TV with his wife Isabel and daughter Kathy in their home in Maplewood, New Jersey.

"I've never seen an athlete show as much emotion as Eddie did after he beat the Canadiens," said Decher. "There he was lying on the ice, kicking his legs and rolling around with a big smile on his face. I think that's why so many fans have come to admire Eddie and can relate so easily to him. Some guys might have considered it unprofessional to act the way he did. Or they would be embarrassed to do what he did before thousands of people. But Eddie didn't care. He felt so good because the Rangers won that he couldn't keep his feelings from showing. He wanted to show everyone how good he felt. It was a beautiful sight."

Eddie was still excited in the dressing room after the game. The smile never left his face and his hands quivered with emotion from the game he had won. His conversation was almost garbled and he kept repeating, "This is the greatest feeling I've ever had."

He laughed when a newsman with a tape-recorder microphone asked about his victory act on the ice in front of the goal.

"I was just so happy that my emotions took over," he said.

"I didn't know what to do but I had to do something to show how good I felt. We finally had beaten the Canadiens —got them off our backs—and I had made that big save on Mahovlich. He beat me on the same kind of play earlier in the series and this time I had beaten him. When the game ended and I saw our guys coming off the bench and heading for me, I was just so thrilled that the next thing I knew I was down on the ice rolling around, kicking and yelling. I guess people must think I'm crazy. But I'm not. I'm just happy. This was my most memorable playoff game."

Eddie was asked if his wife Marg had watched the game on television.

"She was watching and right now she probably thinks her husband is nuts," joked Eddie.

"I certainly did not think he was nuts," said Marg Giacomin. "I sat there at home and looked at the TV and knew how happy he must be. Winning that game was so significant for Eddie and everyone on the team. It meant so much to Eddie because Montreal was so hard to beat and had beaten the Rangers so badly in the previous playoffs."

Mrs. Giacomin paused as she spoke.

"Eddie has taken so much criticism over the years until this game. They said he was not a good playoff goalie. There was that awful word 'choke.' I hated that word as much as he did. There have been so many awful raps at Eddie in the press."

Red Sullivan, who was Giacomin's first Ranger coach, was in the press box watching the game.

"It was a beautiful game by a beautiful guy," said Sullivan. "Eddie's waited so long for this moment. Hell, beating the Montreal Canadiens is just like winning the Stanley Cup."

Eddie and the Rangers faced another great challenge from the Bruins in the Stanley Cup final.

"Orr and Esposito. Those are the two guys we have to stop," Eddie said before the Cup final began. Esposito led the league in scoring with sixty-six goals and 133 points. Orr, generally regarded as the finest all-round player in hockey, finished second with thirty-seven goals and 177 points.

"Esposito is just about the strongest guy in the league," said Eddie. "He just keeps coming at you and has such long arms that he can get shots off that other guys couldn't even attempt. He likes to park himself out in the slot and let his wingers (Ken Hodge and Wayne Cashman) get the puck to him. He's a hard guy to move out of the slot or off the puck. You've really got to double-team him. He gets his shots away quickly and even when his back is to you, you have to be ready for him to shoot."

And Orr?

"He's a defenseman who's also a forward," said Eddie. "He's the best skater in the game. He can take over the game by himself and take the puck behind his own net and lug it all the way down to your end and score a goal. There's really no way to defense him because he's so good."

The Bruins won the opening game in Boston, 6-5, in a game in which both teams played poorly on defense and concentrated on freewheeling, skate-and-shoot hockey. Francis replaced Giacomin with Villemure in the second game, and Gilly played well but lost, 2-1. Eddie was the goaltender in the third game, which the Rangers won, 5-2, and in the fourth game, which they lost, 3-2.

He did not play again. The knee he injured in Chicago still was bothering him and Francis opted for Villemure. He beat the Bruins, 3-2, in the fifth game but lost the sixth and final game, 3-0, when Orr took command and led Boston to the Stanley Cup.

Most of the Rangers insisted that the injury to center Jean Ratelle was the reason why they were unable to beat the Bruins in the Cup final.

"I'm convinced we could have won if Jean had not been hurt," said Gilbert.

Ratelle was leading the league in scoring with 46 goals and 109 points until a shot by teammate Dale Rolfe broke his right ankle on March 1 against California. He missed the final sixteen games of the regular season, as well as the play-offs, against Montreal and Chicago. He played against the Bruins but the injured ankle left him ineffective.

"It was a big blow for us," said Giacomin. That was obvious. Without Ratelle as their center, New York's best line with Gilbert and Vic Hadfield was less effective. Ratelle and his linemates had been the Rangers' chief attacking weapon throughout most of the season. Hadfield became a fifty-goal scorer and Gilbert scored forty-three goals.

Eddie was unhappy for another reason after the Rangers lost in the final to the Bruins. He wanted to play but Francis had selected Villemure as his goalie for the last two games of the series.

"It was a big let down for me after beating Montreal," he said glumly. "I didn't want to be on the bench. I wanted to be out there in goal."

Eddie's low spirits would have been lifted if he had heard what Jean Beliveau said about him after his goaltending brilliance led the Rangers to victory over Montreal.

"No one should every say again that Eddie Giacomin is not a good playoff goalie," said the Canadiens' retired star and member of the Hockey Hall of Fame. "Eddie has earned a place for himself as one of the greatest goalies to play this game. He did it himself by working hard and refusing to give up when things went badly for him and so many people criticized him. He is one of the best examples I can think of to show how much a man can do with dedication and hard work."

Chapter 14

The First Playoff Shutout:
"Eddie! . . . Eddie! . . . Eddie!"

"I WAS SO SURE THIS WAS GOING TO BE OUR
YEAR."

"**I**T'S a great honor to know that people consider you the top goaltender in Ranger history," said Eddie Giacomin.

He was standing in the Madison Square Garden dressing room on the night of January 3, 1973, playfully juggling the game puck in his hands.

"This one goes into the collection, too," he said, gripping the souvenir puck firmly in his hand. "I've got a display case in my basement at home where I keep all the pucks with the dates and scores of the game."

Eddie covered his mouth and coughed. His usually resonant voice was hoarse and raspy. He had a cold that was on the verge of becoming flu and with his gravelly voice reduced almost to a whisper, he sounded as though he were Marlon Brando in *The Godfather*. But he did not mind talking.

The puck in his hand had special significance. It was the game puck he had tucked into his catching glove as the crowd cheered and applauded following his 3-0 shutout of the Los Angels Kings.

The shutout was the forty-first of his National Hockey League career. He had become the Rangers' career shutout leader, surpassing the record of forty shutouts by Dave Kerr from 1934 to 1941.

The crowd knew Eddie was going after the record. He had tied Kerr with his fortieth shutout on December 24, 1972 by defeating Detroit, 5-0. The fans started counting down the final seconds of the game against Los Angeles.

"I heard them," said Giacomin. "I was counting down the last few seconds myself. This is one record I really wanted to get, because it means you have to have been around for a few years and to have done your job pretty well."

New York dominated the game and its 39-26 advantage in shots made it seem that Giacomin spent a relaxed night in the net. Nothing could be further from the truth. Ab De-Marco's first-period goal provided the winning margin, but it was not until Vic Hadfield and Glen Sather scored in the third period that the Rangers were assured of winning.

"One mistake by me and it could have been a tie," said Eddie.

The most dangerous moment for Giacomin was when Juha Widing skated in on a breakaway with 3:05 remaining in the first period. Fast Eddie charged out of the crease and poke checked the puck away from the Kings' center before he could shoot.

"It was a gamble but Widing had beaten me before on breakaways so I decided to do something different," explained Eddie. "I figured I'd use one of Gilles Villemure's old tricks by going for the puck with my stick."

There was one problem: Eddie was 10 feet outside the net when he knocked the puck away from Widing. He also was off balance and vulnerable. Bob Berry, the trailer on the breakaway, retrieved the rebound of Widing's aborted shot and was confronted with the delightful sight of a wide-open goal cage in front of him.

Fast Eddie lived up to his nickname. Regaining his feet quickly, he dived backward into the crease, making a spectacular second save to block Berry's rebound shot with his right hand.

The combination of Berry and Widing almost spoiled Giacomin's shutout record with 10:39 left in the second period. Berry shot from the slot and Eddie kicked out the 12-foot smash with a tumbling skate save. The rebound went to Widing, stationed near the goal post to Giacomin's left. The puck Widing shot appeared to be inside the cage, but before the goal judge could flash the red goal light, Eddie sprawled on his belly in the crease, reached back, and stopped the puck from falling inside the net.

The Kings argued with Referee Bryan Lewis, claiming Giacomin caught the puck behind the goal line and pulled it out.

"They thought I caught the puck over the goal line and brought it back out, but I didn't," insisted Giacomin. "Widing shot along the ice so I reached out with a sweeping motion and the puck hit my left forearm and then went under my leg pads. My hand was definitely behind the goal line in the beginning but the puck didn't hit me until I had brought my arm back out."

Eddie made several other acrobatic saves to break Kerr's record. Twice he stopped Serge Bernier on power-play screen shots. A shot by Don Kozak ticked the goal post. Another shot hopped off Eddie's chest and he caught it in midair as two Kings groped for the rebound with their sticks.

"It definitely wasn't an easy shutout for Eddie," acknowledged Emile Francis. "Eddie got off to a rough start, along with everybody else, but now he's sharp."

A rough start, indeed. Eddie was strafed for nineteen goals in the first four games of the season, and after Montreal beat him, 6-1, on October 14, he was benched for eight games. Villemure took over in goal and brought the Rang-

ers out of their slump. He won six and tied one in the first
seven games, played six consecutive one-goal games and
stopped seven breakaways in beating Chicago, 3-2.

It seemed as though the Rangers' defense automatically
tightened up when Villemure played goal. It often seemed
that the defense let up when Giacomin played.

But by midseason Giacomin had regained his form.

"I don't know what I'm doing differently—except stopping
the puck," he said.

"Eddie just seems more confident than he did at the start
of the year. He's playing more aggressively, covering the
angles better and playing his old stand-up style," suggested
Rod Seiling.

Injuries, as usual, plagued the Rangers. Jim Neilson missed
twenty-six games with two broken bones in his right foot.
Ankle and knee injuries kept Ted Irvine out of fourteen
games. Brad Park was on crutches with a damaged knee and
missed eighteen games. Gene Carr had a broken collarbone.
Steve Vickers, the Rangers' high-scoring rookie left wing, was
sidelined for sixteen games with a knee injury.

Eddie finally brought his goals-against average down below 3.00 on December 31. He was hot. He went on streaks
of 8-1-0, 9-0-2, and 13-1-2. The Rangers fought their way into
second place behind Montreal. They won ten consecutive
games and their undefeated streak reached fifteen games on
February 10.

They were only four points behind the Canadiens when
the teams played on February 11 in Madison Square Garden.

"This is the big one. This is one we've got to win," said
Eddie.

The score was 2-0 Rangers, on goals by Bruce MacGregor
and Vic Hadfield, entering the third period. Then Frank
Mahovlich scored on a power play on which the Canadiens
had a two-man advantage.

The mistake that ended the Rangers' 10-game winning streak came with 9:13 to play in the game. Park had the puck at the blue line on a power play. He was the only man back. He saw Bobby Rousseau cutting toward the net and tried to reach him with a long pass.

Guy Lapointe blocked Park's pass. The puck bounced back over the blue line behind Park. The Montreal defenseman muscled his way past Park, recovered the puck, and skated up the center of the ice for a breakaway.

Eddie came thirty-five feet out of the net to meet Lapointe. The two players collided and slid along the ice. Lapointe pushed the puck behind Giacomin. Chuck Lefley, the trailer, was there to roll the puck into the ungarded goal cage.

Final score: Montreal 2, Rangers 2.

"It was just like we lost," Park said in a Ranger dressing room with the hushed atmosphere of a funeral parlor.

Francis blamed Referee Bruce Hood's penalty calls against the Rangers for the defeat.

"Personally, I think we blew the game," said Dale Rolfe, the candid defenseman. "It was a big game and we had a 2-0 lead. We should have known we couldn't afford to take chances or make a mistake in the last period."

Eddie was nowhere to be found. He had showered, dressed, and slipped out before the horde of interviewers could question him about the play he made that allowed the Canadiens to tie the game.

"You've got to understand Eddie's personality," said Park. "He took it hard. He wanted to win."

Did Eddie make a foolish mistake by leaving the goal cage unguarded on Lapointe's breakaway?

"Oh, no," said Park, defending his teammate. "Eddie made the right move. It was my fault. I made the initial mistake. I didn't get the puck through from the blue line when I had to and that's my job on the power play."

But why had Giacomin left the dressing room in anger?

"Maybe Eddie figures he made a mistake that cost us the game, but he didn't make it, I did," said Park.

"Eddie sort of hesitated and couldn't decide at first to come out of the net or stay back," said Francis. "It's a tough decision that only the goalkeeper can make. Only Eddie knows if he made the right move."

Ken Dryden, the Montreal goalie, defended Giacomin's decision to leave the net.

"I think Eddie made the proper move," he said. "Remember, it's his style to come out of the net. In my own mind, Lapointe just made a fantastic play."

The game the Rangers should have won but did not was costly. Hadfield injured his thumb and MacGregor broke his left ankle and missed the next seventeen games. The Rangers were not the same team after the Montreal game. They were beset by more injuries, fell into a slump, dropped out of first-place contention, and ended the season in third place, eighteen points behind Montreal.

Eddie completed the season in the same manner in which it began: he allowed nineteen goals in his final four games. He was dissatisfied with his 2.91 goals-against average.

He also was still angry at himself about the Montreal game on February 11.

"I don't know. Maybe I made the right move by coming out of the net. Maybe I didn't. I just couldn't stay back there and let the guy come in alone on me. They had another guy coming down, too, so it could have been a two-on-one. I did what I thought I had to do and it backfired. If I make the play, I'm a hero. If I don't, I'm a bum."

The opening round of the Stanley Cup playoffs provided Eddie with a perfect kind of redemption for what he considered a disappointing regular season.

The Rangers wiped out the favored Bruins in five games. Victory was sweet. No longer would critical New York fans and sports writers claim the Rangers lacked the skill and aggressiveness to beat the team that humiliated and intimidated them in the 1970 and 1972 playoffs.

Clearly the difference was in goal. Boston gambled that forty-four-year-old Jacques Plante, a late-season arrival, could do the job. He did not. Francis's strategy was to keep Jake the Snake busy handling and clearing the puck. The Rangers bombarded Plante in the first game. He wilted under fire and put four of his clearing passes on Ranger sticks. New York won, 6-2.

As in all games, there was a turning point, one sequence in the turbulent tempo of play in which action or non-action by a player determined the outcome.

Giacomin skated behind the net to retrieve the puck and was immediately mashed against the dasher-board glass by Ken Hodge. Park sped to his goaltender's rescue and attacked Hodge. Then Ted Irvine stepped in with fists flying.

"Nobody's ever going to run our goalie when I'm on the ice," said Irvine, like Eddie, a fierce competitor and dedicated team player. "For what Eddie means to this club, I'd risk a fine to come off the bench if a guy ever took a cheap shot at him."

Irvine's retaliation inspired the Rangers. A few minutes later Irvine coaxed Bobby Orr into a stick-waving fight. Both men went to the penalty boxes. With the irrepressible Orr out of the game, the Rangers scored three goals to clinch the game.

"Teddy's the guy who got us going and did the most to help us win," Giacomin said of Irvine.

New York won the second game, 4-2, but Giacomin was not around for the finish. He injured his neck and, reluctantly, had to leave the game briefly with 5:13 remaining in the second period. Villemure replaced him. Phil Esposito was not around at the end, either. Ron Harris, whom Francis labeled "our designated hitter," put the Bruins' scoring leader into the hospital with a crunching bodycheck, which resulted in Esposito's falling to the ice and injuring his knee. He was through for the playoffs and underwent surgery.

Eddie was in so much pain from the injury to his neck and shoulder that he had to hold his head to one side and needed help putting on his clothes after the game.

"They tell me it's a pinched nerve," he said, wincing as he tried to move his head.

"Hodge fell on top of me with his full weight [the Bruins' forward weighs 215 pounds]," said Giacomin. "I had gone down to get the puck. I felt something pop and I got a burning sensation. When I went to the bench, I broke into a cold sweat. I couldn't turn my head or move my shoulder so I knew I couldn't go on. I told Emile that I couldn't play. It was my decision to come out."

Villemure had played only forty seconds when Eddie told Francis he felt better and asked to return to the game. He played the final 4:33 of the second period, but the sharp pains in his neck increased and he told Francis he could not play the third period.

Eddie did not allow the pinched nerve to prevent him from playing in the third game. He lost, 4-2, but the next night in Madison Square Garden he achieved his first playoff shutout, making thirty-three saves in a 4-0 victory.

"Let's put it this way: it's the greatest feeling I've ever had," Eddie said of his first shutout in forty-four playoff games. "The third period—that was the toughest for me. What did they get, fifteen shots, right?"

Plante said before the game that no goalie, no matter how young, can play four games in five days.

"Maybe he was trying to psych me out," said Eddie, who had played just that, four games in five nights.

In the final minute of the game, the fans at Madison Square Garden were standing and roaring their approval of Eddie's lightning-fast saves. First they chanted, "Good-by

Boston!" Then it seemed as if every voice in the building were shouting, "Eddie! . . . Eddie! . . . Eddie!"

The noise was deafening.

"Did I hear it?" asked Eddie. "You bet I heard it. I loved it. It gave me goose pimples. I almost wanted to sing along when the fans were chanting my name."

He threw back his head and laughed.

"What do you think 'the Cat' would do if I started singing? Say, has there ever been a singing goalie, eh? Oh, well, I can't sing anyway."

Brad Park did not miss the chance to needle his teammate.

"Maybe you can't sing, Eddie, but you sure can talk—especially after a couple of beers."

When the game ended, Eddie took off his mask and tipped it to the crowd. Then he kissed the puck and held it up toward everyone.

"Giacomin's the big man on their team," Bep Guidolin, the Bruins' coach, said outside the dressing room. "He's not going to beat himself. He's going to make you beat him. It's not easy the way he's played so far in this series."

Mrs. Giacomin was as overjoyed about the shutout as her husband was.

"I knew it was Eddie's first playoff shutout. It was a very sweet victory for him. He was so proud and so was I," said Marg Giacomin.

Eddie could not single out one shot that gave him the most difficulty in his shutout. But he did remember what Boston defenseman Carol Vadnais did to him.

"He gave me a hit right in the back, right here," said Giacomin, pointing to his painful neck and shoulder. "I'm naturally a little sensitive about being hit where I was hurt before."

There was 3:15 remaining in the game when Vadnais slashed at Giacomin with his stick while the goalie was out-

side his crease. Eddie gave Vadnais a stiff-arm blow in retaliation.

He was the goaltender when the Rangers clinched the series by winning the fifth game, 6-3, in Boston Garden, when
Vickers scored a three-goal hat trick. A jubilant but unruly
crowd estimated at 5,000 greeted the Rangers when they
arrived at LaGuardia Airport following the game.

They were chanting: "We want Eddie . . . We want
Eddie! . . . We want Eddie!"

Guidolin said Giacomin was the key to the Rangers' victory. "If we had to lose, I'm glad we lost to an Italian goalie,"
said the Boston coach, smiling.

"Eddie was just superb, just like a third defenseman out
there the way he cleared the puck," said Hodge.

"I've never seen Eddie so sharp or play with so much intensity," observed defenseman Don Awrey.

"We stunk," said Orr. "The Rangers outhustled us."

Eddie Johnston, one of Boston's goalies, called Giacomin's
performance, "just great."

Despite Eddie's sharp goaltending, there was considerably
more attention given to Esposito's injury, Plante's failure,
and Ron Harris's fierce checking. Harris is the player who did
so well in place of injured Rod Seiling.

"I still don't think the Rangers could have won unless
Eddie played the way he did," said Ross Brooks, a Boston
goalie and one of Giacomin's friends from Providence and
the Eastern League. "We counted on Plante to do the job
for us, but he didn't do it. The Rangers counted on Eddie
to do the job for them. And he did. I'm happy for Eddie. I
know how much this means to him."

Considering the ease with which the Rangers disposed of
the Bruins, the Black Hawks looked as though they would
be pushovers for New York in the semifinal playoff.

"I pick Chicago to beat those damned guys," Derek Sanderson said when asked who he felt would win in the New

York-Chicago playoff. Few of those who heard or read Derek's prediction took him seriously. They thought he was just a sore loser bad-mouthing the Rangers.

One thing was certain: Giacomin did not have to worry about Bobby Hull's skating over his hand again. The Black Hawks' star had defected to the new World Hockey Association during the heated bidding war for players between the rival leagues during the summer of 1972.

For one of the few times in their long coaching rivalry, Francis and Chicago's Billy Reay agreed on something.

"A hot goaltender is the most important thing a team can have going for it in the playoffs," said Reay. "If your goalie gets hot at the right time, he can win a playoff for you."

Francis cited Giacomin's play in the Boston playoff as an example of Reay's theory.

"Eddie was hot and he made the big saves. I couldn't ask for any better goalkeeping than Eddie has given us," said the Ranger coach.

The Rangers won the opening game, 4-1. Giacomin was hot. Tony Esposito was not. "I played lousy. It was all my fault," said the Chicago goalie.

Perhaps the Rangers became too confident and subconsciously took victory for granted in the second game. They lost, 5-4. Francis removed Giacomin after he allowed three of Chicago's first eight shots to elude him.

"He didn't say why," said Eddie. "He just said, 'Gilly [Villemure], you're going in for the second period.' I was surprised."

Giacomin was victimized by his teammates' mistakes as much as anything. Two goals he allowed were shots that deflected off the skates of his own defensemen, changed direction, and went into the net. One goal followed a Ranger giveaway. The third goal resulted from a careless clearing pass inside the New York blue line.

Eddie lost again in the third game, 2-1. Jim Pappin scored

the first goal on a two-on-one rush in which his shot glanced off Jim Neilson's skate and spun past Giacomin. Stan Mikita's winning goal was the rebound of a shot by John Marks that Eddie stopped. A bad pass by New York gave Chicago possession of the puck.

Mistakes and Esposito's remarkable goaltending cost the Rangers the fourth game. They lost, 3-1. Brad Park tried to pass the puck between Bill White's legs. The puck bounced off the Black Hawks' defenseman's legs. Pat Stapleton got it and sent Pit Martin in for a breakaway goal. That was the winning one. Dennis Hull put the game out of reach, scoring from a seemingly impossible angle in the corner.

The Rangers outshot Chicago, 38-28, in the third game and lost. They outshot Chicago, 39-21, in the fourth game and lost. They had scored only two goals in 77 shots. Esposito was the hot goaltender and the Rangers could not find a weakness in him to exploit. Chicago's forwards and defensemen bottled up New York's stagnant attack with a cleverly executed and tightly disciplined defensive strategy.

Eddie was frustrated and angry. So were all his teammates.

"They play every game as though it's a 0-0 tie all the time," he said. "They sit back and wait for us to make a mistake and when we do, they take advantage of it. They've got us bottled up and our power play hasn't done a thing. They've frustrated us into gambling, taking chances. When we do, they get too many breakaways, two-on-ones and three-on-ones."

"We have to find a way to get some pucks by that guy Esposito," said Francis, frowning.

The Chicago goalie uses an unorthodox style of guarding his net. He often seems awkward and slow. Critics claim he has more weaknesses than strengths and violates many fundamental techniques of goaltending. He flops and pounces on pucks and often allows rebounds to bounce around perilously close to the net.

"He's different, that's for sure," said Francis. "But I can't criticize him. You can't argue with success. If a guy stands on his head and keeps the puck out of the net, how can you say he's not doing the job?"

"Maybe Tony doesn't do things by the book, but look at his record. That's what counts," said Giacomin. "He uses his body to stop the puck more than most of us do."

The Rangers took 29 shots at Tony in the fifth game. He stopped all but one. Chicago won, 4-1, and captured the playoff from the Rangers in five games. The first goal by Mikita was the third rebound after two point-blank saves by Giacomin. Dennis Hull's winning goal followed a three-on-one rush, with the Rangers far out of position, following a giveaway.

Esposito almost completely stopped the Rangers' offense with his magnificent goaltending. He was the hot goalie who won in the playoff. He allowed New York only three goals in the last three games of the playoff, stopping 88 of 90 shots during one span and 116 of 119 shots since the second game.

It was so quiet inside the Ranger dressing room in Chicago Stadium that you could hear a puck drop.

"I don't understand it. I'm shocked. I'll never understand how or why it could happen," Rod Gilbert said softly. "Five games. They beat us in five games. Esposito was fabulous. He was unreal."

The Rangers' right wing posed a question.

"Do you believe in fate?" he asked. "Sometimes things are just not meant to be. I hope that it isn't fate that says winning the Stanley Cup was never meant to be for us. Maybe fate never intends for us to win the Stanley Cup."

"How can you blame Eddie?" said Hadfield. "Not with all the crazy deflections that ended up as goals or all the breaks we gave them. Not with the way Chicago and Esposito played."

Eddie stared at the floor.

"This was supposed to be our year," he said. "It was supposed to be now or never. We all knew if we didn't win it this year, there would be a lot of changes made the next year. All of us thought this would finally be our year. After we beat Boston in five games, I thought we could go all the way."

He looked up.

"You work so hard for so long and come so close, and then it ends like this," said Eddie. "I'm stunned. I'm shocked. I'm terribly disappointed. I was so sure this was going to be our year."

Chapter 15

Giacomin Speaks His Mind
and the Rangers Get the Message

"EDDIE'S THE LEADER OF THIS TEAM."

EDDIE Giacomin was up on a ladder working on the roof of his new house in Manhasset, Long Island, when his wife called him to the telephone on the afternoon of June 1, 1973.

"What's up?" he asked cheerfully.

He was told that the Rangers had announced they would hold a major news conference on Monday, June 4, at noon in the Madison Square Garden Hall of Fame lounge.

"Do you know what they're going to announce?" Giacomin was asked.

"Maybe they're going to announce they've traded or retired me, eh?" joked Eddie.

"No. They said it was a major news conference," quipped the man from the *New York Post*.

"Thanks a lot," said Eddie, laughing.

Emile Francis was stepping down from his dual role as general manager and coach to concentrate upon the general manager's job. No one, least of all Giacomin, knew that was what the press conference was about.

Eddie said it would be a "tremendous shock" if the press conference were to announce Francis's resignation and the appointment of a new coach for the 1973–74 season. He had visited "the Cat" just the day before and was given no hint of a coaching change.

"I'm sure he would have told me, especially since Marg and I are leaving tomorrow for a vacation in Bermuda," said Eddie. "He never gave me a clue that he wouldn't be coaching us next season. Maybe the press conference is about something else, eh?"

No. It was to announce Francis's resignation and to introduce the new coach.

"I hope that's not it," said the Ranger goaltender. "It would be a big disappointment. How can they knock Emile? When he took over, he took over a bad club. He built us into a contender and we've made the playoffs seven years in a row, right? Any guy on the team would feel the same way I do. But I'd be the guy hurt the most. Emile gave me my chance to play in the NHL. He stuck with me when I was stumbling around. I hope it isn't true he's leaving as coach."

Who might replace Francis as coach?

"My guess would be Larry Popein," said Eddie. "Larry and Emile are similar in a lot of ways. They believe in the same kind of coaching, conditioning, and discipline. Popein has been in our minor-league system for a while, and he and 'the Cat' are very close friends. He's a no-nonsense guy; he can really crack the whip."

Three days later Eddie and Marg Giacomin were sunning themselves on a beach in Bermuda; Francis was out and Popein was in as Ranger coach.

Criticism of the Rangers had reached a new height. They were the highest-paid team in hockey. At least seven of their players had long-term contracts worth more than $100,000 a year. Management had agreed to the exorbitant salaries to prevent many of the players from defecting to the rival World Hockey Association. Each year was supposed to be *the* year for the Rangers. Each year they were beset with injuries and failed to survive in the playoffs.

They were basically a team of highly paid veterans. Many of their promising young players had been traded and achieved success with other teams. The Rangers often seemed to lack intensity and aggressiveness when they played.

There was growing suspicion that some of the players had become self-satisfied and content with their large salaries. Many rival players and coaches made jokes and innuendos about the team from the Big Apple that "tried to buy the Stanley Cup but couldn't." Many Ranger fans had become disenchanted with the team. The words "Fat Cats" began appearing more frequently in newspaper stories critical of the team's repeated playoff failure and the lack of a Stanley Cup champion or first-place hockey team in New York since the 1940s.

"I'm getting sick and tired of reading that crap you've been writing," Vic Hadfield told a *New York Post* writer one day. "Why don't you knock it off?"

"Why do you pick on us?" asked mild-mannered Jean Ratelle. "The Knicks make $200,000 a year, too. Why don't you write about the Knicks and criticize them because they make a lot of money?"

The reason some fans and newsmen could accept the Knicks was simple: they had brought New York two National Basketball Association championships. The Rangers had won nothing.

"I know one thing," said Giacomin. "This better be our year or there's really going to be some changes in this team. A lot of people are really down on us and I'm sure that includes some of the people who own the Garden, too."

The Rangers did not place first or win the Stanley Cup

during the 1973–74 season. Again they were ravaged by injuries to twenty-three of their players and struggled to finish third. Popein coached for only forty-one games before Francis was forced to take charge again of a team some insiders believed to be on the verge of dissension.

Popein was a solemn, humorless man, a loner who seldom said much to his players. He regarded most of them as mature professionals with sufficient pride in themselves and in their team to motivate themselves to do their job.

Some of the players became critical of the new coach Francis called "the perfect man for the job." They complained about him when he benched players and made line-up changes to get the team moving. They said that he failed to communicate with them and that they could only relate to Francis as coach. They mocked the nervous new coach behind his back.

"We're 'the Cat's' people, not his," said one veteran.

"What the hell, we still get our paychecks and we're good enough to collect some playoff money," another player said on the flight home after a particularly distasteful defeat.

The Rangers no longer played the tightly disciplined checking game that had brought their goalies the Vezina Trophy in 1971. Some players only seemed interested in scoring goals to fatten their individual statistics. After one humiliating loss, some seemed more disturbed about assists they thought they deserved than about the team's defeat.

Popein was not blameless himself. He embarrassed Rod Gilbert publicly by suspending him for one game in October because he inadvertently arrived a half-hour late for a team meeting. Gilbert was late because for years he was accustomed to Francis's meeting time, which was thirty minutes later than team meetings scheduled by the new coach.

Gilbert was the highest scorer in Ranger history. He was a dedicated team player. Not the type to disregard team rules. He was hurt and angry by Popein's suspension, but he refused to criticize the coach.

If Giacomin had any complaints about Popein, he, too, kept them to himself. Eddie never aired his team's dirty laundry in public print.

He had reason to complain.

The Rangers' record after eleven games under Popein was 3-6-2. The team defense was horrible, failing repeatedly to protect seemingly secure leads. Eddie and Gilles Villemure felt as though they were going through the London blitz.

"How many breakaways have I had against me?" Eddie asked one morning in the team's hotel in Vancouver.

The man from the *New York Post* who kept such negative statistics looked into his notebook.

"Twenty breakaways in the first nine games. I can't keep up with all the three-on-ones and two-on-ones," Giacomin was told.

"That's too damned many," grumbled the usually docile goalie, who had stopped all but two breakaways.

It got worse. When the season ended, Giacomin had been confronted with sixty breakaways in the fifty-six games he played because teammates continually were out of defensive positions. He stopped forty-seven of the breakaways. Villemure was exposed to fifteen and stopped eleven. Peter McDuffe was the victim of three breakaways, two of which he stopped. The breakaway total: seventy-eight in seventy-eight games for New York.

Popein raised eyebrows and angered many Rangers by leaving Giacomin in goal for the entire game on November 15 when the Bruins made the Rangers resemble a team from the Sudbury midnight leagues in a 10-2 rout. Bobby Orr set a record with three goals and four assists in New York's most one-sided defeat in eight years.

"If it hadn't been for Giacomin, we could have had fifteen goals," a gleeful Bruins' fan said outside Boston Garden.

"Take the poor bastard out; he's exhausted," a fan

shouted down at Popein after Eddie had made four rolling, tumbling saves only to be beaten on the fifth shot of the sequence when his teammates failed to clear the puck.

"I didn't ever consider relieving him," Popein said without emotion after the game.

Why not? It's customary to save a goalie from humiliation when his team is being beaten badly. Villemure was on the bench. He had recovered from the virus attack he suffered a week earlier in Atlanta.

"I'm not 100 percent but I could have played," he said. "I expected he'd send me in. I felt bad for Eddie. He was getting bombed. It wasn't fair. He shouldn't have been made to stay out there and take it."

"I couldn't believe they left the poor guy in there the whole game," said Boston's Phil Esposito.

Brad Park shook his head in disgust. "I never saw the puck in our net so much. We didn't skate. We didn't shoot. We didn't hit. We didn't pass. We didn't check. We didn't get the puck out of our end. We didn't do a goddamn thing. I'm not going to lie to you: this whole [expletive deleted] team stunk. Eddie played super this season, but we haven't done a damned thing to help him out."

"We were horse——. We should all be ashamed to look our goalie in the eye. Eddie should sue us for nonsupport. It was hell for him," Rod Seiling said of the zombielike Rangers' indifferent effort.

Eddie was furious. The Bruins took shot after shot at him without meeting more than token resistance. Finally he could control his anger no longer. After Orr's shot glanced off Seiling's stick and hopped into the net, he flung his stick high in the air and kicked the puck all the way out to the blue line.

"I wasn't mad at Rod Seiling," he said softly in the dressing room. "I was just so disgusted with things in general. It was unbelievable. It was embarrassing. It was humiliating. I never had ten goals scored on me in a game in my life. I threw my stick and kicked the puck because I was like a kettle boiling and the lid had finally blown off."

Tom Fitzgerald and Fran Rosa of the *Boston Globe* wanted to know if Giacomin thought Popein should have removed him from the game to spare him further humiliation. So did Walt MacPeek of the Newark *Star-Ledger*.

"Ask him," snapped Eddie. "I guess he probably could have relieved me. Maybe he didn't want to put the other guy [Villemure] on the spot. I don't know. I won't say. I won't second-guess my coach. But it makes you wonder a bit, eh?"

The Rangers were just as bad on December 6 when they self-destructed in Buffalo, 8-4, and on December 29 in Montreal, 7-1.

Popein's last game as Ranger coach on January 10, 1974 in Buffalo was even worse. The Sabres beat New York, 7-2, scoring almost at will. The Rangers' careless mistakes and lack of hustle were easily recognizable. Although Eddie got support from his teammates, he was fighting the puck and fanned on three long shots.

"The goalie was shaky in spots," said Popein, his face flushed with anger.

The next morning at 8:30, while a blizzard whirled outside, Popein was quietly dismissed as coach and replaced by Francis, the man who hired him. The press conference was considerably less elegant than Popein's June coronation. It was held in the corner of the executive lounge in the Toronto airport. Only John Radosta of the *New York Times*, Wes Gaffer of the *New York Daily News*, radio broadcaster Jim Gordon, and myself were present for the hastily arranged press conference.

Popein seemed almost on the verge of tears. Francis was

boiling with anger inside. The Rangers were in fourth place with an 18-14-9 record. They were in danger of missing the playoffs.

"We better start playing hockey fast or else," snapped Francis.

The Rangers played hockey. In a remarkable comeback, they lost only ten of thirty-seven games with Francis behind the bench, advanced to second place, stumbled in the final week of the season, and settled in third place.

Giacomin was the driving force behind their resurgence. Villemure injured his knee in a December 16 collision with Chicago's Dennis Hull, and Eddie was forced back into his old iron-man role. He played thirteen games in succession. He won fifteen and tied four of his final twenty-four games of the season.

Despite his outstanding play in the second half of the season, Eddie was disappointed.

"If we had played this way in the beginning of the season, think what might have been done," he said. "We might have been able to finish first. We didn't play the kind of hockey we were capable of playing; it hurt us and cost Larry Popein his job."

Eddie still had not lost the sense of humor that he often uses to ridicule himself.

"My goals-against average has been like a toilet seat all season—up one minute, down the next," he said. He was happy the Rangers had finished the season in good form, but he was unhappy with his 3.07 goals-against average. It was his highest after seven consecutive seasons in which his average was below three goals a game. But of the Rangers' forty wins, Fast Eddie was goalie in thirty of them.

Montreal was the Rangers' first opponent in the Stanley Cup playoffs. New York lost two of the first three games and then eliminated the defending Cup champions with a heroic comeback that silenced the critics who were about to cry "choke."

Eddie was the one who turned the playoff around—with his goaltending and with his mouth.

In the first game in the Montreal Forum, he reverted to his old wandering style and drove the Canadiens into fits of frustration by roaming into the corners to trap and clear the pucks they shot deep into the Ranger zone as part of their strategy.

Steve Shutt and Peter Mahovlich decided to do something that might force Eddie to stay near the net instead of wandering boldly into the corners.

Shutt caught Eddie stickhandling like Bobby Orr, 30 feet out of the net in the second period. He charged into Giacomin and knocked him on his backside. In a flash, Seiling came to Giacomin's aid and pummeled the Canadiens' forward with his fists. The usually noncombative defenseman's face was streaked with blood when Referee Ron Wicks escorted him to the penalty box.

Eddie continued to roam from his net and outrace Montreal forwards to the puck. Then, in the third period, Peter Mahovlich used his 6–feet-5–inch, 210-pound body to slam the Ranger goaltender when he was outside of his crease. Again the Rangers came to their goalie's aid. Park retaliated by mugging Mahovlich and sending him crashing against the end boards. Dale Rolfe, who played perhaps his best game of the season, challenged Larry Robinson to a fight.

The Rangers outplayed the Canadiens and won, 4-1.

"I know two of their guys who tried to intimidate Eddie but it didn't work," Park said in the dressing room. "Rod [Seiling] took care of one of them. I think I convinced the other guy to leave Eddie alone. Mahovlich had no business doing what he did to Eddie, so I hit him with a pretty good shot."

Shutt insisted he was not trying to hurt Giacomin. "Do I look like the kind of guy who would take a run at a goalie and try to hurt him?" he asked. "He was out of his net so he was fair game."

Giacomin was angry and went after Shutt when the Canadien cut him down. "He jarred me pretty good," said Eddie, laughing at the incident. "The referee stopped me. I told him he hit me, so why can't I hit him back? The way Seiling and Park got the two guys who nailed me was great. It picked the whole team up."

"Who does that guy Giacomin think he is, a forward?" Montreal defenseman Pierre Bouchard asked after the first game.

"He was like a third defenseman back there," said Francis, beaming. "The Canadiens would shoot the puck in and Eddie would shoot it right back out again."

Eddie minimized his role in the victory. "It was great to see the way my teammates stood up for me," he said.

Rolfe called Giacomin "our secret weapon." "You could see just by looking at their faces how frustrated they became when Eddie kept stealing the puck from them and clearing it out of our end. That's why they tried to get him," said the defenseman.

Mahovlich said he body checked Giacomin "because he was out of the net and he was fair game."

Naturally, the Canadiens denied they had a premeditated plan to try to intimidate the roaming goaltender.

"Bull———," said Scotty Bowman, Montreal's high-strung coach. "Giacomin knows the risk involved when he comes out of the crease to get the puck."

Giacomin said it was no big deal. "I don't think they're deliberately trying to get me or hurt me. I'm fair game when I'm out of the crease. But I know this: every time one of their guys belted me, he got belted back by one of our guys."

Montreal whipped the Rangers, 4-1, in the second game and their slick, quick forward Yvan Cournoyer was almost totally responsible for the Ranger defeat. The player nick-named "Road-runner" because of his deceptive speed was free for seven shots and scored three goals, two on break-aways and one on a two-on-one rush.

"He's the fastest guy on skates in hockey," said Giacomin.

Cournoyer scored two more goals in the third game and now the Canadiens were embarrassing New York's defense. They had broken free for nine breakaways in the last two games and five of them resulted in goals. Unless the Rangers could discover a way to contain "the Road-Runner," they faced playoff elimination.

After the third game, the sports writers and tape-recorder interviewers converged upon the Rangers' dressing room. Most of the downcast players lingered in the shower room to avoid the probing questions by the press. Giacomin was standing in front of his dressing room seat. He exploded at the newsmen who approached him.

"I'm sick and tired of reading and hearing all this junk about how we can't win in the playoffs," he shouted, his voice rising in anger. "You guys are all against us. The head-lines in the papers about the Mets say, LET'S GO METS! and YOU GOTTA BELIEVE! But everybody's always knocking us. I've had enough of it. We've all had enough of it."

Most of the newsmen were shocked at Eddie's angry accusations. He had usually been a cooperative athlete to interview on a team in which many players were suspicious and unfriendly in their relations with the news media. Was Giacomin really like so many other athletes—willing to grant interviews after victory but not after defeat? He never had seemed to be the type of athlete who took out his frustration at losing on the press. Perhaps like so many other athletes he believed sports writers should be a cheer-leading extension of the team and report only the good news, not the bad.

Wes Gaffer of the *New York Daily News* knew exactly what Eddie was doing.

Fast Eddie was using the press to express his anger at his teammates. He knew they heard what he was saying. He knew he would be quoted in the newspapers the next day and that his teammates would read what he had said.

"I'm the oldest guy on this team so maybe it's time I took charge and spoke up," Eddie shouted at the group of newsmen. "It always seems Henri Richard does something to get Montreal going. So I'm going to get this club rolling. We may be behind in this series, but we're going to win the damned thing."

Giacomin continued to rant and rave. By now most of his teammates had emerged from the showers. They pretended not to look at their goaltender, but the sound of his voice made it impossible for them not to hear him.

"We're going to win this series. Put that in the papers," shouted Eddie.

Ted Irvine heard the message Giacomin delivered to the Rangers through the press. "Eddie's a pretty outspoken guy. He says what he thinks. The game and his team means so much to him. He's really sticking his neck out for all of us. If we don't do what he says we're going to do, some of you guys can rip him apart in the sports pages. But sometimes things like he said can psych a team up and bring it back together when it's down and things look pretty hopeless."

It seemed as though Eddie's plan had backfired. Montreal led, 3-1, in the second period of the fourth game. Spectators in Madison Square Garden began to boo the Rangers. Suddenly Giacomin made a series of acrobatic saves that brought his team to life. Rod Gilbert scored. Irvine scored.

Bruce MacGregor scored. Pete Stemkowski scored. The Rangers won, 6-4. Momentum now was on their side.

They won the fifth game in Montreal to take a 3-2 lead in the series. MacGregor, the energetic, red-haired right wing, was assigned to cover Cournoyer. He held "the Road-Runner" scoreless in the final three games of the series and led New York with six goals. He tied the game with a goal with 16 seconds left to play in regulation time after Stemkowski won a critical face-off. Ron Harris won it in overtime with a forty-five-foot wrist shot past Bunny Larocque, Montreal's rookie goaltender.

Giacomin made countless brilliant saves to keep the Rangers in the game. He had been removed from the game and replaced by an extra skater when MacGregor scored the tying goal.

"I was standing on the bench yelling," he said. "My voice was hoarse, I'd been shouting so much. I said a little prayer to myself and then Bruce scored to tie the game. I stood there in a daze. Maybe somebody upstairs is finally on our side."

There was bedlam in Madison Square Garden when the Rangers won the playoff in the sixth game, 5-2. They overcame a 2-1 deficit to win on goals by MacGregor, Bill Fairbairn, Jean Ratelle, and Stemkowski. The crowd chanted, "Eddie! . . . Eddie! . . . Eddie!" and threw streamers on the ice.

"You can't say enough about the guy in the net," said Stemkowski. "Eddie was unreal. He's the guy who got us over the hump when we needed somebody to give us a push."

Irvine smiled. "Good old Eddie. He put his foot in his mouth and then he pulled it out. I remember what he yelled at you guys after Montreal had beaten us for the second time: We're going to win this, you just wait and see, and if we don't win it, then we should all hang it up."

MacGregor called Giacomin "our leader." He said it was too bad goalies were barred from becoming team captain.

"Without a doubt, Eddie's the leader of this team, on or off the ice," said Harris. "Eddie's a fighter and he led the way for us," said Francis.

Steve Vickers smiled his patented John Garfield tough-guy smile.

"Eddie said some things that had to be said and we got the message," he said.

Eddie laughed about the incident in which he had blasted the press while in reality using them to express his anger at his teammates.

"It's easier to yell at one writer than eighteen hockey players to get your point across," he said. "I hope you guys understand I wasn't really taking things out on you."

There was not much time to debate the issue. The Rangers played the Philadelphia Flyers, hockey's most physically intimidating team, in the next playoff series.

It was an emotional and violent playoff. Dave Schultz, the Flyer forward who set a record for sitting in penalty boxes, started the sparks flying by declaring "I'm glad we're playing the Rangers because they always seem to choke in the playoffs."

The Rangers had little love for the Flyers or Schultz. Their hatred increased when they read what Schultz said about them.

"I'm glad for the guy if he thinks he's happy because he's playing us," said Giacomin. "We'll see who chokes."

Eddie was concerned about the Flyers' persistent checking and hustle and the remarkable goaltending of Bernie Parent. He knew Philadelphia would be difficult to beat. He also was concerned about the 16 breakaways against him in the Montreal playoff.

"There were too many breakaways against us," he said. "That means there was too much risk. Too many defensive breakdowns. We've got to avoid giving Philadelphia any breakaways.

The Flyers demolished the Rangers in the first game, 4-0. They had five breakaways. Eddie stopped them all. They had three three-on-ones and two two-on-ones. They battered the Rangers all over the ice and limited their offense to a mere seven shots in the first 45 minutes of the game.

Every time Giacomin left his crease to clear the puck—the style that had so much to do with beating Montreal—the Flyers knocked him down and trapped him from returning to the net.

"Guys were pushing and shoving me all around," he said. "I kept yelling at the ref but it didn't do any good. Gary Dornhoefer is one of the best in the league at screening and interfering with the goalie. He was on me the whole time. I'm just going to have to start cracking a few of their guys with my stick, I guess."

Evidently. The Rangers disgraced themselves by failing to fight back in defense of their goalie who was being mugged by the Broad Street Bullies.

In addition to being bumped, jostled, and harrassed by the Flyers, Eddie was heckled unmercifully by Flyer fans who sat behind his goal cage. A schoolteacher from New Jersey had come to the Spectrum in Philadelphia with a variety of flash cards to taunt the Ranger goalie. "Eddie G. Chokes on the Puck" was one sign. "Eddie Who?" was another. "Today Is Eddie's Choke Day" was a third slogan displayed by the fan.

"If the Flyers are going to come into my crease to get me, then they better know they'll get a piece of lumber," Eddie said angrily. "I'll retaliate. If they want to hit, I'll hit back."

Game two was as rough and turbulent as the first game. The Flyers ran at Eddie when he left his net and crowded and interfered with him while he was in his crease. They got two more breakaways. Eddie stopped the first one. He did not stop the second when New York's power play backfired and Ross Lonsberry beat him for the winning goal in the 5-2 decision.

The goal that annoyed Giacomin and his teammates the most was the one Ed Van Impe scored in the second period. Gilles Marotte, under heavy forechecking pressure, tried to clear the puck. Van Impe intercepted the puck at the blue line and flipped a wobbly 50-foot shot toward Giacomin.

The freakish bad break that followed was reminiscent of the fluke goal on which Bobby Schmautz scored against Giacomin in the Chicago playoffs in 1968.

Van Impe's shot struck Seiling's stick 15 feet from Giacomin and spun over Eddie's right shoulder. The Ranger goalie made a desperate twisting lunge to trap the puck before it fell across the goal line.

Referee Dave Newell raised his arm to signal a goal. Charles Zavorka, the goal judge, pushed the button that made the red goal light glow.

Eddie tore off his mask and screamed, "No!... No...! No!" He appealed to the referee. He flung himself at the protective glass separating him from the goal judge. He screamed and cursed and pounded his fists against the glass. He swung his goaltender's stick toward Newell and, fortunately, he missed.

No one had seen Eddie so enraged in his life.

He skated back to the goal, picked up the puck, and placed it on the goal line—where he insisted he had stopped it. Red-faced and screaming, he kneeled there and pounded the ice with his fists. Over and over again he tried to show the referee how he had stopped the deflected shot from crossing the goal line.

Arms akimbo, Newell shook his head, "No."

Teammates struggled to restrain Eddie. "It never crossed the goal line," screamed Eddie. The words could be heard above the boos of the fans in the Spectrum. The Flyers'

Terry Crisp skated to the net, smiled, and nudged the puck over the line and into the net where the Flyers and the goal judge claimed it had been in the first place.

On and on argued Eddie. He and Francis were furious because they claimed the referee was not in proper position to see if the puck had gone into the net or not. They claimed Newell and linesmen Neil Armstrong and Willard Norris told them, "Sorry, we didn't see it."

"I saw the puck completely over the goal line," said Zavorka, the goal judge.

Giacomin was so enraged that Francis had to send Villemure into the game for twenty-two seconds until Eddie could cool down.. A Flyer fan held up a sign that read "Ed Is Dead!" as Giacomin skated to the bench.

Eddie still was boiling after the game. He stormed out of the shower room and flung a towel into his dressing cubicle. He virtually shook with rage as he spit out the words in a quivering voice.

"I swear on a stack of Bibles that puck did not go over the line," he fumed, emphasizing his opinion of the referee with a string of expletives. "It's a damned good thing Emile took me out to cool off. I was ready to hit anybody, anything. Hell, you saw it. Don't ask me to elaborate. You write what you saw."

He finally calmed down.

"Hey, I'm not mad at you guys. I'm not taking it out on you," he told the last few writers near him.

Seiling was distressed because the puck had deflected accidentally off his stick. He had acquired an unlucky habit of having goals bounce off his stick and into his team's goal cage. "Eddie didn't pull the puck back out of the net with his hand nor did he pull it in," said Seiling.

The Flyers tried to sound sympathetic toward Eddie, but they were too busy enjoying a 2-0 advantage in the playoffs.

"When the puck went off Seiling's stick, it came at Eddie

like a knuckle ball," said Crisp. "He wasn't expecting it. It hit the ice and Eddie scooped at it with his bare hand because his glove had come off. It was in. It was six inches over the line."

Parent shrugged. "I don't blame Eddie for arguing. I would have done the same thing if I were in his place," said the Philadelphia goalie.

"The referee was horse——," shouted Francis, pacing the corridor outside the dressing room. "But we'll get 'em next time. You'll see."

He was correct. Bobby Rousseau scored a disputed goal against Parent with forty-seven seconds to play in the third period, and Gilbert won the game in overtime, 2-1. The Flyers won the fifth game, 4-1, to advance to within one game of eliminating New York. But the Rangers refused to quit and won the sixth game, 4-1, to tie the series.

Giacomin saved his team with breathtaking goaltending and the crowd in Madison Square Garden began to chant, "Eddie! . . . Eddie! . . . Eddie!" The roar started in the mezzanine, rolled down through the lower seats, and soon became a deafening roar. It seemed as though every voice in the arena was shouting Eddie's name.

A man who had watched Ranger fans hurl garbage at a humiliated rookie goalie in 1966 wondered if there was a deeper meaning to the chant of "Eddie! . . . Eddie! . . . Eddie! that echoed through a new Madison Square Garden almost eight years later.

Father Robert McCourt provided insight. He is a young parish priest from Saint Clement the Pope in south Jamaica. He has been a devoted and perceptive hockey follower since boyhood.

"I believe it's a sign which shows that through the years people have come to appreciate Eddie Giacomin for what he is: an honest, hard-working, forthright man who, like all of us, has not found it easy reaching a goal in life," said Father McCourt.

"I think the average person finds Eddie a very easy person to relate to because he has a tough job to do to earn his living. There is nothing false or phony about Eddie. He is recognized as a man of simple values. And despite his fame and fortune, he has maintained a beautiful simplicity that most famous people lose."

The playoff ended May 6, 1974. The Rangers were dead. Philadelphia eliminated them, 4-3, in the seventh game. The Flyers had too much hustle and muscle and played as if every body check were a karate chop to the back of the neck. Parent was brilliant in goal for the eventual Stanley Cup winners. Bobby Clarke, the diabetic center, seemed to be everywhere at once.

"The Rangers have to be the biggest mystery in all of hockey," Parent said of New York's annual spring playoff failure. "Maybe they are overestimated and not so good as they and their fans think they are. They've got good players. They pay them a lot of money but they don't win the playoffs. There has to be something really wrong with them as a team."

Parent was puzzled how, in the crucial seventh game, New York forwards and defensemen could allow an opponent to get thirty-seven shots in the first two periods and forty-six in the game.

"The New York defensemen did not protect their goalie," said Parent. "You would never see a Flyer defenseman stand back and let other teams hit me like they let us hit Eddie."

"The Rangers have too many older guys making too much money," said Andre Dupont. "They traded away too many young players."

Fred Shero questioned the Rangers. The Flyer coach said they failed to protect their goalie the way they should

have. He cited Boston as a team with more courage than
New York.

Giacomin faced 14 breakaways and made the save on 12
of them in the Philadelphia playoff. Including the Montreal
playoff, he faced 29 breakaways and stopped 21. New York
fell behind, 3-1, in the seventh game before goals by Vickers
and Stemkowski provided the illusion of hope.

When the game ended, there was a poignant moment as
teams that had fought with fists and slashing sticks lined up
for the traditional congratulatory handshaking ceremony.

Crisp pushed his way past teammates in the line to reach
Giacomin. The two rivals embraced. Soon Parent was at
Eddie's side. They too embraced. Eddie mussed Bernie's
hair. Almost every Philadelphia player made certain he shook
hands with Giacomin.

"I wouldn't have been much of a man if I hadn't talked
to Eddie," said the red-haired Crisp. "He played his guts
out against us, the way he always does in any game, and he
lost. It had to be awfully tough for him, a guy seeing it end
this way for him. I think every guy on our team came out of
the series with great respect and admiration for Eddie
Giacomin."

Crisp gained new respect for Eddie during the handshaking procession.

"Here's a guy who's never been able to win the Cup and
he's just lost by one goal in the seventh game. It has to be
tough for him. He could have walked away. He could have
stood there and given our guys the cold-fish handshake, put
his head down, and muttered something. That would have
been easy. But Eddie didn't shrink away. He looked all of
us in the eyes and said 'best of luck in the final against
Boston.' He meant it. He was sincere. It took a lot of class.
I always knew Eddie was a classy gentleman. He proved it
to me by what he did."

Crisp read how Giacomin had spoken up and rallied his

team when it was in danger of losing to Montreal.

"You have to admire a guy who had the guts to do that to inspire and shake his team up," he said. "He had enough guts to speak his mind and he took a lot of crap for it. But he came out as the acknowledged leader of his team."

Flyer defenseman Joe Watson said, "God Almighty but Giacomin was good. I can't help but admire the way he played with so little help from the guys in front of him."

"As a goalie, I feel for Eddie," said Parent, sipping a beer in the Flyers' dressing room. "You can only do so much; the rest is up to your forwards and defensemen. I am happy I won, of course, but there is a feeling all goaltenders have between themselves and for that reason I feel sorry for Eddie. I wish I had the talent he has when he skates out of the net to clear the puck. He must have done that fifteen times in one game in Montreal."

Marcel Pelletier is the Flyers' player personnel director. He was a goalie for many years.

"Not many goalies have the courage that Eddie showed when he came out of his net to get the puck, knowing guys were going to run him down," he said. "To me, even though he lost, this was his finest playoff. Eddie is one of the greatest competitors I have seen in the game. He always gives 110 percent."

Shock and disappointment. Disgust and frustration. Bitterness and anger. Shame and humiliation. They were the emotions of failure reflected in the faces of the Rangers in the losers' dressing room.

Eddie searched for the words to describe his eighth consecutive year of playoff failure.

"I wanted it to be now for us. . . . I thought this was the year. . . . maybe it's just not in the cards for us to ever win. . . . Maybe it stems from the trouble we had at the start of the season. . . . All these years in the playoffs and the right card hasn't been in my deck yet. . . . maybe we need a new deck of cards to play with. . . . I tried to give it my best but it wasn't enough."

Rolfe expressed a view shared by many Rangers.

"Let's face it: Eddie took over the leadership of the team when our spirits were down and we needed someone to take charge. He stuck his neck out for us and sounded off in the press when things looked bad against Montreal. He called a spade a spade and backed up what he said. He rallied the whole team around him and inspired us and brought us back together. He's a leader. It's damned unfortunate he had to lose to Philadelphia because he played so well."

Vickers talked about the playoff failure across the room. "On paper we were the better team but as a team in the playoff they were better. We didn't deserve to win the way we played," said the young left wing.

Then he said it.

"We choked. We didn't win the big one."

It was not a nice way to end the season.

Chapter **16**

Eddie Loses a Playoff Game
but Walks away As a Winner

"IT WAS A TOUCH OF CLASS . . ."

EDDIE slipped behind the steering wheel of Walt Tkaczuk's lavish white car on September 19, 1974 and pulled out of the motel parking lot in Kitchener, Ontario.

He was in a cheerful mood.

"See what I mean. The goal scorers drive the big cars, and the goalies? Me, I drive an economy car or a camper," he said with a chuckle.

"You want Italian food or steak?" he asked. The steakhouse won out over spaghetti or linguine with white clam sauce.

When Eddie arrived at the steakhouse, he spotted Ron Wicks, a referee and family friend from Sudbury.

"What are you doing here?" he asked.

Wicks told Eddie that the NHL referees and linesmen had a dinner meeting in an upstairs room of the restaurant. Like the Rangers, the officials' training camp for the 1974–75 season was in Kitchener.

"Let's go up and have some fun," said Giacomin, a gleam in his eyes.

Scotty Morrison, the National Hockey League referee-in-chief, was delivering a serious lecture to the officials when Eddie walked into the room.

"In case some of you young referees and linesmen don't know who this guy is, we have a guest in our midst named Eddie Giacomin," said Morrison. "I think we may have to call for Frank Torpey [the former FBI agent who is NHL security chief]."

The officials looked at Eddie and laughed.

"We can't afford to give you a fee, Eddie, but maybe you'll tell us why you're such a pain in the behind to our linesmen and referees."

Eddie laughed. He stepped up to the microphone and proceeded to throw the roomful of officials into uproarious laughter. He threw one-liners at them as if he were delivering a Don Rickles monologue.

"I see John D'Amico hiding in the back of the room. John, what made a nice Italian boy like you become a linesman? You should have been a barber, eh?"

Eddie then became serious—well, slightly, anyway.

"I know I've given a lot of you referees a few bad times in the past and I'll probably do it in the future. But I mean it when I say it's only been done in the heat of the game: there's nothing personal," said the Ranger goaltender.

"You and me have a lot in common. We love this game so much we're willing to take the toughest jobs there are to be in it—goaltending and officiating. I know my job's tough but your job is even tougher than being a goalie. I think we're alike, because everybody's always putting the blame on goalies and referees."

After a dramatic pause Eddie said: "The referees and linesmen in the league don't get paid what they should be paid.

I'll go on record right here and say the league should pay you guys more money for the job you do."

None of the officials chanted "Eddie! ... Eddie! ... Eddie!" but their cheers and applause were loud and long.

Afterward, Eddie washed his steak down with a beer and said it had not been a put-on; he meant every word he said in his impromptu talk to the officials.

"I don't always agree with those guys but I have a hell of a lot of respect for the tough job they do," he said. "Dave Newell [the referee with whom Giacomin argued about the disputed goal in the Philadelphia playoffs] comes from Sudbury. When I was there this summer, people told me how much abuse he was getting from people in town. I spoke to a group and told them they weren't being fair. I still don't agree with the call he made, but I respect him as a person. It made me mad to hear that people were abusing him."

There was a new face in Ranger training camp: Derek Sanderson. In a surprising trade following the 1973-74 season, Emile Francis acquired the flamboyant Bruins' center who had been suspended by the Boston Bruins.

Derek reported to training camp one week earlier than the Ranger veterans. He wanted to make a good impression on his new teammates. He wanted to show them he was serious. He seemed uneasy in the presence of many of the Rangers whom he had criticized through the years. Many of them had not yet accepted "the Turk" as their new teammate.

One morning at practice, Giacomin noticed how hard Sanderson was working and spoke up.

"Way to go, Turk!" he shouted loud and clear after Derek made a clever passing play. Sanderson smiled. From that moment on he seemed accepted as a Ranger.

"I hated the guy when he was in Boston but now he's

my teammate so I have to like him, eh?" said Eddie.

Eddie and Joe Zanussi were kidding around before practice one morning, imitating the game of odds and evens popular among elderly Italian men. Sanderson joined in the fun and games.

"Where did you learn Italian?" kidded Giacomin.

"I'm half-Italian; I sat next to Esposito in the dressing room in Boston. Phil was my godfather," said Sanderson.

Then Eddie and Derek joked about their feud in the 1970 playoffs.

"I was a dummy when I told you to keep your head up or we'd get you," teased Giacomin. "I should have said that to Bobby Orr. It would have been a hell of a lot better to get him out of the game instead of you."

Sanderson rolled his eyes and pretended his feelings were hurt.

"At least you let your hair grow longer. Man, it was weird then," joked Derek.

"Yeah. Now it's longer and grayer," said Giacomin.

Eddie relaxed in his motel room and talked about the season ahead.

"So many crazy things have gone wrong in the past. Maybe this year we can avoid them," he said.

That was not meant to be: Just before the season opened Gilles Villemure surprised Emile Francis and all of his teammates by walking out in training camp because of a contract dispute. He came back. Then he left again and said he was going to quit hockey and devote himself to his off-season job as a harness-racing driver and trainer. Then he changed his mind and rejoined the Rangers.

Ron Harris was not playing much in the first few games of the season. He said he was retiring from hockey. Then he changed his mind.

Critics in the Madison Square Garden crowd had singled out Rod Seiling as the target of their abuse. The defenseman seldom had been fully appreciated by many Rangers fans who overlooked his subtle skills and disliked him because he was not a fighter.

Seiling lost his starting job and became a benchwarmer to make room for Ron Greschner, a nineteen-year-old rookie. He sensed he was going to be traded. He criticized New York hockey fans in a *New York Post* story, saying they had no understanding or true appreciation of the game of hockey.

Seiling was sold to the Washington Capitals and then traded to Toronto.

The Rangers suffered more injuries than ever before during the season. Team physicians Dr. James Nicholas, Dr. William Liebler, and Dr. John Grozine were kept busier than the medical crew from *M*A*S*H*. Bobby Rousseau was lost for the season and eventually forced to retire from hockey following spinal-fusion surgery. Harris was placed in traction for a broken hip socket. Tkaczuk broke his leg. Rolfe broke his ankle. Brad Park injured his knee. Rookie Rick Middleton, whose flashy style put new life into the offense, broke his leg.

"At least the goalies are healthy," Giacomin said one day.

He spoke too soon.

Eddie damaged his right knee December 19 in Boston when he made a sliding save on a breakaway shot by Terry O'Reilly and Park toppled on him.

That was only part of the disaster. The Rangers already were so badly crippled that eight rookies were in the line-up when the Bruins pulverized them, 11-3. One of them was goalie Curt Ridley, summoned from the Providence farm team. Francis gambled by putting Ridley in goal in hope that the team's weak defense would tighten up. It did not. Boston scored six goals to ruin Ridley's NHL debut, and Eddie was sent in to relieve the struggling rookie.

The Bruins put five more shots into the net behind Giacomin.

New York was not hitting and showed an amazing propensity for dissipating leads late in the game. Eddie decided he was through being Mr. Nice Guy.

"I'm not going to take any more beatings. If I'm not going to get any help from the defensemen, I'll have to start moving out the guys around the net myself. There should be more hitting done in our end of the ice. Our guys get knocked down in the other end. I'd like to see the other guys getting knocked down in our end," he said at lunch in Lenny's Steak House after practice in Long Beach.

The knee injury Eddie suffered in the Boston massacre was more serious than it seemed at first. He was fitted with a brace. He was unable to play from December 22 to January 25 and went from November 27 until February 1 between victories.

"I'd feel a lot worse about not being able to play if the team was playing poorly but we're winning now and Gilly [Villemure] is playing well," said Eddie.

But as the season progressed and Eddie was forced to sit at home and wait until his injured knee permitted him to play, he became depressed. He no longer felt as though he were part of his team. He felt guilty that he was contributing nothing when he was needed.

"I've taken my lumps over the years, but I've always been able to get taped or patched up and keep playing. This is the longest I've been out of action and it's driving me crazy because I can't play. It's the most frustrating time I've ever had," he said dejectedly.

Although Eddie could not play, he was not forgotten. John Davidson, the St. Louis Blues' young goalie who would be a Ranger within a year, said he loved to watch Eddie play because he's "the best in the business." Gary Inness, Pittsburgh's rookie goalie, called Eddie "the old master." He prepared himself for the playoffs by studying video tapes of Giacomin playing goal.

Eddie enjoyed hearing that. But it did not help him as he waited for his wound to heal.

"It's getting to me so much that I'm doing something I've never done, no matter how badly things went: I'm snappy with my wife and kids at home," said the injured goalie.

"I'm having some restless nights," he complained. "It digs into your guts." Eddie had not played in almost six weeks. It was January and the Rangers still were in contention for first place with Philadelphia. Eddie wanted to play but he did not. Villemure remained in the goal.

Eddie made his first appearance since being hurt when he lost in Pittsburgh, 5-2, on January 25. He did not seem sharp following his long layoff. But two games later, in Chicago, he regained his form. He beat the Black Hawks, 4-1. Then he beat the Flyers in Philadelphia, 3-1, with a spectacular performance that evoked cheers of "Eddie! . . . Eddie! . . . Eddie!" from visiting members of the Ranger fan club.

Then the Rangers reverted to their inconsistent play. They lost to Montreal, 7-1, and gave a game away in Washington, losing 7-4, to an expansion team with the worst record in hockey history. Eddie stopped 35 of 36 shots in another marvelous conquest of the Flyers. It was the first time he had played before the New York fans in seven weeks. The fans chanted his name. They did it again three days later, on February 26, when he beat St. Louis, 5-1.

Eddie claimed the Vancouver Canucks as the fiftieth shutout victim in his NHL career on March 19 as the crowd urged him on with its "Eddie!" chant. It should have been a glorious night but it was not.

With 15:36 remaining to play in the second period, Eddie collapsed in front of the goal. Paulin Bordeleau had drawn back his stick to shoot and Greg Polis body-checked him out of the play when Giacomin went down without being touched.

He lunged to his left, dropped to his knees, turned back to his right, tried desperately to get up, and then fell down.

The crowd gasped.

Dr. Grozine was escorted by Trainer Frank Paice to where Eddie lay on the ice, his face masked in agony. The doctor bent over the gray-haired goalie and shined a small flashlight into his eyes.

The crowd started the "Eddie!" chant but the sound drifted away. No one knew what was wrong.

"I wanted to test his eye reflexes and see the response," said the team doctor. "I guess it's the pinched nerve in my neck again. I keep getting it from time to time for no reason at all," said Giacomin.

Francis wanted to take Giacomin out of the game, but Eddie refused to leave. He wanted the shutout. He stood up, pulled his mask down over his face, and went back to work. The Garden reverberated with the "Eddie!" chant.

Giacomin was in pain in the dressing room. He managed a weak smile and touched the back of his neck.

"The shutout feels good but the neck doesn't," he said.

Giacomin's faithfulness to his obligations reminded Sal Messina, analyst on Marv Albert's radio broadcasts of Ranger games, of a vivid aspect of Giacomin's personality.

Messina had asked Eddie to come to Skateland in New Hyde Park to present the awards to a group of eight-year-old hockey players and to drop the first puck for a tournament game. He asked him several weeks in advance of the tournament.

"Eddie just lost a heartbreaker in Atlanta, 3-2, and on the flight home I knew he was feeling bad because the team lost, so I didn't want to remind him that we wanted him to come to Skateland the next day," said Messina, a former goalie himself.

The team did not return home until 3 A.M. and had to

practice at 11 A.M. Messina never expected Giacomin to come to the rink to see the kids.

"Eddie showed up at 3:30 in the afternoon and stayed at least two hours," said Messina. "It made the kids' day."

Although the season that was nearing its end had been disappointing, Eddie never openly sulked or became immersed in his own problems.

Nick Beverley was in his first season with the Rangers. He had come to New York from Pittsburgh in the highly publicized Vic Hadfield trade. He was a quiet, unheralded player who had not been receiving much recognition from the fans or the press for holding the Rangers' injury-ravaged defense together throughout the season.

His name was not that well known throughout hockey. People kidded Beverley by calling him "Nick Who?"

"I call him the goaltender's dream," said Giacomin. "He came in here with a lot of pressure on him and a lot to prove. We'd given up Vic, our captain, for Nick. It was a tough spot for him to be in because a lot of people thought it was a bad trade. Nick Beverley has done a tremendous job in a difficult situation for us. He's been our steadiest guy on defense."

Eddie smiled. "No more 'Nick Who?' eh? I know what that's like. When I came to New York from Providence, they called me 'Eddie Who?' "

The Rangers finished far behind first-place Philadelphia in the new Lester Patrick Division. They were not assured of qualifying for playoffs until the final week of the season. It had not been an outstanding season. New York's defensive record was its worst in ten years.

Eddie was dissatisfied with his season. He had missed too many games because of his knee injury. He played fewer games (thirty-seven) than he had in any of his ten Ranger seasons and his goals-against average (3.48) was the highest since his rookie year. He was the winning goalie in only thirteen games.

"It's been very disappointing for me," he said. "I want to redeem myself in the playoffs."

Under the new playoff format, the Rangers would play a best-two-of-three preliminary series with their first opponent, the New York Islanders.

The Islanders represented a new kind of challenge for the Rangers. They had finished last in their first two seasons since 1972–73 expansion and now they had qualified for the playoffs. They were young and hungry. They played with more vigor and enthusiasm than the established Rangers. Not only were they the Rangers' playoff opponent, they were the neighboring team from Long Island and were challenging the Rangers for regional prestige and news media and spectator appeal.

Some of Giacomin's teammates foolishly took the Islanders for granted, underestimating their ability and determination to surpass the Rangers and become the number-one team in the metropolitan New York area.

It looked easy when the Rangers led the Islanders, 2-0, with only 15 minutes remaining to play in the opening game. Giacomin was sharp. Very sharp.

Then the roof caved in on the overconfident Rangers.

The Rangers relaxed and the Islanders refused to quit trying. Billy Harris skated in from the right corner and not one Ranger bothered to check him. He wristed a 10-foot shot past Giacomin.

"He just walked right in from the corner," snapped Eddie. He was angry.

Jean Potvin outhustled the Rangers to the puck behind the net. It was a case of careless defense by the Rangers. Giacomin sensed trouble and skated around behind the net. Potvin beat Eddie to the puck, scooted around the net, and scored into an unguarded goal cage.

"He knocked the puck over me, it went behind the net, and he got it, came out, and put it in," Giacomin said softly.

Clark Gillies, a twenty-one-year-old rookie, caught Ranger forwards backchecking carelessly and defensemen napping. He skated between Gillies Marotte and Greschner; he challenged Giacomin one-on-one, and he beat him with a perfect 15-foot wrist shot to win the game.

"I didn't have much chance to stop it. He broke through and was in on top of me," said Eddie, excusing himself from the postgame interviewers.

Why had the Rangers made it so easy for Harris to score?

"I guess it was a lack of communication on our part," said Tkaczuk.

Why had Marotte and Greschner not covered the net when Eddie went behind the cage in pursuit of Jean Potvin and the puck?

"I didn't know where the puck was," said Greschner.

Why had Gillies been allowed to skate between the two defensemen without being hit and taken out of the play before he shot and scored the winning goal?

"I don't know what happened," said Marotte.

Giacomin had the answer.

"We didn't do anything in the third period," he said in a voice tight with emotion. "We just stopped working and let them storm us. They deserved to win. We didn't."

Villemure played goal and Giacomin sat on the bench in the second game. It hurt Eddie's pride but he kept his feelings to himself. He could see the logic in Francis's goaltending change. In a game enlivened by fights and penalties in Nassau Coliseum, the Rangers came to life and played with the vigor and aggressiveness they so often lacked. They won, 8-3.

Francis started Villemure in the third game in Madison Square Garden. Some Ranger players were surprised not to see Eddie start the game. He had been the victim of his teammates' errors and the Islanders' inspired play in losing the first game. Some Islanders also were startled when they learned Villemure, not Giacomin, would play goal.

"I don't see how anyone could second-guess the decision to go with Villemure," said Islander Coach Al Arbour. "It was logical. He was the goalie when they beat us badly in the second game. You have to go with a winning combination. But I thought to myself that I wouldn't be at all surprised if 'the Cat' had a trick up his sleeve: bringing Eddie in at the crucial moment to boot the Rangers home."

The Rangers shot fifteen times in the first period at Bill Smith. The Islanders' goalie stopped every shot and was playing as brilliantly as his partner, Glenn (Chico) Resch, had played in the first game. The Islanders had only eight first-period shots at Villemure. They scored on three of them. Gilly did not look sharp. He fanned on a fifty-five-foot medium-speed slap shot by Gillies. He was beaten on a tip-in by Denis Potvin, following a Ranger giveaway, for the second goal. He missed the third goal, a forty-foot drive by Denis Potvin that followed a two-on-one break with the Islanders playing short-handed.

Madison Square Garden fans booed the Rangers.

There was 5:56 remaining in the game when Giacomin climbed over the bench boards and skated toward the Ranger goal. The crowd's jeers changed to cheers and the pounding beat of "Eddie! . . . Eddie! . . . Eddie!" filled the Garden.

The old gunfighter was coming to try to revive his team and win the game. It seemed as though he was too late.

Arbour watched Eddie skate past the Islander bench and take his position in front of the goal.

"I knew exactly what was going to happen," said Arbour. "Eddie was going to do something—anything—to try and pick the club up; stir up his guys in any way he could. Suddenly that three-goal lead we had didn't seem so big to me.

I knew if anybody could get the Rangers going, Eddie could do it."

Eddie did not waste time. With 2:34 left in the second period, Garry Howatt kicked up a spray of ice chips at the crease as he tried to jam the puck past Giacomin but was stopped. Play turned up ice. But suddenly there were Howatt and Eddie face-to-face, twenty feet out in front of the Ranger goal.

Eddie jabbed his big goalie's stick at Howatt's midsection, causing the Islander forward to wince and retreat. Then Eddie threw a flurry of punches at Howatt. They call Garry "the Toy Bulldog" because he is tough and loves to fight. But this time he did not want to fight. He sensed that Giacomin was trying to lure him into the penalty box. He raised his arms and backed away to demonstrate to the referee that it was Giacomin who was the attacker.

"We were losing, 3-0, and I was coming into the game cold. I figured to myself I've got to do something to get myself going, get all of us going before it is too late," said Fast Eddie.

"I didn't really want to fight him. I was just doing something to get us stirred up. That's the way I am; I'm a competitor. I apologized to Howatt after the period was over. I told him I'm no fighter, I'm a lover."

"He speared me and then he cross checked me," said Howatt. "I'm not mad at him. I knew what he was trying to do. I admire him for it. I'd try to do the same thing in his place. He just lost his cool. He told me he was sorry. That took a lot of class on his part."

Eddie accomplished what he set out to do. He got the Rangers moving. They dominated the game in the third period and tied the score on two goals by Bill Fairbairn and one by Steve Vickers. That sent the teams into sudden-death overtime.

Jude Drouin won the opening face-off from Jean Ratelle and passed the puck back to Bert Marshall. He passed the puck to Dave Lewis, who rifled it into the right corner of the Ranger zone.

Vickers recovered the rebound off the end boards. Giacomin shouted at Vickers to skate the puck out of danger around the net. The noise from the crowd was so loud that Vickers did not hear the goalie's instructions. He passed the puck behind him for Beverley to pick up. Beverley did not expect the pass.

Now Drouin had the puck in the corner. He shot it across the goal mouth. Eddie flashed to his right. J. P. Parise was standing three feet away from the far goal post with Brad Park checking him. Parise guided Drouin's centering pass past Giacomin and into the net.

The Rangers were dead. The fastest overtime execution in NHL history was over. It took the Islanders only 11 seconds to win, 4-3.

Eddie got up from the ice and skated directly to the Islanders' bench and extended his hand to congratulate Arbour.

"Such a classy guy," said the rival coach.

Eddie was the first Ranger in line for the handshaking procession with the triumphant Islanders. Several of his teammates chose to ignore the traditional custom of congratulating the winning players.

"Eddie told me he wished me luck in the playoffs and said how well he thought I had played," said Smith, the Islanders' goaltender.

Giacomin took the blame for the winning goal. He did not mention the mixed-up pass exchange between Vickers and Beverley that set up the goal. He said he had no chance to stop Parise's point-blank tip-in.

"I don't think any goalie could have stopped the shot," said Parise. "The whole thing happened so fast that nobody expected it. Giacomin never touched the puck. He had no time to cover the side of the net where I put the puck."

"We have nothing to be ashamed of coming back after being down, 3-0," said the beaten goaltender.

Some of Giacomin's teammates were less than complimentary in their comments about losing to the Islanders. They said they felt "embarrassed" to loose to a team like them. They indicated the Islanders won by luck and were not really the better team.

"The Islanders won't win another game in the playoffs," said Sanderson.

It sounded like sour grapes.

"I know one thing. The Rangers sure won't win another game in the playoffs," said Parise. "Tell that to Derek."

Vickers blamed himself for the accidental giveaway and broken play that sent the Rangers to defeat.

"I gave it to them. It was my fault. Don't blame Nick [Beverley] or Eddie," he said.

The season was over for the Rangers. The players dressed and went home.

Everyone except Eddie Giacomin.

He walked out of the dressing room and down the runway beneath Madison Square Garden to where the Islanders were seated on their team bus.

"We were all sitting there in the dark in the bus when the driver heard someone outside rapping on the door," said Eddie Westfall, the Islander captain.

The Islanders thought it was one of their fans or one of their players for whom they were waiting. The driver opened the door. In stepped Eddie.

"Congratulations, guys," he said in a voice that carried to the rear of the bus. "You deserved to win the way you played. Good luck against Pittsburgh. I'm going to be rooting for you guys to go all the way and win it."

Eddie stepped out of the bus and the door closed behind

him. He and his wife Marg walked out into the night and went home.

"Eddie Giacomin left a lasting impression with me for what he did," said Bob Bourne, a twenty-year-old Islander rookie with a boyish face. "How many guys do you know who would do that after they'd just lost their final playoff game in overtime?"

"Every guy inside that bus was deeply moved by what Eddie did and said to us. I think it was a good example for all our young players to see what a man like Eddie is really like," said Arbour.

"It was a touch of class by a man who has always been all class in everything he did," said Westfall.

Eddie may have lost the game but he went out as a winner.

Chapter 17

A Talk with Eddie Giacomin

"You learn to pray a lot."

Is there a great deal of personal satisfaction in being a goaltender?

Yes. Definitely. I think there is. I suppose it's a lot like being a catcher in baseball or a quarterback in football. You're always involved in the outcome of the game. You know you're always making a contribution to your team. Knowing that you have this responsibility makes every game a personal challenge and keeps you mentally sharp and competitive.

But doesn't the pressure and responsibility of playing a position that most people believe is the most difficult in all sports sometimes get to you?

Oh, sure it does. I think a goalie gets himself more keyed up before the game than, say, the defensemen or forwards. Let's face it: a forward or a defenseman can make a mistake and get away with it and have plenty of opportunities to make up for it. They put a red light on for everyone to see when the goalie makes a mistake. Any mistake the goalie makes means a goal for the other team and that can be the difference between winning or losing. After a game, if you happen to have lost, it's always hard not to feel it was your fault because you didn't stop the puck enough.

Sometimes the goals scored against you are more the fault of one of your teammates.

Right. But that still doesn't make you feel any better when you lose. You know you're the last man back there, and it's your job to stop the puck. A goaltender always feels personally responsible when his team loses, no matter how or why the other guys score the goals.

Is being a goaltender the position with the most pressure and responsibility in all sports?

Overall, I think so. I think you could compare the constant pressure and responsibility of being a goalie to that of being a pitcher or a quarterback. The big difference, to me at least, is that a pitcher has eight guys who can catch his mistakes while a quarterback can do something himself to get points for his team while a goalie can't.

Coaches, players, and sports writers talk about playoff pressure. Does it really exist? Is there that much extra pressure in the playoffs?

Definitely. You can feel the extra pressure building up inside you in the playoffs. With so much at stake in a short series, a goaltender has to play much more cautiously. You know that if you make one mistake it can mean everything. You know that the first goal in a playoff game is especially important. You know that no matter what you do, or don't do, as soon as that red light goes on behind you, about 20,000 people watching you in the arena and thousands watching on TV are convinced it was all your fault.

You can try to tell yourself to stay relaxed but before a game I'll be uneasy. But I don't get the butterflies or get sick the way some guys do. I've never been that kind of person. There's nothing wrong with feeling pressure before a game. It's normal and it helps get you keyed up so you can play your best. You just can't let the pressure get the best of you.

What's the first thing a young goalie must learn to accept?

That no matter how well he plays, he's going to give up a certain amount of goals and that fans are going to blame him. A goal net is six feet wide and a goaltender isn't. But we do have certain things we can do to make ourselves look larger than we are.

Like what?

Moving out to meet the guy with the puck is one thing. The further you move out of the net, the bigger you look to the shooter. Often you can make him rush his shot by moving out to cut down the area of the net he has to shoot at. The shooter has four main targets he'll usually go for: the two upper and the two lower corners of the net. A goalie has two arms and two legs to stop shots to each of those areas.

Of course, if the goaltender moves out too far, the shooter may try to go around him and he'll have to use a poke check or maybe throw out a leg to block the shot. If the goaltender makes his move too soon, the shooter will be able to go right by him and shoot at the empty net.

The more a shooter is off to the side, the less net he has to shoot at. A goalie has a strong side and a weak side. His weak side is the side on which he holds his stick, because all he has on that side is the blocker on the back of his stick-hand for high shots and the blade of his stick for low shots. On the strong side, he's got the blade of his stick, his skate, and his catching glove. Goalies try to get the shooter to shoot for the strong side. We do this by leaving a larger amount of the net uncovered on our strong side than on our weak side, daring the shooter to go for it, just like a bullfighter holds his cape, daring the bull to charge it.

After the goalie gives the shooter the target, he waits for the shooter to shoot before he makes his move. If you move too soon, the shooter has time to make a correction and shoot for the other side.

The main thing for a goalie to do is to challenge the shooters. Never make it easy for them. And never get caught backing into your net or making your move too soon.

What is the most difficult kind of shot for you to stop?

All of them. No, seriously, I'd have to say tip-ins and deflections are the worst for any goalie. You get set to handle a shot that's coming at you, and suddenly somebody cruising by the net deflects the puck and it changes direction. There's almost no way to stop a tip-in or a deflection, except by luck. Pucks that accidentally bounce off one of your defensemen's sticks or legs are awfully tough, too.

Rebounds? They're always tough. You make the initial save and you're usually off balance or down and trying to get back up, and before you can, some guy gets the rebound and puts it by you. That's why it's so important for a goalie to clear rebounds away from the net, steer them to the corners, or when there's a scramble in front of you, catch or smother the puck, and freeze it for a stoppage in play.

Screen shots can drive a goalie nuts. You see the guy with the puck and then guys cut in front of you and you're screened and can't see it any longer. You have to anticipate. You have to guess. Should you go to the right or the left? You know where the puck's coming from but, for an instant, you don't see it. It only takes a second for some of the shooters they have today to pull the trigger. Suddenly the puck comes out of nowhere, through a lot of legs and bodies, and you don't see it until it's too late.

You are described as a stand-up goalie, but you seem to crouch more than some goaltenders. Why?

Maybe I'm trying to hide, eh? No, really, it's much easier to straighten up than it is to fall down so I use the stand-up style with a crouch. It's important for a goalie to stay on his feet as much as possible because, once he's down, flopping on the ice, a lot of net is wide open and he's pretty defenseless in covering it.

Obviously, there are times when a goalie must dive, sprawl, or fall to stop the puck.

Sure. But he must make certain he can get back up on his feet as quickly as possible. That's why a goalie needs strong legs, quick reactions, a natural sense of anticipation.

What does it mean when a goalie complains about giving up a "bad goal"?

Every goal is a bad goal. No, not really. There are a lot of goals where the goalie just didn't have a chance because the shot was too good. The bad goals are the ones you give up but know you should have stopped. It can be a little lapse in concentration or carelessness. You hate to get beaten on a routine shot from the blue line or on a soft shot that should have been an easy save.

How does the goaltender defend against a two-on-one rush?

You have to play the puckhandler, the guy who may shoot, but you have to be ready for the guy coming down the other side looking for the pass so he can shoot. You want the one defenseman back to play in the middle and try to force the puckhandler to the outside or make him pass.

What about a three-on-one rush?

You learn to pray a lot. There are three guys coming down on you and only one of your defensemen is back. You've still got to concentrate on the guy who has the puck, but in the back of your mind you know there are two other guys who may get the puck at any second. The best way to avoid two-on-ones or three-on-ones is to have defensemen who don't get caught up ice out of position.

Why have you been so effective stopping breakaways? You always seem to get a lot of breakaways against you.

I'm just lucky, I guess. The important thing on a break-away is to know the shooter's moves, come out, cut down the angle, challenge him, and make him make his first move before you make your first move. Derek Sanderson was always one guy who got a lot of breakaways on me. He beat me quite a few times. But now that he's on my side I don't have to worry about him anymore.

You have the best record of any goaltender in the NHL for stopping penalty shots and yet some people favor the shooter over the goalie on a penalty shot.

I don't agree that the shooter has the edge. I think any good goaltender should stop the majority of ten penalty shots. I know Rod Gilbert doesn't agree with me. He feels a good shooter should be able to score on six or seven out of ten penalty shots. But I say the odds favor the goal-tender, and if you look at the record over the years I think you'll see I'm right.

When a penalty shot is called, the first thing I do is go over in my mind everything I know about the guy taking the shot: what his moves and little tricks are; what his habits are shooting and handling the puck; what I think his weak-nesses may be; little habits he has; and how he tries to fool a goalie. The worst thing a goalie can do on a penalty shot is to make the first move or stay back in his net. You have to come out and make the shooter commit himself first.

There's no greater pressure in the game than the penalty shot—both for the shooter and for the goalie—because the play doesn't happen that often.

Bill Chadwick, among many others, says he would like to see referees call more penalty shots because it creates an exciting, dramatic moment for hockey fans.

Bill Chadwick was never a goaltender. All the forwards would love to see more penalty shots. You won't find any goaltender who wants them to call more. We've got enough trouble doing our job as it is.

Who are the hardest shooters in hockey?

I always hate to answer that question. If I fail to mention some guy, he reads it, gets mad at me, and then scores a goal against me. There are so many hard shooters, more than there used to be because of the curved sticks and the fact that the younger guys coming into the league today seem to be bigger and stronger. Some of the guys who come to mind are Bobby Orr, Ken Hodge, Yvan Cournoyer, Mickey Redmond, and Bill Goldsworthy. They've all got hard shots but so do a lot of other guys. Dennis Hull has what I call a "heavy" shot. When the puck reaches you, it's got an awful lot of impact behind it.

If I had to pick one guy, though, it would be Bobby Hull. He's the hardest shooter I ever saw and he has given me a lot of trouble over the years. It only took Bobby a second to get his shot away. I wasn't too sorry to see him go over to the other league.

Why did you stop keeping your little black book on the shooters in the league?

I gave that up a few years ago because, being in the league for so long, I developed a pretty good mental book on most shooters. With all the new teams and players today, I may have to start keeping a book on them again.

Emile Francis used to give you a $100 bonus for each shutout.

He did at first but not any more. "The Cat" stopped doing that when hockey players' salaries started going up because of expansion and the new league.

Since the adoption of the two-goalie system by the Rangers, when do you usually find out whether you are playing or not?

Sometimes Emile Francis would tell me the day of the game at the noon team meeting. Sometimes he would tell me the night before. I like to be told as early as possible, at least the night before a game.

Why do you do so much talking to your teammates during a game?

I've got a big mouth, I guess. It's important for a goalie to communicate with the other guys on his team during the game. A goalie is like a catcher in baseball. He sees the play developing in front of him and has the best view of the game. I can see things happening that other players can't see. I yell to guys to warn them if their back is turned and a checker is coming in on them or I shout and tell them if they've got plenty of time or room to make a play. A goalie should help his team out by telling guys to pick up a man on the other team who isn't covered or which defenseman should go for the puck. It keeps everyone, including the goalie, alert and on his toes.

Some goalies relax in practice and seldom exert themselves trying to stop practice shots. You're not that way.

The habits you get into in practice can carry over into games. I like to have guys like Rod Gilbert give me their best shots in practice. If I can't stop a guy in practice, how am I going to stop a guy in a game? It's too easy for a goalie to get into bad habits, and go into a slump, just like a baseball hitter. There are so many little things you can do wrong and not even know it. Since I don't play sixty or seventy games a year any more, I have to work even harder in practice to keep sharp mentally and physically.

What has given you your biggest satisfaction in ten years with the Rangers?

Beating Montreal and Boston in the playoffs was probably the most satisfying thing for me. If you recall, we'd been getting beaten pretty regularly in the opening round of the playoffs for quite a while. A lot of people said we weren't a good playoff team and that I was a lousy playoff goalie.

Do you think you were a lousy playoff goalie?

No. But enough people sure wrote or said I was. They said I choked in the playoffs. It was not very pleasant to hear or read that kind of stuff. I don't think I was a lousy playoff goalie and I know I never choked. I know I didn't play that well but I don't believe I was the only one who did or that I was the whole reason why we got beaten. But, as you know, everyone always blames the goalie when a team loses.

Some people believe the reason you and the Rangers could not survive the opening round in the playoffs for so long was that you played so many games in the regular season and were physically and mentally exhausted in the playoffs.

That always bothered me. I was always hearing I was tired, worn out by the time the playoffs started. Only I never felt I was tired. What was I supposed to do? Say I'm tired and don't want to play? Looking back, though, I can see now that I might have been a little tired and didn't know it at the time. All the travel, practices and games, and the longer schedule wear down a lot of guys and I feel now that occasional rest does help. But I never felt that we lost because I was tired or overworked.

Did you really like it when Emile Francis introduced the two-goalie system to the Rangers in 1970–71 and you and Gilles Villemure shared the goaltending?

At first I didn't care for it. I hated to sit on the bench. I took a lot of pride in playing every game. I don't think any guy who likes sitting on the bench is worth much to himself or his team. But Emile explained to me that not playing every game would benefit me, lengthen my career, and in the long run would help the Rangers. Now I can see he was right. I feel more relaxed now that I get rested more often. I can see that it helped me and helped the team. With all the travel and the long season, the day of one goalie playing all the games is over. I like it now. But I still don't like sitting on the bench. I never will.

What has been the biggest disappointment during your career?

It has to be the 1972–73 season. Everybody picked us to finish first and maybe win the Stanley Cup. It was finally supposed to be our year but it wasn't. After we beat Boston in the playoffs, we figured we could walk over Chicago. But we didn't. It was too quick an ending.

Does it bother you when you read that the Rangers are the highest-paid team in the NHL but have failed to finish first since 1942 or win the Stanley Cup since 1940?

Sure it does. It bothers all of us on the Rangers. But I guess we're going to keep on hearing it until we finally win something, eh? We've had teams capable of finishing first and winning the Cup but we just haven't been able to do it. We always seem to get so many injuries at just the wrong time or run into other teams that happen to be hot in the playoffs. But you never give up hope. You never quit trying until you finally make it. Life is a lot of roadblocks. I've always had to come in through the back door. I'm waiting until I walk through the front door. I'm going to stay with it until that day comes.

What's the answer to the Rangers' inability to win a championship?

I wish I knew. We've had some injuries and our share of bad luck but even so we just haven't done what we thought we could do. It's very frustrating.

You have the reputation of being an outstanding stick-handler and skater, which is rare for a goaltender.

I work on my stickhandling and skating a lot. A goalie can help his team, and himself, if he's a good skater and knows how to use his stick to clear the puck out of danger and get it away from the net and out to his forwards.

You have come close several times to becoming the first goalie to score a goal into an empty net in NHL history. Will it ever happen?

I think someone will do it someday. I hope I'm the one. I've missed by inches a couple of times. I'll keep trying whenever the chance is there.

Why did you wait so long before you started wearing a mask in 1970?

If you don't grow up wearing a mask, then you're not used to it and the adjustment is difficult. I just reached the point where I finally felt the mask had become an important part of a goalie's equipment and felt it was better to wear one than to risk injury. It hasn't changed my style, but, psychologically, a goalie is probably more confident wearing a mask. Now we all do.

Which goaltenders influenced you the most in the formative stages of your career?

When I was starting out, I always admired the styles of Glenn Hall and Jacques Plante, and I adopted some of their techniques.

You have been named to the All Star team five times, led the league in shutouts three times, shared the Vezina Trophy with Gilles Villemure, and broken Dave Kerr's Ranger record for career shutouts. Which means the most to you?

Probably breaking Kerr's shutout record and having a share in winning the Vezina Trophy. But I wish I could have won it by myself.

At what point in a game do you start thinking about the possibility that you might get a shutout?

As soon as I go in goal for the opening face-off. You have to go out there believing you are not going to give up a goal. Of course, it doesn't happen that way very often. It depends upon how sharp you feel and how well your team is playing in front of you. If everything seems to be going well, I'll begin to think shutout when there are about ten minutes left in the game. But I try to block the thought out of my mind; I've lost too many shutouts in the last couple of minutes of a game.

Winning the game is the most important thing, no matter

how many goals you give up. But, of course, every goalie loves to get a shutout. It's the ultimate thing for a goalie. I'm sure a pitcher feels the same way in baseball.

Shutouts are funny, though. Sometimes it's a matter of luck. I've played games where I've given up two or three goals, had to make a lot of saves, and know I played well. Then I've had shutouts where I had to handle fewer tough shots and didn't really feel I played that well. I think most goalies have a tendency to play their best games when the score is close and they have to handle a lot of shots.

What is your opinion of the World Hockey Association? Is the WHA here to stay? Is it good for hockey?

I was skeptical about the WHA at first. Now I feel the WHA has proved itself. Having a second league is good for the players because it means more jobs and more money. The NHL is still *the* league. Maybe there will be a merger eventually, but I don't see one coming in the near future.

Hockey salaries have skyrocketed. Is this good for the sport?

It's great for the players, that's for sure. There was a time, not too long ago, when most of us didn't make much money. I do think, though, that some of the money being tossed around for kids who haven't yet proved themselves can hurt their motivation and desire to some degree.

You have had a lot of adversity in your life. You were told you were not good enough to play Junior A hockey. You were badly burned and told you might not play again. You spent a long time in the minor leagues. It wasn't easy getting to the NHL.

I look back at it now and it gets me up. It helps me keep going and stay on top. I'll always remember my days in the minor leagues and how long it took for me to get a chance to play in the NHL. I think it's made me appreciate where I am more than some guys who made it easier than I did. I guess I'm kind of unique.

What disturbs you most about hockey fans? You've taken a lot of abuse and criticism from them.

The few who throw objects on the ice at games and use dirty language are very disturbing. By and large most fans are good and are important to the game. I like to think I've some good fans on my side.

Some professional athletes refuse to sign autographs and are surly and unfriendly toward fans.

I don't think it's right for an athlete to be that way. We owe a lot to the fans. I enjoy meeting and talking with fans and signing autographs. But you can't always stand there talking and signing autographs when you have to get to the game or catch a bus or a plane, and sometimes when you have to leave, fans don't understand and become annoyed.

Autographs? I always sign as many as I can. But I wish some fans would not be so rude. You like to be asked, not told, to sign an autograph. It never hurts to say please. It's natural for kids to want autographs and it's flattering, but some people are really rude. I've seen older guys asking the same player for his autograph day after day. I know outside the hotel in Chicago the guys who demand your autograph only want it so they can sell it.

What do you think of the youth sports?

I'm all for kids playing as many sports as they can. But I'd like to see more parents and coaches remember that it's for the kids, not for themselves, and that having fun and learning the game is more important than winning for young kids. The big thing is to see that every kid on a team gets a fair chance to play.

Are you a sports fan?

Oh, yeah. I follow baseball and pro football. I like to watch it on TV and I like to get to Shea Stadium as much as I can in the summer to see the Mets or Yankees.

Would a job as a sportscaster interest you?

Marv Albert let me do his sports show on WNBC radio

one time. Maybe I wasn't so hot because he never asked me back again. I thought it would be easy but sitting there reading all the scores was a lot tougher than I imagined. I enjoyed doing it, though.

Do you do much public speaking?

I've been doing more in the last few years. I like doing it. I enjoy getting out and meeting people.

A lot of your teammates like to kid or tease you about your prematurely gray hair. Is this what goaltending has done to you?

That's what everybody thinks. Who knows? Maybe that's why I turned gray so young. Harry Howell had a lot of gray hair when he was young, too, and then when he got older his hair got darker. I always accused Harry of using black shoe polish on his hair. I don't really think you get gray hair from worrying. I think it's heredity. Both my father and my mother were gray at a young age and my two brothers, Rollie and Jiggs, probably would be, too, if they had any hair to show it.

You have had your share of arguments with referees.

Now when did you ever see me dispute a referee's decision? Seriously, yeah, I fight for what I think is right, and I've had a few pretty good arguments with referees. But it's part of the game. Nothing more than that. I've got tremendous respect for referees and linesmen. They've got the toughest job in hockey and they don't get paid as much as they should. They're a lot like goaltenders. Everybody's always blaming them.

Do you have any special hobbies or interests outside of hockey?

Camping. I've really gotten into camping. I do a lot of it with my family during the off-season. I like to spend as much time together with my wife and family as I can in the summer because there isn't much time during the season. We took the camper out west one summer. We went to Bermuda one summer and I just sat on the beach and relaxed and got away from it all. I like to work with my hands, building things at home, doing woodworking, gardening, and yardwork. I guess I just like the simple life, even if it doesn't sound that exciting to some people.

Does being a professional athlete create an added burden for you as a family man?

Definitely. It's tough for a wife with young children when her husband is gone most of the time from September to almost June playing hockey. She has to be a combination mother-father. When the kids get sick or something breaks down in the house, she's the one who's on the spot. We practice or play almost every day in the season and are away on the road so much.

I try to make the most of what little time we have together during the season. I try not to be moody when I'm not playing well or the team is going badly. Being the wife of a hockey player isn't easy.

Through hockey, you have come into contact with some prominent people. Correct?

Well, let's see. I know Secretary of State Henry Kissinger came to the Garden to see us play. I remember that because we were playing badly and someone mentioned that maybe Mr. Kissinger could help. I said, "Yeah, if he can stop the bombing going on in the Middle East, maybe he can stop the bombing going on in the Rangers' end of the ice."

I went on Johnny Carson's "Tonight Show" once and he shot pucks at me. Yogi Berra has become quite a hockey fan because one of his boys plays hockey. Yogi has come down to the dressing room to see me, along with one of his coaches, Joe Pignatano. Tiny Tim used to come to our games but I never met him. I did, however, meet Bob Hope once.

My biggest thrill has to be meeting Joe DiMaggio. They invited me to a dinner honoring Italian athletes a couple of years ago. That's where I met Joe. He was always one of my heroes as a kid.

Are you sorry Emile Francis resigned as Ranger coach?

Very definitely. He did so much for all of us. I wouldn't be where I am today if he had not stuck by me when things were going badly. I'm disappointed we couldn't win the Stanley Cup for him. He built the Ranger organization. He wanted to win the Cup so badly.

Do you ever see Johnny Gagnon, the scout who recommended you to the Rangers?

Johnny comes around for training camp and drops in a few times during the season. He's a quiet little guy who stays in the background, but I owe so much to him for all he did in my behalf. They had a testimonial dinner in Providence for Johnny a couple of years ago. There was no way in the world I would have missed going to Johnny's testimonial dinner.

Did your not playing junior hockey in Canada as a youth hamper your career?

There's no question that not playing junior hockey hurt my career. There are lots of valuable points that I would have picked up. I would have been playing in better competition than I did. It really set me back at first. Other guys played four years of junior hockey.

Have hockey players changed noticeably since you entered the NHL?

The modern players are bigger, stronger, and shoot the puck harder, in most cases, but I don't know that all of them have as much desire or hunger for the game or are as willing to work as hard as guys had to be when I started out. It's a whole new life style today. A lot of the old values have changed. The big money in hockey today has taken away some of the motivation. You don't see that many guys around with a great hunger or love for the game. To some guys today, playing hockey is strictly a business.

What disturbs you most about sports writers and sports broadcasters?

Nothing very much. Writers have a job to do, just like players do. Occasionally, someone will write something you didn't say or take a rip at you that you consider too personal or uncalled for. Every player likes to read good things about him. We've all got egos and pride. No one likes to see something written about him that isn't favorable. But honest criticism is part of the game and part of life. And the writer has an obligation to his newspaper and to the fans to tell it like it is.

I believe the sports writers have played an important part in publicizing hockey and the players. They've got a tough job, too: long hours and spending a lot of time away from their families. It's a pressure job, just like goaltending. The goalie has to stop the puck; the writer has to make his deadline.

There have been times after bad games when I didn't feel like talking or probably sounded grumpy. But mostly I've always tried to cooperate with the press. Every player has that obligation. After all, it's the writer who communicates from the player to the fans. And the fans have a right to know what's going on and what the players have to say about a game.

I like to think I've got some friends among the sports writers. Guys like Tim Moriarty, Bob Gockley, Hugh Delano, Wes Gaffer, Sid Payne, Gerry Eskenazi, Hal Bock, Frank Brown, Marty Lader, Dana Mozley, and Dave Anderson from New York and the guys from the suburban newspapers, Walt MacPeek, Mark Ruskie, and Dick Yerg.

There are other writers I've enjoyed talking with over the years: John Hanlon and Ted Mulcahey from my days in Providence. Red Fisher, Jacques Beauchamp, Bert Raymond, and Tim Burke in Montreal. Red Burnett, Milt Dunnell, Jim Proudfoot, and Frank Orr in Toronto. Tom Fitzgerald, Fran Rosa, and Leo Monahan in Boston. Bill Libby in Los Angeles. And Mark Mulvoy and Norm McLean.

Hockey gets much more TV and radio coverage than it used to. So I can't overlook guys like Marv Albert, Jim Gordon, Sal Messina, Bill Chadwick, Keith Morris, Tim Ryan, Sal Marchiano, Dan Kelly, Bill Mazer, Gene Stuart, Spencer Ross, Bob Wilson, and Brian MacFarlane.

I know he never covered hockey but one of my biggest thrills when I joined the Rangers was being interviewed by Mel Allen. I always listened to him broadcast Yankee games. How about that!

Is there too much violence in hockey?

I think the word "violence" is often overused. Hockey is a rough game, a fast game, and a certain amount of fighting is part of the game. But I don't go for the senseless fighting and brawling or the cheap, dirty play and stick swinging. Being a goon doesn't take much talent or win games. I don't like to see the game sold on violence. It's too great a game for that and it gives the sport a bad image, especially for kids.

The Philadelphia Flyers often are accused of being overly violent and yet they have won two straight Stanley Cups.

The Flyers play a very physical game but that's not the only reason they've won the Stanley Cup. They've got a great goalie in Bernie Parent and a great player and leader in Bobby Clarke. They check and work hard for sixty minutes and stick to their system of play as well as any team and they've got a hell of a coach in Freddie Shero. That's why they've been successful. Plus they've got the talent. Sure, I don't like a lot about some of the tactics they use, especially the way they try to bounce me around, but I know one thing: They won't ever see me back down.

Does it surprise you that few former goalies ever become hockey coaches?

Yes. Goalies are behind everything. They see the overall

picture of the whole game. We know the other teams better than the forwards or defensemen do. We're the first to see when a man is out of position. I think goaltenders would make excellent coaches.

At thirty-six, are you beginning to think of retiring as a player? What do you want to do when you retire?

I hope to play three or four more years, if I can, mainly because I enjoy playing hockey. When I do quit, I definitely want to coach more than anything else.

How would you like to be remembered as a hockey player?

As one who always worked hard, tried to do his best, never gave up, and helped his team.

What do you want most that you have been unable to achieve in hockey?

I think you know the answer, eh?—to win the Stanley Cup.

EDDIE GIACOMIN LOOKS AT THE GOALIES

Tony Esposito, Chicago: He has a unique style that's unorthodox, not the kind you teach a young goalie, but he stops the puck and that's what counts the most. Tony's a nervous guy but he's been so successful that he's one of the best. He likes to use his knees a lot and is good going down in the V with his legs. He's a blocker who'll use his hands or his body to knock down pucks and pounce on them. He likes to flop and his catching hand isn't as strong as some.

Bernie Parent, Philadelphia: Probably the best goalie going today and the best example for anyone to copy. He's a perfect example of the style of goaltending they stress: standup and challenge the shooter. He doesn't have the lightning reflexes but he's great playing the angles and great with his skates. Bernie's a relaxed guy and very durable. We were rookies together in 1965. If he's got any weakness, it's that he doesn't always clear the puck that well.

Rogie Vachon, Los Angeles: We have one thing in common —Punch Imlach used to say the two of us were nothing more than Junior B goalies. To me, he's one of the quickest goalies in the league. He's small and plays from a crouch, and the book on him is that you have to try to beat him with high shots because he stays low.

Glenn Resch, Islanders: Chico the Man. What a playoff he had last season. He's the spunkiest goalie I've seen and I hope he never loses that quality. He's got so much confidence and he thinks he's the best. Someday he will be. He's not afraid to take a chance and wander or use his stick. I like Chico.

Bill Smith, Islanders: He's my type of goalie, too. He's a fighter. He's a hell of a competitor. He hates to lose. He seems to get down on himself after a bad goal or a bad game, and he has to get over that. If I were a coach, I'd want him to be my goalie.

Ken Dryden, Montreal: The educational goalie. I wish I were as smart as he is. He's so big that he has the best long reach of any goalie and he uses it so well. He'll tease the shooter by giving him the far side to shoot at, and because he's so agile for a big man and has quick legs, he can come back over and cover the other side of the net. He uses the V very well and he's starting to maneuver around the net more. He's got one of the best glove-hands in the league. I'll bet he makes 85 percent of his saves with it.

Phil Myre, Atlanta: The Ranger killer. Boy, does he thrive on us. I compare him to Parent because he's a standup goalie. But his style is a little different. Most goalies keep their catching hands near their sides. He likes to hold his glove out in front of him.

Eddie Johnston, St. Louis: One of the really nice guys in this game. An old pro who's been around. I call him "the Director" because he runs the club when he's in goal. He'll even swat one of his own guys on the butt with his stick to wake him up. Eddie is still quick and maneuvers well around the net. He's a hell of a good man and he helps young goalies a lot. He'll make a good coach someday.

Gilles Meloche, California: He's so quick. If he were with a top-notch club, he'd be number one in the league right now. I've got to say he's the quickest goalie in the league. It's tough for him since he's young and gets 40 or 50 shots a game because he's with a weak club. He'll make the unbelievable save but sometimes he'll miss the easy one, and you can beat him with shots through the legs.

Doug Favell, Toronto: They say he's a flake. Hell, you've got to be a little flaky to be a goalie. He's the flashy-type goalie. Quick reflexes. Good skater. Uses his stick like it's a magic wand. He plays lacrosse in the off-season and I think sometimes he forgets he's playing hockey instead of lacrosse. He just needs to get that one good year to find his groove.

Jimmy Rutherford, Detroit: Another guy who plays for a team with defensive weaknesses. He's small, like Vachon, and plays a stand-up style, and he's quick and scrappy. His lack of size hinders him. He seems to get beaten a lot because he's not set up for screen shots.

Peter McDuffe, Detroit: I felt sorry for Peter. He sat in the press box or on the bench and only got to play one game the full year he spent with the Rangers. I always kept on him to work hard in practice and keep himself in shape because someday he'd get his chance. He played some good goal for an expansion team, Kansas City, last season. I'd like to see him show a little more fire and aggressiveness.

Gary Inness, Pittsburgh: I read a story in the *New York Post* that he studies the way I play on film. I'm flattered, but after the season I had last year, maybe he's making a mistake watching me. He really came on in the playoffs last season. He plays the angles well and he's a strong, determined guy. I see him using my wandering style, and I only hope he has better luck with it than I did in the beginning. He seems to want to make himself the best. I can see he's a quality guy.

Bunny Larocque, Montreal: I remember him in the 1974 playoffs. He was a rookie and they put him under all that pressure. I only wish I could have played half as well as he did when I was a rookie.

Gilles Gilbert, Boston: I remember him with Minnesota when he was just a kid and I figured he'd be a good one. You can score on him early and he doesn't get down on himself. In fact, he seems to get stronger as the game goes on. That's important for a goalie. He seems to get beaten a lot on shots between the legs.

Roger Crozier, Buffalo: He's the acrobatic goalie. He's not big and he's not strong, but he's always bouncing up and down, making saves no goalie has any business making. He can make saves 80 percent of the other goalies can't. He's been hospitalized for ulcers and stomach troubles and has had a problem with his nerves, but he keeps coming back. An old pro who's at his best under pressure, very quick and good on rebounds.

Cesare Maniago, Minnesota: My old friend, Cesare. One of the great Italians in the game. Right? He's tall and likes to throw that big body down across the goal mouth. He was getting bombed in Minnesota last season, like the two of us were our first year together in New York, but he stood up to it. He's definitely a flopper, a blocker, like Esposito. He has a tendency to throw that right leg of his out, and a shooter can take advantage of it and get the puck by him. He's one of the nice guys in the game.

Ross Brooks, Boston: Ross and I are old buddies from Providence and the Eastern League. We suffered together a lot, and it took both of us a long time to get to the NHL. I was glad to see Ross make it. He's amazing. He's so relaxed for a goalie and he works so hard. He changed himself into a straight stand-up, angle goalie, and now he doesn't beat himself any more. Another nice guy. And a great team man with a great attitude.

Gary Smith, Vancouver: They call him "the Ax" because he uses that big stick to clear guys out around his crease. I like that. I wish I were as big as he is because then when I use my stick, guys would be scared and leave me alone. I guess he's a flake. He undresses after each period in the dressing room. He really lifted up Vancouver last season. He was an iron man and played almost every game. I think he deserved to be MVP in the league, but he didn't get the award. He's got lots of energy and he plays well under pressure. He uses his knees and body well. And he's quick with the glove. He seems to get beaten a lot on deflections, though.

Ron Low, Washington: With the kind of team he played for last season, it's hard to judge him as a goalie. Washington won only eight of eighty games and was the weakest defensive club in the league with 446 goals scored against it. He showed me a lot of guts just by sticking it out. A lot of guys would have lost all their confidence in his situation.

Jacques Plante: I guess I never agreed with a lot of the things he said or did, but I can't argue with his record. He was "Mr. Everything" as a goalie. He proved you don't have to be a dummy to be a goalie. He was smart and made a science of goaltending. He developed the wandering style of clearing the puck and really revolutionized the art of goaltending to what it is today. A lot of goalies, including myself, copied his style.

Glenn Hall: They called him "Mr. Goalie." He once played 502 consecutive games in goal. He got sick and threw up before games. That tells you something of what goaltending is like and what the pressure can do to a man. He was the master. One of the best ever, if not *the* best. He was instrumental in developing the V spread with the legs. I admired him and copied a lot of his style. Year after year he was the best. I don't know how he did it or lasted as long as he did, with all that torture going on inside him.

Gump Worsley: Small in size but big in heart. A real character but a super guy. He always had that quick wit about him and he kind of played goal that way, if it's possible. It was hell for him during those bad years in New York, but when he went to Montreal he won the Vezina Trophy and proved he was one of the best. I was happy for him. I guess "the Gump's" biggest problem was always too many rebounds.

Terry Sawchuk: A unique man. Tough and mean, on and off the ice. No one ever got to know him well. He was a loner. But he was a great goalie. Maybe *the* greatest. No goalie had more shutouts than he did. He was an innovator. One of the few goalies who ever put both styles together and mastered them. He could play stand-up style or be an acrobat. He was in New York with me for his last season before he died. I loved to watch him play, but I never got to know him too well. I wish I could have.

Gilles Villemure, Chicago: How can I forget Gilly? My former partner. We've followed each other around for years in the Eastern League, the American League, and up to the NHL. It was great working with Gilly. We got along so well. We are two opposite goalies in style and that always helped the Rangers and made it tougher for our opponents. I caught with the left hand, Gilly caught with the right. I was the acrobat. He was the stand-up goalie. He plays the angles so well and is strong with his hands, feet, and stick. Very good on breakaways, too, and always relaxed. He's improved a lot in using his stick. Like me, he suffered for a long time in the minors until he finally got his chance.

Rollie Giacomin: O.K. So he never played in the NHL. But he's my brother and when you talk about goalies, we have to talk about Rollie. I think he could have made it in the NHL, but he had to work to support his family in Sudbury. Rollie played junior hockey and in the old Eastern Pro League. He's the one who got me to become a goalie and taught me a lot. He was a stand-up guy with a good catching hand. One hell of a tough competitor. He wouldn't hesitate to use his stick to clear guys out from the crease. Guys used to drop their gloves and challenge Rollie. They'd do it only once. He was a big guy, around 200 pounds, and he was a good fighter. Rollie the Goalie! Headline writers would have loved him if he'd played in the NHL.

Epilogue

"THE END OF AN ERA: THEY THREW ME TO THE WOLVES."

EDDIE Giacomin reported to the Rangers' new training camp in Long Beach, Long Island, on September 15, 1975 to begin preparations for his eleventh season as a National Hockey League goaltender.

It was almost ten years ago to the day that he had reported as a nervous rookie to his first Ranger training camp in Kingston, Ontario.

Now he was thirty-six years old—the oldest player on the team—and many of the new young faces in Ranger uniforms were only four- and five-year-old kids when Eddie had gone to Washington in 1959 to begin his long, difficult climb to stardom as a hockey goalie.

There had been two significant changes made that would greatly effect Giacomin's career since the 1974–75 season ended so abruptly five months ago in the demoralizing overtime loss to the Islanders in the Stanley Cup playoffs.

Emile Francis, the man who brought Eddie from Providence to New York in 1965 and nursed him through his troubled formative years as Ranger goalie, no longer was coach. He resigned after the last season to devote full time to his job as general manager.

Ron Stewart was the Rangers' new coach. He had played against Giacomin as a forward for the Toronto Maple Leafs, Boston Bruins, St. Louis Blues, Vancouver Canucks, and New York Islanders. He had been one of Eddie's Ranger teammates between 1967 and 1972. He was a defense-oriented coach, who played for twenty-two years in the NHL.

"Ron Stewart is a winner," Eddie said of his new coach. "He was always a top-class guy when I played against him and with him. He's stern and tough but he's fair-minded and he'll be good for us as a coach. I remember Stewie as a guy with magic legs—he was one of the most graceful skaters in the game—and as the defensive specialist who always shadowed Bobby Hull. If it hadn't been for Stewart, who knows how many goals Hull would have scored on me."

Giacomin said that Stewart's background as a defensive player would help the Rangers. "Let's face it: we've got to improve our goals-against average. Ron Stewart is the kind of guy who'll see that we do. It's up to all of us to accept Ron as our coach and as our boss and pull together with him. I know that's what I'll be doing."

The second significant change was the presence of a new goaltender—twenty-two-year-old John Davidson. The Rangers acquired him from St. Louis in a trade for Ted Irvine, Jerry Butler, and Bert Wilson. Big, strong, and agile, Davidson is regarded as a young goaltender with immense potential.

His presence in Ranger training camp was no surprise: he is the young goalie of the future for the Rangers. He is heir apparent to the job Giacomin has held or shared for ten years.

"I've always admired John as a goalie since he came into

the league in 1973," said Giacomin. "He's got great talent. But he's still young and just learning. They say he has trouble maneuvering around the net and with rebounds. I'll help him in every way I can."

Giacomin laughed.

"I know he's big. Remember the brawl we had in St. Louis last year? He ran into me so I know he hits hard."

"It was a logical move, getting a top young goalie like John," said Eddie. "Gilles Villemure and I are getting older. The Rangers have to think of the future and get the best young goalie they can."

The light-hearted tone in Eddie's voice changed to one of grim determination.

"I'm in the best shape I've ever been in for training camp and the season ahead. I've been running and riding a bicycle all summer. I've always worked hard to keep myself in shape but this year is a little different."

The advancing years and the arrival of a new goaltender with star potential made the 1975–76 season different.

"Last season was definitely a very disappointing one for me, maybe one of the most disappointing years I've had," said Eddie. "I had the knee injury. I couldn't play for quite a while. I wasn't proud of my record. I don't feel I contributed enough to the team."

And the new goaltender?

"He's going to have to work hard to win my job," said Eddie. "Anybody who wants to take my job away from me is going to have a hell of a fight on his hands. No one's going to push me out of my job without a fight. I may be getting older, but I'm not ready or about to step aside for anyone yet."

Eddie chose his words carefully.

"I've got a lot to prove after last season. And I'll never be content until we win the Stanley Cup," he said.

Giacomin's dream of helping the Rangers win the Stanley

Cup for the first time since 1940 ended on October 31, 1975. He was sold to the Detroit Red Wings on waivers for $30,000. The transaction shocked and angered many of his teammates and many of the popular goaltender's fans.

It was not so much that Eddie had played poorly during the first three weeks of the season as it was that the Rangers were afflicted by their most dreadful start in ten years. The team and its management were under extreme pressure from fans and the press. Management decided a shake-up of player personnel was in order.

Giacomin was in the net for the eleventh consecutive opening game when New York started the 1975–76 season on October 8, against Chicago in Madison Square Garden. He played well but was forced to accept a 2-2 tie. His team let him down. One goal followed a giveaway in the Ranger defensive zone. The second came with two Rangers in the penalty box.

Eddie lost his second game to Los Angeles, 6-4, three goals being scored with the Kings on the power play and four following giveaways by the Ranger defense. He lost his third game, 4-1, on two power-play goals and a giveaway goal in Toronto. But the worst came on October 26 in Madison Square Garden against the defending Stanley Cup champion Philadelphia Flyers. Giacomin and his struggling teammates were badly embarrassed in a 7-2 defeat in which spectators subjected Eddie and the Rangers to some of the most vicious booing directed toward a New York team.

Many of the crowd's jeers and curses were directed at Eddie. His error-prone teammates gave him little defensive support but he looked weak and seemed to be fighting the puck on two or three of Philadelphia's goals.

"I stood out there and thought about all the times the fans were shouting 'Eddie! . . . Eddie! . . . Eddie!' in the past. It can go the other way for you, too, like it did in this game," Eddie said in the dressing room after the game.

"We're not playing up to expectations as a team. I'm not playing up to expectations as a goaltender. You can't pick one department; we've been lousy in all of them so far."

Jean Ratelle shook his head. "This is the worst it's ever been for us," he said. "We've never taken setbacks this bad before. We're not giving our goaltenders any help at all."

The Rangers were in last place with a 3-5-1 record. They had been humiliated in three straight games, Davidson, the new goaltender, being overwhelmed by 9-1 and 7-1 scores to Buffalo and the Islanders, respectively, before the 7-2 rout by the Flyers.

Stewart, the new coach, used a stream of profanities to describe the poor effort the Rangers put forth against Buffalo. "It was a shameful exhibition. Our goaltenders could sue for non-support," he said, his face flushed with anger, his voice tight with emotion.

"I've never seen such lack of effort by the Rangers," observed Brian Spencer, a Buffalo forward. "It was the worst effort I've ever seen by a Ranger team," commented teammate Don Luce.

The Flyers had essentially the same thoughts about the Rangers following their 7-2 conquest.

"They just seemed to quit," said defenseman Joe Watson.

"It's the worst I've ever seen them play and it's certainly not all the goaltender's fault," said forward Ross Lonsberry.

Many spectators in Madison Square Garden chanted "Refund! . . . Refund! . . . Refund!" as the passive Rangers self-destructed before the Flyers. They chanted "We want a hit!" and sarcastically mocked Giacomin when he stopped an easy shot.

"Very inept," Stewart said in a voice that was more of a hiss. "All it takes is a little guts, but we haven't found anyone yet who has any."

Francis was enraged by his team's dreadful play and successive losses by 9–1, 7–1, 7–2 scores. At practice on October

27 in Long Beach, he read the riot act to his players. He told them he was placing every player on waivers, making them available to be claimed by any other team in the league.

" 'The Cat' let us have it pretty good," said Giacomin. "We deserved it."

Eddie had played four games for the Rangers. He had surrendered nineteen goals. His record was 0–3–1. His goals-against average was an unattractive 4.75. He did not know at the time that he would never play another game as a Ranger.

On October 28 Ranger management began its shake-up and purge of high-salaried veterans. Gilles Villemure, who had not played in a single game, was traded to Chicago for defenseman Doug Jarrett.

"It's the end of an era," said Giacomin, referring to the five seasons he and Villemure shared the Ranger goaltending. "I'm sad to see Gilly leave. But I'm happy because he'll get a chance to play."

On October 30 Derek Sanderson was traded to St. Louis for a first-round draft choice. The trade incensed many Ranger fans. The colorful "Turk" was popular among New York hockey fans. The trade seemed to make no sense until William Jennings explained why Sanderson had been traded.

"When the coach tells you a man is damaging the team, he has to go," said the Rangers' team president. Derek left New York in a huff, criticizing the team's management policies.

Friday, October 31, 1975, started out like any other day in Eddie's eleven years as a Ranger. He went to practice in the morning and returned home to pack for the team flight at 5:45 P.M. which would take the Rangers to Montreal for a game the following night against the Canadiens.

At 4 P.M. the telephone rang in the Giacomins' home. Emile Francis was calling.

"Something's in the making but I can't say what until six-thirty. You better come down to Long Beach and see me then," the general manager told Eddie.

"What about Montreal?" Giacomin asked Francis.

"You won't be going to Montreal," Francis told Eddie.

Giacomin was confused and worried. He knew something important was up. Why else would Francis want to see him and tell him not to accompany the team to Montreal?

"I was lost. I didn't know why he wanted to see me," said Giacomin.

Eddie's oldest son Mark was preparing to ride his bike to St. Mary's Church to serve as an altar boy at the 5:15 Mass.

"Hold it! C'mon, I'll drive you to Mass," the father told his son.

After mass, Eddie drove twenty-two miles from Manhasset to Long Beach. It was Halloween Night and he passed children in their costumes going from door-to-door on his way to Nassau Arena and his meeting with Francis.

It was dark outside the arena when Eddie pulled his car into the gravel parking lot. He could not see a light in the arena.

"It was eerie," he said. "I had to fumble my way around in the dark to find a side door that was unlocked. There was nobody else around. Then I had to feel my way around in the dark until I got to where the dressing room is and could see the light in 'the Cat's' office."

Francis gave Eddie the bad news.

"He told me I had been put on waivers, that Detroit claimed me and that now I belonged to them," said Giacomin. "It was a very cold atmosphere. There were no harsh words. I had a thirteen-minute interview. Eleven years with the Rangers and all it took was thirteen minutes to end it."

Eddie was stunned by the news that he no longer was a Ranger. His pride was hurt when he realized that his value on the hockey market seemed worth only the minimal $30,000 waiver price and that the Rangers were willing to give him up without getting at least one player in exchange.

"I was so mixed up I almost drove my car into the water when I left," he said, referring to the inlet behind the arena parking lot.

Eddie's mind was filled with a million different thoughts as he drove back to Manhasset. How would he break the news to his wife that he had been sold to Detroit? One of his first thoughts was that the bad news would spoil the Halloween party his children had planned that night. He stopped at a bar on the way home to have a beer and collect his thoughts.

"I was just sitting there at the bar having a beer and thinking what I'd do," he said. "Nobody recognized me. Then a guy comes in and starts telling the bartender that he just heard on the radio that the Rangers got rid of Giacomin, the old guy who was a goalie."

Eddie left his unfinished beer on the bar and walked out.

The scene near midnight in the Giacomins' home had the tragic, somber atmosphere of family and friends grieving together at a funeral parlor. Marg Giacomin sat near her husband. The day of agony was almost over. The kids, Mark, thirteen, David, ten, and Nancy, six, had gone to bed following a Halloween night they could not enjoy. Sparky, the family's small, fluffy white dog, was waiting to be walked. No one said much and when they spoke their voices were hushed. Paul Levine, Eddie's close friend from Port Washington, had come over to be with Eddie and handle the incoming telephone calls from friends, relatives and sports writers who learned of Giacomin's departure from the Rangers.

"He's taking it hard. He's pretty depressed. It's a very difficult time for him," said Levine.

"I'm sitting here completely numb, hardly functioning.

I walk around and feel like I'm embalmed or dead," Eddie began. "I don't want to sound bitter. God, I don't want to be bitter. I'm trying like hell not to be bitter."

He spoke in a soft whisper, his voice choked with emotion.

"Tell me why? Tell me why they did it this way? Tell me why they had to do it to me in a way that hurt, a way that makes a man feel like he's dirt, a piece of garbage?" asked Giacomin.

He thought about how Madison Square Garden fans used to chant: "Eddie! . . . Eddie! . . . Eddie!"

"I can still hear them. It always sent chills up and down my spine. Now I'll never hear it again," he said. An emotional man, Eddie was on the verge of tears.

"Am I shocked? That's a calm word. I did everything I could to help this club for eleven years. I had one more year left in my contract. I would have retired if they didn't want me. Why wouldn't they let me go out gracefully as a New York Ranger? Why wouldn't they give me that much respect?" A tinge of bitterness was creeping into Giacomin's voice.

"They threw me to the wolves. All these years with the New York Rangers and they throw you out like a piece of garbage and wait for someone to pick it up. I'm not a horse, I'm not some dirty piece of cattle."

Eddie excused himself. He needed time to compose his thoughts.

"They threw me out. They told me I was not on waivers. Why did they lie? I'm not some kid who was here for just a couple of years. Why couldn't they have told me at practice in the morning? They make me drive all the way down to Long Beach at night and tell me after the team has gone. I don't even get a chance to see the guys on the team to say goodbye and wish them luck."

Eddie's wife and children took the news hard. "They cried," he said. Eddie was disturbed at the manner in which his sale to Detroit was released to the news media. "It was flashed around all over New York and Canada before I had a chance to call my friends and relatives to let them know," he said.

"For the rest of my life, I'll always remember the statement he [Francis] made," said Giacomin. "As long as I'm with New York, you'll always be with me."

Times change. Attitudes change. It is business as usual for the people who run hockey teams. Perhaps it cannot be helped.

Despite the shock of being discarded by the Rangers with no advance warning and the concern that he must uproot and move his family, Eddie displayed his class in a difficult time. He refused to blame Francis or to criticize Ranger management.

The relationship between Francis and Giacomin had been compared to a father-son relationship. "The Cat" rescued Eddie from the minor leagues and brought him into the National Hockey League. He stuck with him through the hard times.

"I know it had to be tough for him to do what he did," said Eddie. Still, that did not help ease the pain of leaving the Rangers.

"Not one call from anybody on the team. The fact that none of the guys called me hurts," said Eddie.

There was a reason why none of the goalie's Ranger teammates telephoned him. Eddie's teammates arrived in Montreal not knowing that their goaltender had been sold to Detroit.

Walt MacPeek of the *Newark Star-Ledger* contacted Jean Ratelle by telephone in his Montreal hotel room.

"I need your reaction to the trade," said the New Jersey writer.

"I was surprised because I thought Derek was playing pretty well," Ratelle began.

"No, I don't mean the Sanderson deal," corrected Mac-

Peek. "I'm talking about Eddie Giacomin."

"Don't fool me like that," replied Ratelle. "It can't be true. We knew Eddie was not on the team bus or the plane but we thought he was coming up the next day. I'm shocked they got rid of Eddie. It wasn't his fault. Maybe I'm next to go."

The prophesy was correct. One week later, on November 7, 1975, Ratelle and Brad Park, along with Joe Zanussi, were traded to the Boston Bruins in a stunning trade which brought Phil Esposito, the highest goal-scorer in hockey history, and defenseman Carol Vadnais to New York.

Giacomin's departure produced shock waves throughout the National Hockey League.

"I can't believe they'd do this to Eddie," former Ranger Rod Seiling said in Toronto. "How can they get rid of Gilles Villemure and Eddie within one week? It makes absolutely no sense, especially when they get nothing in return for one of the best goalies in hockey. It has to be the bottom line people at the Garden trying to save money. It's a lousy way to treat a guy who did so much for so long for the Rangers."

"Are you kidding me?" asked Denis Potvin, the Islanders' young all-star defenseman. "My goodness. What are the Rangers doing? What do they gain by this? When you think of the Rangers, you think of Eddie Giacomin. He's synonomous with the Rangers. All of New York has to be sorry to see him go this way. Derek Sanderson one day, Eddie Giacomin the next. It's unreal."

"Who do they have left now who can bail them out, get them going when they need it?" asked Bob Plager of St. Louis. "Eddie's the best damned goaltender around when it comes to handling the puck."

Eddie Johnston, the Blues' veteran goaltender, questioned the logic of giving up Giacomin.

"Eddie may be getting older but he hasn't lost his ability. I'm surprised they wouldn't keep him around as backup goalie and have him work with John Davidson. Eddie could teach John a lot about playing goal."

"A real shocker," was the reaction of the Minnesota North Stars' Glen Sather, a former Ranger.

General Manager Keith Allen of the Flyers was asked for his reaction by Don Wilno of New Jersey's *Trenton Times.*

"If there was one guy on the Rangers who positively fought us through the years, it was Eddie Giacomin. It should be obvious they [Madison Square Garden management] thought they could buy a championship with long-term contracts and big salaries. Obviously it didn't work. Obviously now they're getting rid of guys to save money."

This was denied by Michael Burke, the president of Madison Square Garden Center. "To deduce that these moves were to save money is entirely and absolutely incorrect," he said.

The Madison Square Garden executive did agree that the Giacomin transaction might have been handled differently, considering Eddie's popularity among fans and long, meritorious service to the Rangers.

"I agree the timing and handling left a great deal to be desired. He had to be hurt emotionally and his reaction was very natural. We didn't handle this very well. We at the Garden are responsible," said Burke. "Eddie Giacomin had a very special place in the hearts of New York fans and in the Ranger organization. On the human level he deserved greater courtesy from us. We owed it to him to do it in the most graceful way."

Francis said he had tried to make a trade for Giacomin since the end of the 1974–75 season but that he had been unable to do so. "If I knew of any better way to do it, any better way to tell him, you can be sure I would have done it," said the general manager.

It was obvious Francis disliked discarding Giacomin and did not intentionally handle the matter in a way to upset Eddie.

"It was one of the toughest decisions I ever had to make," he said, alluding to their close relationship and his fondness for Eddie. "But I've got to put the interests of the New York Rangers ahead of my personal interests," he said. "In this business you have to make decisions. I didn't want Eddie to go to Montreal and then have to call him and tell him what had happened."

Francis made it clear he was deeply disturbed by the performance of the Rangers. "There is no such thing as an untouchable player on this team when it comes to getting traded," he said.

Dunc Wilson was summoned from the American League Baltimore Clippers to replace Giacomin and share the goaltending with Davidson.

"What this comes out to is that John Davidson is our number one goalkeeper and is going to play a lot of games for us. This move is a vote of confidence for Davidson on our part. As for Wilson, he's nine years younger than Eddie."

Was Eddie being made the scapegoat for the Rangers' poor play?

"We're not pinpointing Eddie," said Francis. "In no way was it a shove at him. He gave us outstanding service for many years. I have the greatest respect for Eddie Giacomin. There's not a finer competitor in the game. But, we've got to rebuild the team."

On the morning after the trade, the switchboard at the *New York Post* was clogged with telephone calls from Ranger fans protesting the sale of Giacomin. *New York Daily*

News columnist Phil Pepe, serving as guest host on John Sterling's sports talk show on radio station WMCA, was deluged with calls from fans who wanted to talk about Giacomin.

Meanwhile, in Detroit, Alex Delvecchio was trying to contact Eddie by telephone.

"What a bonus for us to get him," said the general manager of a last-place team which had won only once in ten games. "Eddie is one of the most competitive guys in hockey. He's far from being over the hill. Look at Gump Worsley, Jacques Plante, Terry Sawchuk, Johnny Bower; they were still great goaltenders when they were older than Giacomin. I think it's kind of foolish for the Rangers to give up a guy as great as Eddie. They're not that strong in goal to be able to afford losing him."

Ironically, Detroit's next game was on Sunday, November 2, 1975—in Madison Square Garden against the Rangers.

"I just talked with coach Doug Barkley and we'll definitely play Eddie Giacomin in goal against the Rangers, if there are no complications in his joining us," said Delvecchio.

On the day following his sale to Detroit, it seemed as though there might be complications. Eddie was still in an emotional state of shock. But reality was finally beginning to sink in. He was concerned about the effect upon his family of going to Detroit. He was thinking about retiring. He telephoned an old friend from Sudbury, New York Islanders' coach Al Arbour.

"I had to talk to someone," he said. "Al had given me a lot of good advice in the past and I always respected him. He'd been traded a lot during his career. For me, this was the first time I'd been traded. Al helped me a lot. I was pretty mixed up in my thinking. He helped me straighten myself out."

Giacomin spoke with Delvecchio by telephone. They

agreed to meet on Sunday at 1:30 P.M. in the hotel in which the Red Wings were staying across the street from Madison Square Garden.

"If Detroit wants me to play against the Rangers, I'll play," said Eddie.

When Eddie was walking from his car in the parking lot to the hotel, he accidentally encountered Ratelle, Bill Collins and Greg Polis of the Rangers.

"It was hard to bear," he said. "It brought tears to my eyes. I hoped they didn't notice."

Before he agreed to join the Red Wings, Eddie wanted assurance that he figured in Detroit's plans beyond the 1975–76 season. Like so many highly paid hockey players (Giacomin's salary is estimated to be $150,000), he was fearful the Red Wings might not be interested in extending his contract at the end of the season.

Eddie walked across the street to Madison Square Garden and for the first time went to the visiting team's dressing room instead of the dressing room used by the Rangers. He was greeted warmly by his new teammates as he undressed and put on his bright red Detroit Red Wings' uniform with the white numerals 31 across the back. He felt strange. He thought to himself that throughout his long goaltending career he had never worn any number but one. Scrawled on a blackboard in the dressing room was an anonymous message from some of the Madison Square Garden personnel whom Eddie had befriended through the years. It read: "Go Get 'Em, Eddie. Shut 'Em Out!" It was signed: "The Boys from MSG."

Gradually, Ranger players walked down the corridor and entered the Detroit dressing room to shake Giacomin's hand, wish him well, and express sadness that he was no longer their teammate. John Bednarski stopped by. So did Rod Gilbert and Ratelle. Then Davidson, the young man who had replaced Giacomin as New York's goaltender, appeared.

Big John and Fast Eddie had roomed together on the road. Even though they were rivals for the same job, they became friends. They stayed up late at night in their hotel room and talked about goaltending. Giacomin, the veteran, worked with Davidson, the young goalie, teaching him some of the finer points of the goaltending craft.

"I wanted to wish him well before the game and thank him for all the help he had given me," said Davidson. "Do you know what he said to me before the game? He wished me luck. He said he'd be pulling for me to have a great career with the Rangers. Eddie Giacomin is a man who is all class. He's a competitor. He personifies what goaltending is all about."

In the press lounge before the game, Delvecchio was drinking coffee and talking about Giacomin.

"He wants to play," said the Red Wings' former star center. "He's chomping at the bit. What a competitor he is. He's putting himself on the spot. He's putting himself in the pressure-cooker. We didn't expect him to play because it might be too emotional for him and he might face embarrassment if he doesn't do well."

Bob Gockley of the *Long Island Press* remarked to Lawrence Sacharuk that Eddie was displaying a lot of guts by playing against his former teammates only two days after being sold.

"That's what Eddie Giacomin has more of than any of us—guts," said the Rangers' young defenseman.

Outside in the arena the crowd was filing in. Signs and banners paying homage to Eddie and criticizing the Rangers for selling him to Detroit were being strung from the mezzanine.

Some of them read:

"Eddie—Still No. 1."

"The Rangers Without Eddie Is Like the Cup Without Champagne."

"Steady Eddie, We Miss You Already."

"Eddie, Whether You Are Near or Far, You'll Always Be Our No. 1 Star."

When Giacomin appeared on the ice in his new crimson uniform for the pregame warmup, Madison Square Garden spectators cheered and applauded him. When he stepped into the crease and pulled his white mask down over his eyes for shooting practice, the cheers grew louder. He stopped the first nineteen practice shots he faced and the crowd began to chant: "Eddie! . . . Eddie! . . . Eddie!"

The best was yet to come.

The Rangers emerged from the runway beneath the stands and skated out on to the ice. The New York crowd booed its own team. Then the visiting Red Wings appeared on the ice. The crowd cheered them as though they, not the Rangers, were the home team.

Eddie Giacomin positioned himself between the twin face-off circles as the teams lined up for the playing of the National Anthem and the Madison Square Garden public-address announcer, Carl Martin, asked the crowd to rise. The chanting and cheering began in the seats in the upper level of the arena and spilled down to the lower seats. Soon the noise became a deafening, thunderous roar that virtually shook the building.

"Eddie! . . . Eddie! . . . Eddie! . . . Eddie! . . . Eddie!" the crowd roared.

Eddie Giacomin stood at attention on the ice in front of the goal crease and stared up through misty eyes at the American flag. The tears rolled down his cheeks.

"Eddie! . . . Eddie! . . . Eddie!" The roar of the crowd drowned out the recorded rendition of the National Anthem.

"Eddie! . . . Eddie! . . . Eddie!" The chanting of the crowd and the standing ovation lasted five minutes and delayed the start of the game.

Eddie shuffled nervously on his skates. He swallowed hard. He was proud but embarrassed by the fans' outpouring of affection for him. He looked as out of place in his bright red Detroit uniform as a man arriving late at a black-tie dinner in a sports jacket.

"Eddie! . . . Eddie! . . . Eddie!"

The gray-haired goaltender blinked to fight back the tears but he could not. The emotion was too great, too overwhelming. He reached up with his gloved left hand and wiped away the tears. Then he waved to the crowd to show his appreciation.

"Eddie! . . . Eddie! . . . Eddie!"

The chant grew louder. Even some of the Rangers at the other end of the ice tapped their stick blades gently on the ice in tribute to the crowd's emotional reaction to their friend and former goaltender.

Eddie bit his lower lip to squelch the smile beginning to crease the corners of his mouth. He blinked his watery eyes. Strange thoughts raced through his mind. Forty-eight hours earlier he had been a Ranger. Now he was a Detroit Red Wing, playing his first game for his new team against his old team.

"The reception I got was amazing, unbelievable," said Eddie. "I stood there before the game. . . . I couldn't hear 'The Star-Spangled Banner.' . . . I was shaking. . . . I thought I might faint. I thought it was sweat in my eyes but it was tears. God bless those people."

"I had a dream the night before the game," he said. "I thought about it when the people were cheering for me. I thought: Stop the game, shake hands, thank them for the privilege of stepping on the ice. I even thought about going to the Ranger bench to shake hands. Then walking off the ice, ending it all right then and there."

That is not how Giacomin does things.

"I owed Detroit a debt; at least a one-game debt," he said. "They wanted me when the Rangers didn't want me anymore."

Finally the chanting and the cheering stopped and the game started. Eddie covered his face with his mask, crouched in front of the net and shouted to his new teammates: "O.K. . . . O.K. . . . O.K., guy's, let's go."

Bill Fairbairn was the first Ranger to challenge his former teammate. He skated full speed along the right sideboards, broke behind the Red Wings' defense, veered into the face-off circle on a breakaway and drove a rising wrist shot toward the net. Eddie came fifteen feet out of his crease and flicked the shot aside with the blocking pad covering his right hand and forearm.

He stopped Steve Vickers with a sliding save. He stopped Vickers again one-on-one. He blocked Pat Hickey's shot in his midsection. He made leaping, twisting saves and dived to smother rebounds on two slap shots by John Bednarski that flew at him through a maze of arms, legs and sticks in front of the net. He embarrassed the Rangers by boldly skating out of his crease to trap and clear loose pucks.

The sound of "Eddie! . . . Eddie! . . . Eddie!" filled the building. The crowd cheered and applauded every move Eddie made. They cheered the Red Wings. They booed the Rangers each time they touched the puck. They cheered Ranger mistakes.

Bill Hogaboam scored. Nick Libett scored. Danny Grant scored. Barry Salovaara scored. Detroit was beating the Rangers, 4-0. The Rangers could not beat Eddie. He shut them out for twenty-seven minutes and until Fairbairn scored it seemed as though he might achieve his fiftieth regular-season career shutout at the expense of the team that had given up on him. The Red Wings won, 6–4, and Eddie stopped forty-two of forty-six shots by his former teammates.

It was enough that he had played. That he played and won seemed suitable for a Hollywood script.

"It was the hardest thing I ever had to do, go against my old teammates, my friends, and try and beat them," he said as newsmen with notebooks, tape-recorders and cameras surrounded him after the emotional and dramatic game.

"It's a good thing I wear a mask or you would have seen me cry a few times," he said, smiling. "I felt sorry for the Rangers, the way the fans were for us, for me, against them."

Several of his former teammates told Eddie, "Good luck . . . we wish you well. . . . it's a damned shame, what they did to you," during play stoppages. One of the Rangers said, "I'm sorry," after scoring a goal. Eddie declined to identify the player. "I don't want to embarrass him or get in any trouble," he explained.

Giacomin praised his new teammates for the way they played in front of him. "I don't even know all their names yet but they went out and got me four quick goals," he said.

He went to Jim Rutherford and Peter McDuffe, Detroit's other goalies, and said, "Hey, gents, I'm sorry about this. I didn't cause it to happen." Eddie did not want either goalie to resent his presence on the team.

He looked down at his sweat-soaked Detroit uniform and smiled. "Well, I finally made it to Detroit, eh?" He referred to his youth when he twice was rejected while trying out for the Red Wings' junior teams. "No," he said softly, "I'm not bitter about what happened. I don't hold a grudge against the Rangers or their brass. It was a shock to leave New York. I loved the guys on the Rangers. I'm going to miss New York and miss playing for the Rangers. But you've got to think positively. It's not the end of the world for me. I was lucky to play for the New York Rangers for eleven years. I'm thankful for that. They felt they had to make changes and I was one of the changes they made. That's part of being a professional athlete."

The Rangers had mixed emotions after the game. They hated to lose but they felt good for Eddie.

"I was glad to see Eddie get the tribute from the fans that he deserved," said Davidson.

"He didn't just beat us with his goaltending; he beat us with his very presence in the building," said Park.

"It was a great night for him," said Gilbert. "I'll miss Eddie. He was a great goaltender and a good friend, always full of spirit and enthusiasm."

The fans' reception to Giacomin had an adverse effect upon the Rangers. "You could see it in their eyes," agreed Eddie.

"Eddie's presence in the game made us the visitors in our own rink," said Pete Stemkowski.

"I can honestly say that the fans' reaction to Giacomin caused us to lose this game," said Stewart.

"I hope the fans don't miss those two points in the final standings," Ranger president William Jennings told *New York Times* sports columnist Dave Anderson.

"It was a bizarre, incredible night," Marv Albert told his listeners on WNEW Radio and viewers on WNBC television.

"I've never seen anything like it," Herb Goren of WCBS, a former Ranger publicist and New York sports writer, said of the fans' emotional reaction to Giacomin.

Terry Harper, a Detroit defenseman, was deeply touched by Giacomin's courageous game and the fans' affection for him.

"This was one of the nicest, most beautiful, warmest feelings I've ever felt in sports in terms of tribute to a man and an athlete," he said.

Eddie was touched by two strange events that happened to him after the game.

A young man wearing a service station attendant's uniform was waiting for Giacomin in the parking lot outside Madison

Square Garden. He had heard on the radio that Eddie was playing goal against his former Ranger teammates. "I just came down and took a chance that I could meet you," he told Eddie. "All I want to do is shake your hand and say thanks for all the great moments you gave me."

The youth had driven all the way to Manhattan from Tarrytown, New York.

Eddie and his friend Paul Levine got into their car and drove toward the Midtown Tunnel leading to Long Island. They were a short distance from the toll booth when a car pulled up beside them and the driver leaned out the window.

"Are you Eddie Giacomin?" the man asked.

"That's right," said Eddie, puzzled by the stranger in the car.

"I want to do something for you for all the great years you gave the Rangers and Ranger fans. Follow me to the tunnel; I'd like to pay the toll for you. It's the least I can do to say thanks," said the man.

When Eddie arrived home, Brad Park, Walt Tkaczuk, their wives and several close friends were waiting for him.

"They say people in the world today are cold and unfeeling," said Eddie. "That's not true. Believe me, I know. I've had feelings and memories from people I know and people I don't know that I'll remember as long as I live."

APPENDIX

Career Highlights and Statistics

CAREER HIGHLIGHTS

Traded by Providence Reds of American Hockey League to New York Rangers for goalie Marcel Paille, defenseman Aldo Guidolin, and forwards Sandy McGregor and Jim Mikol, May 17, 1965.

Named to NHL All Star first team 1966–67, 1970–71; second team 1967–68, 1968–69, 1969–70.

Selected to play in NHL All Star game 1967, 1968, 1969, 1970, 1971, 1973.

Led NHL goaltenders in games and minutes played 1966–67, 1967–68, 1968–69, 1969–70.

Led NHL in shutouts 1966–67, 1967–68, 1970–71.

Led NHL goaltenders in games won 1966–67, 1967–68, 1968–69.

Shared Vezina Trophy with Gilles Villemure for best goals-against average in NHL 1970–71.

Set NHL record for most assists (2) in one game by a goaltender, March 19, 1972.

Tied NHL record for most assists (3) in one season by a goaltender, 1971–72.

Holds New York Ranger career goaltending record for most shutouts (49), wins (266), assists (8), one-goal games (94), playoff games (65), playoff wins (29) and playoff series (9).

Holds New York Ranger record for most goaltending wins (38) in one season, 1968–69.

Shares New York Ranger record with Gump Worsley and Johnny Bower for most games played (70) in one season, 1968–69, 1969–70.

Tied NHL record for most games played (70) by a goaltender in one season, 1968–69, 1969–70.

Shares New York Ranger record with Gump Worsley for most seasons as a goaltender (10).

Holds New York Ranger goaltending record for most playoff games in one season (13), 1973–74.

Led NHL goaltenders in playoff games (10) and minutes played (600), 1971–72.

Shares New York Ranger goaltending record with Dave Kerr and Chuck Rayner for most one-goal games in one season (16), 1969–70.

Won West Side Association Award as New York Rangers' Most Valuable Player in 1966–67, 1968–69, 1970–71.

Won New York Ranger Fan Club Frank Boucher Trophy in 1968–69.

Led American Hockey League goaltenders in games played, shutouts, and penalty minutes, 1963–64.

Sold to Detroit Red Wings by New York Rangers, October 31, 1975.

EDDIE GIACOMIN

Born: June 6, 1939; Sudbury, Ontario, Canada
Home: Manhasset, Long Island, New York
Height: 5'11"   Weight: 175   Shoots: Left

GOALTENDING RECORD

Season	Team	League	Games	Minutes Played	Goals Against	Shutouts	1-Goal Games	Avg.	Record Won	Record Lost	Record Tied
1958–59	Washington Presidents	EHL	4	—	13	0	—	3.25	4	0	0
1959–60	NY Rovers-Clinton Comets	EHL	51	—	206	3	—	4.04	—	—	—
1959–60	Providence Reds	AHL	1	60	4	0	0	4.00	1	0	0
1960–61	NY Rovers	EHL	12	—	54	0	—	4.50	—	—	—
1960–61	Providence Reds	AHL	43	—	183	0	—	4.26	16	25	0
1961–62	Providence Reds	AHL	40	—	144	2	—	3.60	19	20	1
1962–63	Providence Reds	AHL	*39	—	102	4	—	2.62	22	15	2
1963–64	Providence Reds	AHL	*69	—	*232	*6	—	3.37	30	34	5
1964–65	Providence Reds	AHL	59	—	*226	0	—	3.84	18	38	2
1965–66	NY Rangers	NHL	36	2,096	128	0	3	3.66	7	19	6
1965–66	Baltimore Clippers	AHL	7	420	21	0	—	3.00	—	—	—
1966–67	NY Rangers	NHL	*68	*3,981	173	*9	11	2.61	*30	27	10
1967–68	NY Rangers	NHL	*66	*3,940	*160	*8	12	2.44	*36	20	10
1968–69	NY Rangers	NHL	*70	*4,114	175	7	14	2.55	*38	24	7
1969–70	NY Rangers	NHL	*70	*4,148	163	6	16	2.36	35	21	14
1970–71	NY Rangers	NHL	45	2,641	95	*8	5	2.15	27	10	7
1971–72	NY Rangers	NHL	44	2,551	115	1	12	2.70	24	10	9
1972–73	NY Rangers	NHL	43	2,580	125	4	3	2.91	26	11	6
1973–74	NY Rangers	NHL	56	3,286	168	5	9	3.07	30	15	10
1974–75	NY Rangers	NHL	37	2,069	120	1	9	3.48	13	12	8
	NHL Totals		535	31,406	1,422	49	94	2.72	266	169	87

* Indicates led league.

PLAYOFF RECORD

Season	Team	League	Games	Minutes Played	Goals Against	Shutouts	1-Goal Games	Avg.	Record Won	Record Lost
1962–63	Providence Reds	AHL	6	360	31	0	0	5.17	2	4
1963–64	Providence Reds	AHL	3	180	12	0	0	4.00	1	2
1966–67	NY Rangers	NHL	4	246	14	0	0	3.41	0	4
1967–68	NY Rangers	NHL	6	360	17	0	2	2.83	2	4
1968–69	NY Rangers	NHL	3	180	10	0	0	3.33	0	3
1969–70	NY Rangers	NHL	5	276	19	0	0	4.13	2	3
1970–71	NY Rangers	NHL	12	759	28	0	*4	2.21	7	5
1971–72	NY Rangers	NHL	*10	*600	*27	0	0	2.70	6	4
1972–73	NY Rangers	NHL	10	539	23	1	1	2.56	5	4
1973–74	NY Rangers	NHL	13	788	37	0	3	2.82	7	6
1974–75	NY Rangers	NHL	2	86	4	0	0	2.79	0	2
NHL Totals			65	3,834	179	1	10	2.82	29	35

* Indicates led league.

ALL STAR GAME RECORD

Season	Team	Games	Periods Played	Goals Against	Avg.	Record Won	Lost	Tied
1966–67	NHL All Stars	1	1	1	1.00	0	0	0
1967–68	NHL All Stars	1	1	1	1.00	0	0	0
1968–69	East All Stars	1	2	2	2.00	0	0	0
1969–70	East All Stars	1	1½	1	1.00	1	0	0
1970–71	East All Stars	1	1½	2	2.00	0	1	0
1972–73	East All Stars	1	1½	3	3.00	1	0	0
	Totals	6	8½	10	1.67	2	1	0

SCORING AND PENALTY RECORD

Season	Team	League	Assists	Penalty Minutes
1960–61	Providence Reds	AHL	0	8
1961–62	Providence Reds	AHL	1	4
1962–63	Providence Reds	AHL	0	12
1963–64	Providence Reds	AHL	2	41
1964–65	Providence Reds	AHL	0	6
1965–66	NY Rangers	NHL	0	10
1966–67	NY Rangers	NHL	0	8
1967–68	NY Rangers	NHL	0	4
1968–69	NY Rangers	NHL	0	2
1969–70	NY Rangers	NHL	2	0
1970–71	NY Rangers	NHL	0	4
1971–72	NY Rangers	NHL	3	4
1972–73	NY Rangers	NHL	2	6
1973–74	NY Rangers	NHL	1	4
1974–75	NY Rangers	NHL	0	20
	NHL Totals		8	62

PLAYOFF SCORING AND PENALTY RECORD

Season	Team	League	Assists	Penalty Minutes
1963–64	Providence Reds	AHL	0	4
1966–67	NY Rangers	NHL	0	0
1967–68	NY Rangers	NHL	0	0
1968–69	NY Rangers	NHL	0	5
1969–70	NY Rangers	NHL	0	0
1970–71	NY Rangers	NHL	0	2
1971–72	NY Rangers	NHL	0	2
1972–73	NY Rangers	NHL	0	4
1973–74	NY Rangers	NHL	0	6
1974–75	NY Rangers	NHL	0	4
	NHL Totals		0	23

NHL SHUTOUT RECORD

No.	Date	Opponent	Score	Saves	Winning Goal	Opposing Goalie
			1966–67			
1.	Oct. 23, 1966	Toronto (H)	1–0	29	W. Hillman	Bower
2.	Nov. 27, 1966	Toronto (H)	5–0	23	Hadfield	Bower
3.	Nov. 30, 1966	Chicago (A)	5–0	32	Kurtenbach	Hall
4.	Dec. 25, 1966	Chicago (A)	1–0	27	Geoffrion	Dejordy
5.	Jan. 12, 1967	Boston (A)	3–0	21	Neilson	Johnston
6.	Jan. 15, 1967	Detroit (A)	2–0	27	Nevin	Crozier
7.	Feb. 22, 1967	Detroit (H)	1–0	26	Nevin	Gardner
8.	Feb. 25, 1967	Montreal (A)	5–0	31	Kurtenbach	Vachon
9.	Mar. 26, 1967	Toronto (H)	4–0	31	Kurtenbach	Bower
			1967–68			
10.	Nov. 1, 1967	California (A)	2–0	16	Kurtenbach	Hodge
11.	Dec. 20, 1967	Detroit (H)	2–0	27	Gilbert	R. Edwards
12.	Dec. 31, 1967	Toronto (H)	4–0	22	Hadfield	Gamble
13.	Jan. 20, 1968	California (A)	3–0	15	Neilson	Hodge
14.	Feb. 4, 1968	Montreal (H)	3–0	23	Hadfield	Vachon
15.	Mar. 2, 1968	Philadelphia (H)	4–0	18	Hadfield	Favell
16.	Mar. 3, 1968	Chicago (H)	4–0	13	Hadfield	D. Dryden/DeJordy
17.	Mar. 17, 1968	Pittsburgh (H)	3–0	20	Ratelle	Bassen

#	Date	Opponent	Score		Goyette	Rutledge/Desjardins
18.	Oct. 20, 1968	Los Angeles (H)	7–0	26	Goyette	Rutledge/Desjardins
			1968–69			
19.	Oct. 26, 1968	Minnesota (A)	3–0	19	Nevin	Maniago
20.	Jan. 25, 1969	Chicago (H)	3–0	15	A. Brown	DeJordy
21.	Jan. 29, 1969	Detroit (H)	2–0	23	Hadfield	Sawchuk
22.	Feb. 8, 1969	St. Louis (H)	2–0	29	D. Marshall	Plante
23.	Feb. 23, 1969	Boston (H)	9–0	21	Tkaczuk	Johnston
24.	Mar. 30, 1969	Toronto (H)	4–0	15	R. Stewart	Bower
			1969–70			
25.	Oct. 19, 1969	Toronto (H)	1–0	17	Hadfield	Gamble
26.	Nov. 22, 1969	St. Louis (A)	5–0	20	D. Marshall	Plante
27.	Nov. 26, 1969	Boston (H)	3–0	24	Fairbairn	Johnston
28.	Feb. 15, 1970	Montreal (H)	2–0	19	D. Marshall	Myre
29.	Mar. 8, 1970	Pittsburgh (H)	0–0	25	—	A. Smith
30.	Mar. 18, 1970	Pittsburgh (A)	2–0	30	Nevin	A. Smith
			1970–71			
31.	Oct. 14, 1970	Buffalo (H)	3–0	15	Gilbert	Crozier
32.	Oct. 18, 1970	Montreal (H)	1–0	25	Tkaczuk	Vachon
33.	Dec. 5, 1970	Toronto (A)	1–0	38	Stemkowski	Plante
34.	Dec. 16, 1970	Buffalo (H)	4–0	20	Irvine	Daley
35.	Feb. 20, 1971	Pittsburgh (A)	2–0	37	Neilson	A. Smith
36.	Feb. 27, 1971	Pittsburgh (A)	4–0	26	B. MacGregor	Binkley
37.	Mar. 14, 1971	Toronto (H)	1–0	33	B. MacGregor	Parent
38.	Apr. 4, 1971	Detroit (H)	6–0	33	Nevin	D. McLeod

No.	Date	Opponent	Score	Saves	Winning Goal	Opposing Goalie
			1971–72			
39.	Feb. 27, 1972	St. Louis (H)	2–0	28	B. MacGregor	Wakely
			1972–73			
40.	Dec. 24, 1972	Detroit (H)	5–0	24	Ratelle	R. Edwards/ A. Brown
41.	Jan. 3, 1973	Los Angeles (H)	3–0	26	DeMarco	Vachon
42.	Jan. 7, 1973	Pittsburgh (H)	3–0	24	Tkaczuk	Rutherford
43.	Feb. 7, 1973	Islanders (H)	6–0	25	B. MacGregor	Desjardins
			1973–74			
44.	Oct. 17, 1973	St. Louis (H)	4–0	21	B. MacGregor	Stephenson
45.	Nov. 18, 1973	Pittsburgh (H)	7–0	33	Ratelle	A. Brown
46.	Nov. 21, 1973	California (H)	3–0	24	Ratelle	Meloche
47.	Nov. 25, 1973	Vancouver (H)	5–0	29	Vickers	G. Smith
48.	Feb. 6, 1974	Islanders (H)	6–0	16	Hadfield	B. Smith
			1974–75			
49.	Mar. 19, 1975	Vancouver (H)	3–0	18	Vickers	G. Smith
			PLAYOFFS			
			1972–73			
1.	Apr. 8, 1973	Boston (H)	4–0	33	Gilbert	Johnston

H—Home game.   A—Away game.

RANGERS' ALL-TIME SHUTOUT LIST

	Seasons	Games	Regular Season Shutouts	Playoff Shutouts	Total
ED GIACOMIN	10	535	49	1	50
Dave Kerr	7	324	40	7	47
John Ross Roach	4	180	30	5	35
Chuck Rayner	8	377	24	1	25
Gump Worsley	10	582	24	0	24
Lorne Chabot	2	80	21	2	23
Andy Aitkenhead	3	106	11	3	14
Gilles Villemure	8	184	13	0	13
Johnny Bower	3	77	5	0	5
Jacques Plante	2	98	5	0	5
Jim Henry	4	109	4	1	5
Cesare Maniago	2	34	2	0	2
Marcel Paille	7	107	2	0	2
Hal Winkler	1	8	2	0	2
Bill Beveridge	1	17	1	0	1
Ken McAuley	2	96	1	0	1
Jack McCartan	2	12	1	0	1
Terry Sawchuk	1	8	1	0	1
Joe Miller	1	3	0	1	1

NHL ALL-TIME SHUTOUT LEADERS

	Seasons	Games	Shutouts
Terry Sawchuk	21	971	103
George Hainsworth	11	464	94
Glenn Hall	18	906	84
Jacques Plante	18	837	82
Tiny Thompson	12	552	81
Alex Connell	12	416	80
Lorne Chabot	11	412	73
Harry Lumley	16	803	71
Roy Worters	12	488	66
Turk Broda	12	628	62
John Ross Roach	14	492	58
Clint Benedict	13	360	58
*Tony Esposito	7	378	52
Dave Kerr	11	427	51
*ED GIACOMIN	10	535	49

* Active player.

EDDIE GIACOMIN'S RECORD
AGAINST OPPONENTS

	Won	Lost	Tied	Shutouts
Atlanta Flames	3	2	1	0
Boston Bruins	26	24	11	3
Buffalo Sabres	9	5	0	2
California Seals	20	4	3	3
Chicago Black Hawks	18	27	12	4
Detroit Red Wings	34	20	11	6
Kansas City Scouts	0	0	1	0
Los Angeles Kings	13	6	7	2
Minnesota North Stars	14	6	7	1
Montreal Canadiens	22	31	10	4
New York Islanders	6	2	1	2
Philadelphia Flyers	15	5	8	1
Pittsburgh Penguins	20	6	3	7
St. Louis Blues	21	8	3	4
Toronto Maple Leafs	32	21	8	8
Vancouver Canucks	12	2	1	2
Washington Capitals	1	0	0	0
Total	266	169	87	49

EDDIE GIACOMIN'S RECORD AGAINST
PLAYOFF OPPONENTS

	Won	Lost	Shutouts
Boston Bruins	7	6	1
Chicago Black Hawks	7	11	0
Montreal Canadiens	8	11	0
New York Islanders	0	2	0
Philadelphia Flyers	3	4	0
Toronto Maple Leafs	4	1	0
Total	29	35	1

EDDIE GIACOMIN'S PENALTY-SHOT RECORD

Date	Penalty Shot	Goal	Score
Dec. 21, 1966	Dallas Smith	No	Rangers 5, Boston 1
Feb. 4, 1967	John Bucyk	Yes	Rangers 4, Boston 3
Oct. 31, 1967	Ed Joyal	No	Rangers 6, Los Angeles 1
Nov. 24, 1968	Norm Ferguson	Yes	Rangers 3, California 2
Feb. 5, 1969	Charlie Burns	No	Pittsburgh 3, Rangers 2
Mar. 18, 1970	Keith McCreary	No	Rangers 2, Pittsburgh 0
Mar. 15, 1972	Stan Mikita	No	Chicago 3, Rangers 1
Mar. 10, 1973	Ron Schock	No	Rangers 5, Pittsburgh 4
Mar. 31, 1973	Jacques Lemaire	Yes	Montreal 5, Rangers 1
Dec. 29, 1973	Yvan Cournoyer	No	Montreal 7, Rangers 1

EDDIE GIACOMIN'S ALL STAR YEARS

First Team		*Second Team*
	1966–67	
Ed Giacomin, Rangers	Goal	Glenn Hall, Chicago
Pierre Pilote, Chicago	Defense	Tim Horton, Toronto
Harry Howell, Rangers	Defense	Bobby Orr, Boston
Stan Mikita, Chicago	Center	Norm Ullman, Toronto
Ken Wharram, Chicago	Right Wing	Gordie Howe, Detroit
Bobby Hull, Chicago	Left Wing	Don Marshall, Rangers
	1967–68	
Gump Worsley, Montreal	Goal	Ed Giacomin, Rangers
Bobby Orr, Boston	Defense	J. C. Tremblay, Montreal
Tim Horton, Toronto	Defense	Jim Neilson, Rangers
Stan Mikita, Chicago	Center	Phil Esposito, Boston
Gordie Howe, Detroit	Right Wing	Rod Gilbert, Rangers
Bobby Hull, Chicago	Left Wing	John Bucyk, Boston
	1968–69	
Glenn Hall, St. Louis	Goal	Ed Giacomin, Rangers
Bobby Orr, Boston	Defense	Ted Green, Boston
Tim Horton, Toronto	Defense	Ted Harris, Montreal
Phil Esposito, Boston	Center	Jean Beliveau, Montreal
Gordie Howe, Detroit	Right Wing	Yvan Cournoyer, Montreal
Bobby Hull, Chicago	Left Wing	Frank Mahovlich, Detroit
	1969–70	
Tony Esposito, Chicago	Goal	Ed Giacomin, Rangers
Bobby Orr, Boston	Defense	Carl Brewer, Detroit
Brad Park, Rangers	Defense	Jacques Laperrière, Montreal
Phil Esposito, Boston	Center	Stan Mikita, Chicago
Gordie Howe, Detroit	Right Wing	John McKenzie, Boston
Bobby Hull, Chicago	Left Wing	Frank Mahovlich, Detroit
	1970–71	
Ed Giacomin, Rangers	Goal	Jacques Plante, Toronto
Bobby Orr, Boston	Defense	Brad Park, Rangers
J. C. Tremblay, Montreal	Defense	Pat Stapleton, Chicago
Phil Esposito, Boston	Center	Dave Keon, Toronto
Ken Hodge, Boston	Right Wing	Yvan Cournoyer, Montreal
John Bucyk, Boston	Left Wing	Bobby Hull, Chicago

NEW YORK RANGER GOALTENDING HISTORY

1926–27

	Games	Goals-Against	Shutouts	Average
Lorne Chabot	36	56	10	1.56
Hal Winkler	8	16	2	2.00

1927–28

	Games	Goals-Against	Shutouts	Average
Lorne Chabot	44	79	11	1.80

1928–29

	Games	Goals-Against	Shutouts	Average
John Ross Roach	44	65	13	1.48

1929–30

	Games	Goals-Against	Shutouts	Average
John Ross Roach	44	143	1	3.25

1930–31

	Games	Goals-Against	Shutouts	Average
John Ross Roach	44	87	7	1.98

1931–32

	Games	Goals-Against	Shutouts	Average
John Ross Roach	48	112	9	2.33

1932–33

	Games	Goals-Against	Shutouts	Average
Andy Aitkenhead	48	107	3	2.23

1933–34

	Games	Goals-Against	Shutouts	Average
Andy Aitkenhead	48	113	7	2.35

| 1934–35 | | | |
Games	Goals- Against	Shutouts	Average
Dave Kerr	37	94	4	2.54
Andy Aitkenhead	10	37	1	3.70
Percy Jackson	1	8	0	8.00

| 1935–36 | | | |
Games	Goals- Against	Shutouts	Average
Dave Kerr	47	95	8	2.02
Bert Gardiner	1	1	0	1.00

| 1936–37 | | | |
Games	Goals- Against	Shutouts	Average
Dave Kerr	48	106	4	2.21

| 1937–38 | | | |
Games	Goals- Against	Shutouts	Average
Dave Kerr	48	96	8	2.00

| 1938–39 | | | |
Games	Goals- Against	Shutouts	Average
Dave Kerr	48	105	6	2.19

| 1939–40 | | | |
Games	Goals- Against	Shutouts	Average
Dave Kerr	48	77	8	1.60

| 1940–41 | | | |
Games	Goals- Against	Shutouts	Average
Dave Kerr	48	125	2	2.60

| 1941–42 | | | |
Games	Goals- Against	Shutouts	Average
Jim Henry	48	143	1	2.98

NEW YORK RANGER GOALTENDING HISTORY

1942–43

	Games	Goals-Against	Shutouts	Average
Jimmy Franks	23	103	0	4.48
Bill Beveridge	17	89	1	5.24
Steve Buzinski	9	55	0	6.11
Lionel Bouvrette	1	6	0	6.00

1943–44

	Games	Goals-Against	Shutouts	Average
Ken McAuley	50	310	0	6.20
Harry Lumley	1	0	0	0.00

1944–45

	Games	Goals-Against	Shutouts	Average
Ken McAuley	46	227	1	4.94
Doug Stevenson	4	20	0	5.00

1945–46

	Games	Goals-Against	Shutouts	Average
Chuck Rayner	41	150	1	3.75
Jim Henry	11	41	1	4.10

1946–47

	Games	Goals-Against	Shutouts	Average
Chuck Rayner	58	177	5	3.05
Jim Henry	2	9	0	4.50

1947–48

	Games	Goals-Against	Shutouts	Average
Jim Henry	48	153	2	3.19
Chuck Rayner	12	42	0	3.65
Bob DeCourcy	1	6	0	6.00

1948–49

	Games	Goals-Against	Shutouts	Average
Chuck Rayner	58	168	7	2.90
Emile Francis	2	4	0	2.00

1949–50

	Games	Goals-Against	Shutouts	Average
Chuck Rayner	60	181	6	2.62
Emile Francis	1	8	0	8.00

1950–51

	Games	Goals-Against	Shutouts	Average
Chuck Rayner	66	187	2	2.83
Emile Francis	5	14	0	2.80

1951–52

	Games	Goals-Against	Shutouts	Average
Chuck Rayner	53	159	2	3.00
Emile Francis	14	42	0	3.00
Lorne Anderson	3	18	0	6.00

1952–53

	Games	Goals-Against	Shutouts	Average
Gump Worsley	50	153	2	3.06
Chuck Rayner	20	58	1	2.90

1953–54

	Games	Goals-Against	Shutouts	Average
Johnny Bower	70	182	5	2.60

1954–55

	Games	Goals-Against	Shutouts	Average
Gump Worsley	65	197	4	3.03
Johnny Bower	5	13	0	2.60

| | | *1955–56* | | |
| | | *Goals-* | | |
	Games	*Against*	*Shutouts*	*Average*
Gump Worsley	70	203	4	2.90

| | | *1956–57* | | |
| | | *Goals-* | | |
	Games	*Against*	*Shutouts*	*Average*
Gump Worsley	68	220	3	3.23
Johnny Bower	2	7	0	3.50

| | | *1957–58* | | |
| | | *Goals-* | | |
	Games	*Against*	*Shutouts*	*Average*
Gump Worsley	37	86	4	2.32
Marcel Paille	33	102	1	3.10

| | | *1958–59* | | |
| | | *Goals-* | | |
	Games	*Against*	*Shutouts*	*Average*
Gump Worsley	67	205	2	3.08
Bruce Gamble	2	6	0	3.00
Marcel Paille	1	4	0	4.00
Julian Klymkiew	1	2	0	2.00

| | | *1959–60* | | |
| | | *Goals-* | | |
	Games	*Against*	*Shutouts*	*Average*
Gump Worsley	39	137	0	3.57
Marcel Paille	17	67	1	3.94
Al Rollins	10	31	0	3.10
Jack McCartan	4	7	0	1.75
Joe Schaefer	1	5	0	7.50

| | | *1960–61* | | |
| | | *Goals-* | | |
	Games	*Against*	*Shutouts*	*Average*
Gump Worsley	59	193	1	3.29
Jack McCartan	8	36	1	4.91
Marcel Paille	4	• 16	0	4.00
Joe Schaefer	1	3	0	3.61

1961–62

	Games	Goals-Against	Shutouts	Average
Gump Worsley	60	174	2	2.90
Marcel Paille	10	28	0	2.80
Danny Olesevich	1	2	0	4.00
Dave Dryden	1	3	0	4.50

1962–63

	Games	Goals-Against	Shutouts	Average
Gump Worsley	67	219	2	3.30
Marcel Paille	3	10	0	3.33
Marcel Pelletier	2	4	0	2.00

1963–64

	Games	Goals-Against	Shutouts	Average
Jacques Plante	65	220	3	3.38
Gilles Villemure	5	18	0	3.60

1964–65

	Games	Goals-Against	Shutouts	Average
Marcel Paille	39	135	0	3.58
Jacques Plante	33	109	2	3.37

THE GIACOMIN YEARS

1965–66

	Games	Goals-Against	Shutouts	Average	Won	Lost	Tied
Ed Giacomin	36	128	0	3.66	7	19	6
Cesare Maniago	28	94	2	3.50	9	15	4
Don Simmons	10	37	0	4.63	2	7	1

1966–67

	Games	Goals-Against	Shutouts	Average	Won	Lost	Tied
Ed Giacomin	68	173	9	2.61	30	27	10
Cesare Maniago	6	14	0	3.84	0	1	2

1967–68

	Games	Goals-Against	Shutouts	Average	Won	Lost	Tied
Ed Giacomin	66	160	8	2.44	36	20	10
Don Simmons	5	13	0	2.60	2	1	2
Gilles Villemure	4	8	1	2.00	1	2	0

1968–69

	Games	Goals-Against	Shutouts	Average	Won	Lost	Tied
Ed Giacomin	70	175	7	2.55	38	24	7
Don Simmons	5	8	0	2.33	1	1	1
Gilles Villemure	4	9	0	2.25	2	1	1

	Games	Goals-Against	Shutouts	Average	Won	Lost	Tied
1969–70							
Ed Giacomin	70	163	6	2.36	35	21	14
Terry Sawchuk	8	20	1	2.91	3	1	2
1970–71							
Ed Giacomin	45	95	8	2.15	27	10	7
Gilles Villemure	34	78	4	2.29	22	8	4
1971–72							
Ed Giacomin	44	115	1	2.70	24	10	9
Gilles Villemure	37	74	3	2.08	24	7	4
1972–73							
Ed Giacomin	43	125	4	2.91	26	11	6
Gilles Villemure	34	78	3	2.29	20	12	2
Peter McDuffe	1	1	0	1.00	1	0	0

1973-74

	Games	Goals-Against	Shutouts	Average	Won	Lost	Tied
ED GIACOMIN	56	168	5	3.07	30	15	10
Gilles Villemure	21	62	0	3.53	7	7	3
Peter McDuffe	6	18	0	3.18	3	2	1

1974-75

	Games	Goals-Against	Shutouts	Average	Won	Lost	Tied
ED GIACOMIN	37	120	1	3.48	13	12	8
Gilles Villemure	45	130	2	3.16	22	14	6
Dunc Wilson	3	13	0	4.33	1	2	0
Curt Ridley	2	7	0	5.19	1	1	0

NEW YORK RANGER PLAYOFF GOALTENDING

	Games	Goals-Against	Shutouts	Average	Won	Lost	Tied
1926–27							
Lorne Chabot	2	3	1	1.50	0	1	1
1927–28							
Lorne Chabot	6	8	1	1.50	2	2	1
Joe Miller	3	3	1	1.00	2	1	0
Lester Patrick	1	1	0	1.49	1	0	0
1928–29							
John Ross Roach	6	5	3	0.83	3	2	1
1929–30							
John Ross Roach	4	7	0	1.75	1	2	1
1930–31							
John Ross Roach	4	4	1	1.00	2	2	0

		Games	Goals-Against	Shutouts	Average	Won	Lost	Tied
1931–32	John Ross Roach	7	27	1	3.86	3	4	0
1932–33	Andy Aitkenhead	8	13	2	1.63	6	1	1
1933–34	Andy Aitkenhead	2	2	1	1.00	0	1	1
1934–35	Dave Kerr	4	10	0	2.50	1	1	2
1936–37	Dave Kerr	9	10	4	1.11	6	3	0

1937-38

	Games	Goals-Against	Shutouts	Average	Won	Lost	Tied
Dave Kerr	3	8	0	2.67	1	2	0

1938-39

	Games	Goals-Against	Shutouts	Average	Won	Lost	Tied
Bert Gardiner	6	12	0	2.00	3	3	0
Dave Kerr	1	2	0	2.00	0	1	0

1939-40

	Games	Goals-Against	Shutouts	Average	Won	Lost	Tied
Dave Kerr	12	20	3	1.67	8	4	0

1940-41

	Games	Goals-Against	Shutouts	Average	Won	Lost	Tied
Dave Kerr	3	6	0	2.00	1	2	0

1941-42

	Games	Goals-Against	Shutouts	Average	Won	Lost
Jim Henry	6	13	1	2.16	2	4

1947-48

	Games	Goals-Against	Shutouts	Average	Won	Lost
Chuck Rayner	6	17	0	2.83	2	4

	Games	Goals-Against	Shutouts	Average	Won	Lost
1949–50						
Chuck Rayner	12	29	1	2.42	7	5
1955–56						
Gump Worsley	3	15	0	5.00	0	3
Gordie Bell	2	9	0	4.50	1	1
1956–57						
Gump Worsley	5	22	0	4.19	1	4
1957–58						
Gump Worsley	6	28	0	4.60	2	4
1961–62						
Gump Worsley	6	22	0	3.44	2	4

THE GIACOMIN PLAYOFF YEARS

	Games	Goals-Against	Shutouts	Average	Won	Lost
1966–67						
Ed Giacomin	4	14	0	3.41	0	4
1967–68						
Ed Giacomin	6	17	0	2.83	2	4
1968–69						
Ed Giacomin	3	10	0	3.33	0	3
Gilles Villemure	1	4	0	4.00	0	1
1969–70						
Ed Giacomin	5	19	0	4.13	2	3
Terry Sawchuk	3	6	0	4.51	0	1
1970–71						
Ed Giacomin	12	28	0	2.21	7	5
Gilles Villemure	2	6	0	4.51	0	1

	Games	Goals-Against	Shutouts	Average	Won	Lost
1971–72						
Ed Giacomin	10	27	0	2.70	6	4
Gilles Villemure	6	14	0	2.33	4	2
1972–73						
Ed Giacomin	10	23	1	2.56	5	4
1973–74						
Ed Giacomin	13	37	0	2.82	7	6
Gilles Villemure	1	0	0	0.00	0	0
1974–75						
Ed Giacomin	2	4	0	2.79	0	2
Gilles Villemure	2	6	0	3.83	1	0

NEW YORK RANGER HOCKEY HISTORY

	Games	Won	Lost	Tied	Points	Finished	Playoffs
1974–75	80	37	29	14	88	2nd	Lost Quarterfinal
1973–74	78	40	24	14	94	3rd	Lost Semifinal
1972–73	78	47	23	8	102	3rd	Lost Semifinal
1971–72	78	48	17	13	109	2nd	Lost Final
1970–71	78	49	18	11	109	2nd	Lost Semifinal
1969–70	76	38	22	16	92	4th	Lost Quarterfinal
1968–69	76	41	26	9	91	3rd	Lost Quarterfinal
1967–68	74	39	23	12	90	2nd	Lost Quarterfinal
1966–67	70	30	28	12	72	4th	Lost Semifinal
1965–66	70	18	41	11	47	6th	Out of Playoffs
1964–65	70	20	38	12	52	5th	Out of Playoffs
1963–64	70	22	38	10	54	5th	Out of Playoffs
1962–63	70	22	36	12	56	5th	Out of Playoffs
1961–62	70	26	32	12	64	4th	Lost Semifinal
1960–61	70	22	38	10	54	5th	Out of Playoffs
1959–60	70	17	38	15	49	6th	Out of Playoffs
1958–59	70	26	32	12	64	5th	Out of Playoffs
1957–58	70	32	25	13	77	2nd	Lost Semifinal
1956–57	70	26	30	14	66	4th	Lost Semifinal
1955–56	70	32	28	10	74	3rd	Lost Semifinal
1954–55	70	17	35	18	52	5th	Out of Playoffs
1953–54	70	29	31	10	68	5th	Out of Playoffs
1952–53	70	17	37	16	50	6th	Out of Playoffs
1951–52	70	23	34	13	59	5th	Out of Playoffs
1950–51	70	20	29	21	61	5th	Out of Playoffs

Season	GP	W	L	T	Pts	Finish	Result
1949–50	70	28	31	11	67	4th	Lost Final
1948–49	60	18	31	11	47	6th	Out of Playoffs
1947–48	60	21	26	13	55	4th	Lost Semifinal
1946–47	60	22	32	6	50	5th	Out of Playoffs
1945–46	50	13	28	9	35	6th	Out of Playoffs
1944–45	50	11	29	10	32	6th	Out of Playoffs
1943–44	50	6	39	5	17	6th	Out of Playoffs
1942–43	50	11	31	8	30	6th	Out of Playoffs
1941–42	48	29	17	2	60	1st	Lost Semifinal
1940–41	48	21	19	8	50	4th	Lost Quarterfinal
1939–40	48	27	11	10	64	2nd	Won Stanley Cup
1938–39	48	26	16	6	58	2nd	Lost Semifinal
1937–38	48	27	15	6	60	2nd	Lost Quarterfinal
1936–37	48	19	20	9	47	3rd	Lost Final
1935–36	48	19	17	12	50	4th	Out of Playoffs
1934–35	48	22	20	6	50	3rd	Lost Semifinal
1933–34	48	21	19	8	50	3rd	Lost Quarterfinal
1932–33	48	23	17	8	54	3rd	Won Stanley Cup
1931–32	48	23	17	8	54	1st	Lost Final
1930–31	44	19	16	9	47	3rd	Lost Semifinal
1929–30	44	17	17	10	44	3rd	Lost Semifinal
1928–29	44	21	13	10	52	2nd	Lost Final
1927–28	44	19	16	9	47	2nd	Won Stanley Cup
1926–27	44	25	13	6	56	1st	Lost Quarterfinal

STANLEY CUP CHAMPIONS

1974–75—Philadelphia Flyers
1973–74—Philadelphia Flyers
1972–73—Montreal Canadiens
1971–72—Boston Bruins
1970–71—Montreal Canadiens
1969–70—Boston Bruins
1968–69—Montreal Canadiens
1967–68—Montreal Canadiens
1966–67—Toronto Maple Leafs
1965–66—Montreal Canadiens
1964–65—Montreal Canadiens
1963–64—Toronto Maple Leafs
1962–63—Toronto Maple Leafs
1961–62—Toronto Maple Leafs
1960–61—Chicago Black Hawks
1959–60—Montreal Canadiens
1958–59—Montreal Canadiens
1957–58—Montreal Canadiens
1956–57—Montreal Canadiens
1955–56—Montreal Canadiens
1954–55—Detroit Red Wings
1953–54—Detroit Red Wings
1952–53—Montreal Canadiens
1951–52—Detroit Red Wings
1950–51—Toronto Maple Leafs
1949–50—Detroit Red Wings
1948–49—Toronto Maple Leafs
1947–48—Toronto Maple Leafs
1946–47—Toronto Maple Leafs
1945–46—Montreal Canadiens
1944–45—Toronto Maple Leafs
1943–44—Montreal Canadiens
1942–43—Detroit Red Wings
1941–42—Toronto Maple Leafs
1940–41—Boston Bruins
1939–40—New York Rangers
1938–39—Boston Bruins
1937–38—Chicago Black Hawks
1936–37—Detroit Red Wings
1935–36—Detroit Red Wings
1934–35—Montreal Maroons
1933–34—Chicago Black Hawks
1932–33—New York Rangers
1931–32—Toronto Maple Leafs

STANLEY CUP CHAMPIONS

1930–31—Montreal Canadiens
1929–30—Montreal Canadiens
1928–29—Boston Bruins
1927–28—New York Rangers
1926–27—Ottawa Senators
1925–26—Montreal Maroons
1924–25—Victoria Cougars
1923–24—Montreal Canadiens
1922–23—Ottawa Senators
1921–22—Toronto St. Pats
1920–21—Ottawa Senators
1919–20—Ottawa Senators
1918–19—No Champion
1917–18—Toronto Arenas
1916–17—Seattle Metropolitans
1915–16—Montreal Canadiens
1914–15—Vancouver Millionaires
1913–14—Toronto Blueshirts
1912–13—Quebec Bulldogs
1911–12—Quebec Bulldogs
1910–11—Ottawa Senators
1909–10—Montreal Wanderers
1908–09—Ottawa Senators
1907–08—Montreal Wanderers
1906–07—Montreal Wanderers (March)
1906–07—Kenora Thistles (January)
1905–06—Montreal Wanderers
1904–05—Ottawa Silver Seven
1903–04—Ottawa Silver Seven
1902–03—Ottawa Silver Seven
1901–02—Montreal A. A. A.
1900–01—Winnipeg Victorias
1899–00—Montreal Shamrocks
1898–99—Montreal Shamrocks
1897–98—Montreal Victorias
1896–97—Montreal Victorias
1895–96—Montreal Victorias (December)
1895–96—Winnipeg Victorias (February)
1894–95—Montreal Victorias
1893–94—Montreal A. A. A.
1892–93—Montreal A. A. A.

Hugh Delano is a sports writer and columnist for the New York Post *and covers the games of the New York Rangers. During his career as a newspaper writer, his assignments have run the gamut of sports from dog shows and college rowing to college football and basketball and from the Stanley Cup playoffs to the New York Mets' World Series championship in 1969. He started his newspaper career as a general-news reporter with the* Plainfield (New Jersey) Courier-News *and first became acquainted with Eddie Giacomin in 1969 when he covered the Rangers, Mets, and Yankees for the* Newark (New Jersey) News. *He attended Washington College and served three years in the Far East as a Marine Corps sergeant. His first book,* Power Hockey, *was coauthored in 1975 with Ken Hodge and Don Awrey. He and his wife, Marylou, live in Cranford, New Jersey, with their four sons, Buzz, Jon, Peter, and Craig.*